HARDPRESS.NET
HOME OF HARD-TO-FIND BOOKS

Louis' School Days
by Edith J. May

Louis' school days

Edith J. May

Arthur Rotch.

With Mama's love

October 27th 18

The meeting with Mrs. Paget.   Page 218.

LOUIS' SCHOOL DAYS

Master Louis on Section Hill. Page 76

NEW YORK:
D. APPLETON & CO. 346 & 348 BROADWAY.
1855.

LOUIS' SCHOOL DAYS.

A STORY FOR BOYS.

By E. J. May.

Louis and Meredith on Brandon Hill.   Page 76.

NEW YORK:

D. APPLETON & CO., 346 & 358 BROADWAY.

1856.

LOUIS' SCHOOL DAYS:

A STORY FOR BOYS.

BY E. J. MAY.

NEW-YORK:
D. APPLETON & COMPANY,
443 & 445 BROADWAY.
M.DCCC.LXI.

PREFACE.

It was originally my intention to leave the child of my imagination to make its way where it would, without any letter of introduction in the form of the usual prefatory address to the reader; but having been assured that a preface is indispensable, I am laid under the necessity of formally giving a little insight into the character of the possible inmate of many a happy home.

Reader, the following pages claim no interest on the score of authenticity. They are no fiction *founded on facts*. They profess to be nothing but fiction, used as a vehicle for illustrating certain broad and fundamental truths in our holy religion.

It has often struck me, in recalling religious stories (to which I acknowledge myself much indebted), that many of them fell into an error which might have the effect of confusing the mind of a thinking child, namely, that of drawing a perfect character as soon as the soul has laid hold of Christ, without any mention of those struggles through which the Christian must pass, in order to preserve a holy consistency before men. This would seem to exclude the necessity of maintaining a *warfare*.

The doctrine I have endeavored to maintain in the following pages is, that man being born in "sin, a child of wrath," has, by nature, all his affections estranged from God; that, when by grace, through faith in Christ, a new life has been implanted within him, his affections are restored to their rightful Lord, every thought and imagination is brought into captivity to the obedience of Christ; and his whole being longs to praise Him who has called him "out of darkness into light"—to praise Him "not only with his lips, but in his life." Then commences the struggle between light and darkness, between the flesh and the spirit, between the old and new man; and the results of this conflict are seen in the outward conduct of the Christian soldier.

The character of the child of God does not essentially alter, but a new impulse is given him. Whatever good quality was in his natural state conspicuous in him, will, in a state of grace and newness of life, shine forth with double lustre; and he will find his besetting sin his greatest hindrance in pressing forward to the attainment of personal holiness. The great wide difference is, that he *desires* to be holy, and the Lord, who gives him this desire, gives him also the strength to overcome his natural mind; and the more closely he waits on his heavenly Father for His promised aid, the more holily and consistently he will walk; and when, through the deceits of his heart, the allurements of the world, or the temptations of Satan, he relaxes his vigilance, and draws less largely from the fountain of his strength, a sad falling away is the inevitable consequence. This warfare, this danger of backsliding, ends only with the life, when, and when *only*, he will be perfect, for he shall be like his Saviour.

As a writer for the young, I dare not plead even the humble pretensions of my little volume in deprecation of the criticism which ought to be the lot of every work professing to instruct others. In choosing the arena of a boy's school for the scene of my hero's actions, I have necessarily been compelled to introduce many incidents and phrases to which, perhaps, some very scrupulous critics might object as out of place in a religious work; but my readers will do well to recollect, that to be useful, a story must be attractive, and to be attractive, it must be natural; and I trust that they who candidly examine mine will find nothing therein that can produce a wrong impression. It has not been without an anxious sense of the great responsibility dependent on me in my present capacity, that this little effort has been made. Should it be the instrument of strengthening in one young one the best lessons he has received, it will, indeed, not have been in vain. To the service of Him who is the strength and help of all His people, it is dedicated.

> " Be Thou alone exalted :
> If there's a thought of favor placed on me—
>   THINE be it all !
> Forgive its evil and accept its good—
> I cast it at Thy feet."

E. J. M.

LOUIS' SCHOOL-DAYS:

A STORY FOR BOYS.

CHAPTER I.

DOLEFUL were the accounts received from time to time of Louis Mortimer's life with his tutor at Dashwood Rectory; and, if implicit credence might be yielded to them, it would be supposed that no poor mortal was ever so persecuted by Latin verses, early rising, and difficult problems, as our hero. His eldest brother, to whom these pathetic relations were made, failed not to stimulate him with exciting passages of school life—and these, at last, had the desired effect, drawing from Louis the following epistle:

" My dear Reginald,

" Your letter was as welcome as usual. You cannot imagine what a treat it is to hear from you. Mr. Phillips is kind, but so very different from dear Mr. Daunton. What I dislike most is, that he says so often, ' What *did* Mr. Daunton teach you? I never saw a boy so ignorant in my life!' I do not care how much he says of me, but I cannot bear to hear him accuse dear Mr. Daunton of not teaching me properly. I believe I am really idle often,

but sometimes, when I try most, it seems to give least satisfaction.   The other day I was busy two hours at some Latin
verses, and I took so much pains with them—I had written
an 'Ode to the Rising Sun,' and felt quite interested, and
thought Mr. Phillips would be pleased; but when I took
it to him, he just looked at it, and taking a pen dashed out
word after word, and said, so disagreeably, 'Shocking!
Shocking, Louis!   Disgraceful, after all that I said yesterday—the pains that I took with you.'   'Indeed, sir,' I said,
'I tried a great deal.'   'Fine ideas! fine ideas! no doubt,' he
said, 'but I have told you dozens of times that I do not
want *ideas*—I want *feet*.'   I wish those same feet would
run away to Clifton with me, Reginald; I hope I have not
been saying any thing wrong about Mr. Phillips—I should
be very sorry to do so, for he is very kind in his way: he
tells me I do not know what I am wishing for, and that
school will not suit me, and a great deal about my having
to fag much harder and getting into disgrace; but never
mind, I should like to make the experiment, for I shall be
with you; and, dear as Dashwood is, it is *so* dull without
papa and mamma—I can hardly bear to go into the Priory
now they are away.   I seem to want Freddy's baby-voice
in the nursery; and sober Neville and Mary are quite a
part of home—how long it seems since I saw them!   Well,
I hope I shall come to you at Easter.   Do you not wish it
were here?   I had a nice letter from mamma yesterday—
she was at Florence when she wrote, and is getting quite
strong, and so is little Mary.   I have now no more time;
mamma said papa had written to you, or I would have told
you all the news.   I wanted to tell you very much how
our pigeons are, and the rabbits, and Mary's hen, which I

shall give in Mrs. Colthrop's care when I leave Dashwood. But good bye, in a great hurry. With much love, I remain your very affectionate brother,

"Louis Francis Mortimer.

"P. S. Do you remember cousin Vernon's laughing at our embrace at Heronhurst? I wonder when I shall have another—I am longing so to see you."

It would not concern my readers much were I to describe the precise locality of the renowned Dr. Wilkinson's establishment for young gentlemen—suffice it to say, that somewhere near Durdham Down, within a short walk of Clifton, stood Ashfield House, a large rambling building, part of which looked gray and timeworn when compared with the modern school-room, and sundry dormitories, that had been added at different periods as the school grew out of its original domains. Attached to the house was a considerable extent of park land, which was constituted the general play-ground.

At the time of which I am writing, Dr. Wilkinson's school consisted of nearly eighty pupils, all of whom were boarders, and who were sent from different parts of the kingdom; for the doctor's fame, as an excellent man, and what, in the eyes of some was even a greater recommendation, as a first-rate classical scholar, was spread far and wide. At the door of this house, one fine April day, Louis presented himself; and, after descending from the vehicle which brought him from Bristol, followed the servant into the doctor's dining-room, where we will leave him in solitary grandeur, or, more correctly speaking, in agitating expectation, while we take a peep at the room on the opposite side of the hall. In this, Dr. Wilkinson was giving audience to a gentleman who had brought back his little boy a few minutes before Louis arrived. Having some private business to transact, the child was sent to the school-room, and then Mr. Percy entered into a discussion respecting the capabilities of his son, and many other particulars, which, however interesting to himself, would fail of being so to us.

At length these topics were exhausted, and it seemed nearly decided how much was to be done or discontinued in Master Percy's education. Mr. Percy paused to consider if any thing were left unsaid.

"Oh! by the by, Dr. Wilkinson," he said, letting fall the pencil with which he had been tapping the table during his cogitations, "you have one of Sir George Vernon's grandsons with you, I believe?"

"Two of them," replied the doctor.

"Ah! indeed, I mean young Mortimer, son of Mr. Mortimer of Dashwood."

"I have his eldest son, and am expecting another to-day."

"Then it was your expected pupil that I saw this morning," said Mr. Percy.

"May I ask where?" said the doctor.

"At the White Lion. He came down by the London coach. I saw his trunk, in the first place, addressed to you, and supposed him to be the young gentleman who attained to some rather undesirable notoriety last year."

"How so?" asked the doctor.

"Oh! he very ungenerously and artfully endeavored

to retain for himself the honor of writing a clever little essay, really the work of his brother, and actually obtained a prize from his grandfather for it."

"How came that about?" asked Dr. Wilkinson.

"Oh! there was some mistake in the first instance, I believe, and the mean little fellow took advantage of it."

Mr. Percy then gave a detailed account of Louis' birthday at Heronhurst, and concluded by saying—

. "I was not present, but I heard it from a spectator; I should be afraid that you will not have a little trouble with such a character."

"It is extraordinary," said the doctor; "his brother is the most frank, candid fellow possible."

"I hear he is a nice boy," said Mr. Percy. "There is frequently great dissimilarity among members of the same family; but of course, this goes no further. It is as well you should know it,—but I should not talk of it to every one."

Dr. Wilkinson bowed slightly, and remained silent, without exhibiting any peculiar gratification at having been made the depository of the secret. Mr. Percy presently rose and took his leave; and Dr. Wilkinson was turning towards the staircase, when a servant informed him that a young gentleman waited to see him in the dining-room.

"Oh!" said the doctor to himself, "my dilatory pupil, I presume."

He seemed lost in thought for a minute, and then slowly crossing the hall, entered the dining-room.

Louis had been very anxious for the appearance of his master, yet almost afraid to see him; and when the door opened, and this gentleman stood before him, he was seized with such a palpitation as scarcely to have the power of speech.

Dr. Wilkinson was certainly a person calculated to inspire a school-boy with awe. He was a tall, dignified man, between fifty and sixty years of age, with a magnificent forehead and good countenance : the latter was not, however, generally pleasing, the usual expression being stern and unyielding. When he smiled, that expression vanished ; but to a new-comer there was something rather terrible in the compressed lips and overhanging eyebrows, from under which a pair of the keenest black eyes seemed to look him through.

Louis rose and bowed on his master's entrance.

" How do you do, Mortimer ?" said the doctor, shaking hands with him. " I dare say you are tired of waiting. You have not seen your brother, I suppose ?"

" No, sir," replied Louis, looking in the stern face with something of his customary simple confidence. Doctor Wilkinson smiled, and added, " You are very like your father,—exceedingly like what he was at your age."

" Did you know him then, sir ?" asked Louis, timidly.

" Yes, as well as I hope to know you in a short time. What is your name ?"

" Louis Francis, sir."

" What ! your father's name—that is just what it should be. Well, I hope, Louis, you will now endeavor to give him the utmost satisfaction. With such a father, and such a home, you have great privileges to account for ; and it is your place to show to your parents of what use their care and instruction have been. In a large school you will find many things so different from home, that, unless you are constantly on your guard, you will often be likely to do things which may afterwards cause you hours of pain. Remember that you are a responsible creature sent into the world to act a part assigned to you by your Maker; and to Him must the account of every talent be rendered, whether it be used, or buried in the earth. As a Christian gentleman, see, Louis, that you strive to do your part with all your might."

Dr. Wilkinson watched the attention and ready sympathy with his admonition displayed by Louis; and in spite of the warning he had so lately received, felt very kindly and favorably disposed towards his new pupil.

"Come with me," he said, "I will introduce you to your school-fellows; I have no doubt you will find your brother among them somewhere."

Louis followed Dr. Wilkinson through a door at the further end of the hall, leading into a smaller hall which was tapestried with great-coats, cloaks, and hats; and here an increasing murmur announced the fact of his near approach to a party of noisy boys. As the doctor threw open the folding-doors leading into the noble school-room, Louis felt almost stupefied by the noise and novelty. A glass door leading into the play-ground was wide open, and, as school was just over, there was a great rush into the open air. Some were clambering in great haste over desks and forms; and the shouting, singing, and whistling, together with the occasional overthrow of a form, and the almost incessant banging of desk-lids, from those who were putting away slates and books, formed a scene perfectly new and bewildering to our hero.

The entrance of Dr. Wilkinson stilled the tumult in a

slight degree, and in half a minute after, the room was
nearly cleared, and a passage was left for the new-comers
towards the upper end.   Here was a knot of great boys
(or, rather, craving their pardon, I should say *young men*),
all engaged in eager and merry confabulation.   So intent
were they that their master's approach was wholly unno-
ticed by them.   One of these young gentlemen was sitting
tailor fashion on the top of a desk, apparently holding forth
for the edification of his more discreet companions, to whom
he seemed to afford considerable amusement, if the peals of
laughter with which his sallies were received might be considered any proof.   A little aloof from this party, but within hearing, stood a youth of about seventeen, of whom nothing was remarkable, but that his countenance wore a
very sedate and determined expression.   He seemed struggling with a determination not to indulge a strong propensity to laugh ; but, though pretending to be occupied
with a book, his features at length gave way at some irresistible sally, and throwing his volume at the orator, he exclaimed—

"How can you be such an ass, Frank !"

"There now," said Frank, perfectly unmoved, "the cen-
tre-of gravity is disturbed,—well, as I was saying,—Here's
the doctor !" and the young gentleman, who was no other
than Frank Digby, brother of Louis' cousin Vernon, dismounted from his rostrum in the same instant that his auditors turned round, thereby acknowledging the presence of
their master.

"I have brought you a new school-fellow, gentlemen,"
said the doctor ; "where is Mortimer ?"

"Here, sir," cried Reginald, popping up from behind a

desk, where he had been pinned down by a short thick-set boy, who rose as if by magic with him.

"Here is your brother."

Louis and Reginald scrambled over all obstacles, and stood before the doctor, in two or three seconds.

In spite of Louis' valiant protestations the preceding mid-summer at Heronhurst, he did not dare, in the presence of only a quarter of the hundred and twenty eyes, to embrace his brother, but contented himself with a most energetic squeeze, and a look that said volumes; and, indeed, it must be confessed, that Reginald was not an inviting figure for an embrace; for, independently of a rough head, and dust-bedecked garments, his malicious adversary had decorated his face with multitudinous ink-spots, a spectacle which greatly provoked the mirth of his laughter-loving school-fellows.

Dr. Wilkinson made some remark on the singularity of his pupil's appearance, and then, commending Louis to the kind offices of the assembled party, left the room.

He had scarcely closed the door behind him, when several loiterers from the lower part of the room came up; and Reginald and his brother were immediately assailed with a number of questions, aimed with such rapidity as to be unanswerable.

"When did you come?" "Who's that, Mortimer?" "Is that your brother?" "What's his name?" "Shall you be in our class?" "Why didn't you stay longer in Bristol?—If I had been you I would!"

Louis was amused though puzzled, and turned first one way, and then another, in his futile attempts to see and reply to his interrogators.

"Make way!" at last exclaimed Frank Digby; "you are quite embarrassing to her ladyship. Will the lady Louisa take my arm? Allow me, madam, to interpose my powerful authority." And he offered his arm to Louis with a smirk and low bow, which set all the spectators off laughing; for Frank was one of those privileged persons, who, having attained a celebrity for being *very funny*, can excite a laugh with very little trouble.

"Don't, Frank!" said Reginald.

"*Don't!* really, Mr. Mortimer, if you have no respect for your sister's feelings, it is time that I interposed. Here you allow this herd of *I don't know what to call them*, to incommode her with their senseless clamor. I protest, she is nearly fainting; she has been gasping for breath the last five minutes. Be off, ye fussy, curious, prying, peeping, pressing-round fellows; or, I promise you, you shall be visited with his majesty's heaviest displeasure."

"How do you do, lady Louisa? I hope your ladyship's in good health!" "Don't press on her!" was now echoed mischievously in various tones around Louis, whose color was considerably heightened by this unexpected attack.

"Now do allow me," persisted Frank, dragging Louis' hand in his arm, in spite of all the victim's efforts to prevent it, and leading him forcibly through the throng, which made way on every side, to Edward Hamilton, the grave youth before mentioned:—"His majesty is anxious to make the acquaintance of his fair subject. Permit me to present to your majesty the lovely, gentle, blushing lady Louisa Mortimer, lately arrived in your majesty's kingdom; your majesty will perceive that she bears loyalty in her— hey! what! excited!—hysterics!"

The last exclamations were elicited by a violent effort of Louis to extricate himself.

"Frank, leave him alone!"

"What is the will of royalty?" said Frank, struggling with his refractory cousin.

"That you leave Louis Mortimer alone," said Hamilton. "You will like us better presently, Louis," added he, shaking hands with him: "my subjects appear to consider themselves privileged to be rude to a new-comer; but my royal example will have its weight in due time."

"Your majesty's faithful trumpeter, grand vizier, and factotum is alive and hearty," said Frank.

"But as he had a selfish fit upon him just now," returned Hamilton, "we were under the necessity of doing our own business."

"I crave your majesty's pardon," said Frank, stroking his sovereign tenderly on the shoulder; for which affectionate demonstration he was rewarded by a violent push that laid him prostrate.

"I am a martyr to my own benevolence," said Frank, getting up and approaching Louis, "still I am unchanged in devotion to your ladyship. Tell me what I can do,"— and whichever way Louis turned, Frank with his smirking face presented himself;—"Will you not give your poor slave one command?"

"Only that you will stand out of my sunshine," said Louis good-temperedly.

"Very good," exclaimed Hamilton.

"Out of your sunshine! What, behind you? that is cruel, but most obsequiously I obey."

Louis underwent the ordeal of a new scholar's introduction with unruffled temper, though his cousin took care there should be little cessation until afternoon school, when Louis was liberated from his tormentors to his great satisfaction—Frank's business carrying him to a part of the school-room away from that where Louis was desired to await further orders. In the course of the afternoon, he was summoned to the presence of Dr. Wilkinson, who was holding a magisterial levee in one of two class-rooms or studies adjoining the school-room. The doctor appeared in one of his sternest humors. Besides the fourteen members of the first class, whose names Louis knew already, there was in this room a boy about Louis' age, who seemed in some little trepidation. Doctor Wilkinson closed the book he held, and laying it down, dismissed his pupils; then turning to the frightened-looking boy, he took a new book off the table, saying, " Do you know this, Harrison ?"

" Yes, sir," faintly replied the boy.

" Where did you get it ?"

" I bought it."

" To assist you in winning prizes from your more honorable class-fellows, I suppose," said the doctor, with the most marked contempt. " Since you find Kenrick too difficult for you, you may go into the third class, where there may be, perhaps, something better suited to your capacity; and beware a second offence : you may go, sir."

Louis felt great pity for the boy, who turned whiter still, and then flushed up, as if ready to burst into tears.

" Well, Louis, I wish to see what rank you will be able to take," said the doctor, and he proceeded with his examination.

" Humph !" he ejaculated at length, " pretty well— you

may try in the second class. I can tell you that you must put your shoulder to the wheel, and make the most of your powers, or you will soon be obliged to leave it for a less honorable post; but let me see what you can do—and now put these books away on that shelf." As he spoke, the doctor pointed to a vacant place on one of the shelves that lined two sides of the study, and left the room. Louis put the books away, and then returned to the school-room, where he sought his brother, and communicated his news just before the general uproar attendant on the close of afternoon school commenced.

Reginald was one of the most noisy and eager in his preparations for play; and, dragging Louis along with him, bounded into the fresh air, with that keen feeling of enjoyment which the steady industrious school-boy knows by experience.

" What a nice play-ground this is !" said Louis.

" Capital !" said Reginald. " What's the fun, Frank ?" he cried to his cousin, who bounded past him at this moment, towards a spot already tolerably crowded.

" Maister Dunn," shouted Frank.

" Oh, the old cake-man, Louis," said Reginald ; " I must go and get rid of a few surplus pence."

" Do you like to spend your money in cakes ?" asked Louis ; " I have plenty, Mrs. Colthrop took care of that."

" In that case I'll save for next time," said Reginald, " but let's go and see what's going on."

Accordingly Reginald ran off in the cake-man's direction. Louis followed, and presently found himself standing in the outer circle of a group of his school-fellows, who formed a thick wall round a white-haired old man and a boy, both of whom carried a basket on each arm, filled with dainties always acceptable to a school-boy's palate.

Were I inclined to moralize, I might here make a few remarks on waste of money, &c., but my business being merely to relate incidents at present, I shall only say that there they stood, the old man and his assistant, with the boys in constant motion and murmur around them.

Frank Digby and Hamilton were in the outer circle, the latter having *walked* from a direction opposite to that from which Frank and Reginald came, but whose dignity did not prevent a certain desire to purchase if he saw fit, and if not, to amuse himself with those who did so. He stood watching the old man with an imperturbable air of gravity, and, hanging on his arm in a state of listless apathy, stood Trevannion, another member of the first class.

Frank Digby took too active a share in most things in the establishment to remain a passive spectator of the actions of others, and began pushing right and left. " Get along, get away ye vagabonds !" he politely cried : "you little shrimps ! what business have you to stop the way ?— Alfred, you ignoramus ! Alfred, why don't you move ?"

"Because I'm buying something," said the little boy addressed, looking up very quietly at the imperious intruder.

" *Da locum melioribus*, Alfred, as the poet has it. Do you know where to find that, my boy ?—the first line of the thirteenth book of the Æneid, being a speech of the son of Anchises to the Queen of Carthage. You'll find a copy of Virgil's works in my desk."

"I don't mean to look," said Alfred, "I know it's in the Delectus."

Maister Dunn.   Page 22.

"Wonderful memory!—I admire that delectable book of yours," cried Frank, who talked on without stopping, while forcing himself to the first rank. "How now, Maister Dunn!" he said, addressing the old man, "I hope you b'aint a going to treat us as e did last time. You must be reasonable ; the money market is in a sadly unflourishing condition at present."

"You always talk of the *money market*, Frank," said little Alfred: "what do you mean by the money market?"

"It's a place, my dear—I'll explain it in a moment. Here, Maister Dunn ;—It's a place where the old women sell sovereigns a penny a measure, Alfred."

"Oh, Frank!" exclaimed Alfred.

"Oh! and why not?" said Frank; "do you mean to say you don't believe me ? That's it,—isn't it, maister ?"

"Ah, Maister Digby! ye're at yer jokes," said the old man.

"Jokes!" said Frank, with a serious air. "Pray, Mr. Dunn, did you ever happen to notice certain brass, or copper, or bronze tables, four in number, in front of the Bristol Exchange !"

"Ay sure, maister !"

"Well, I'll insense you into the meaning of that, presently. That, my good sir, is where the old women stood in the good old times, crying out, ' Here you are ! sovereigns a penny a measure!' And that's the reason people used to be so rich !"

"Oh, Frank! now I know that's only your nonsense," said Alfred.

"Well, I can't give you a comprehension, and if I could buy you one, I couldn't afford it," answered Frank. "Now here's my place for any one; Louis, I'll make you a present of it, as I don't want it."

"I don't want to buy any thing," said Louis.

"Rubbish!" cried Frank. "Every one does. Don't be stingy." And so Louis allowed himself to be pushed and pulled into the crowd, and bought something he would much rather have been without, because he found it inconvenient to say *no*.

The two upper classes were privileged to use the largest of the class-rooms as their sitting-room in the evenings; and here Reginald introduced his brother after tea; and, when he had shown him his lessons, began to prepare his own. Most of the assembled youths were soon quietly busy, though some of the more idly disposed kept up a fire of words, while turning over leaves, and cutting pens to pieces. Among the latter class was Frank Digby, who was seldom known to be silent for a quarter of an hour, and who possessed the singular power of distracting every one's attention but his own; for, though he scarcely ever appeared to give his lessons a moment's attention, he was generally sufficiently prepared with them to enable him to keep his place in his class, which was usually two from the bottom.

Louis saw that he must give his whole mind to his work; but being unused to study in a noise, it was some time before he was well able to comprehend what he wanted to do; and found himself continually looking up and laughing at something around him, or replying to some of Frank's jokes, which were often directed to him. When, by a great exertion, he had at last forced himself to attend to Reginald's repeated warnings, and had begun to learn in earnest, the door softly opened, and the little boy he had noticed in the crowd that afternoon came in.

"Halloa! what do you want?" cried one of the seniors; "you have no business here."

"Is Edward here, Mr. Salisbury?"

"No."

"Do you know where he is, please?"

"With the doctor," replied the young gentleman.

"Oh dear!" sighed the little boy, venturing to approach the table a little nearer.

"What's the matter with you?" asked Reginald.

"I can't do this," said the child: "I wanted Edward to help me with my exercise."

"My little dear, you have just heard that sapient Fred Salisbury declare, in the most civil terms chooseable, that your fraternal preceptor, Edwardus magnus, *non est inventus*," said Frank, pompously, with a most condescending flourish of his person in the direction of the little boy.

"And, consequently," said the afore-mentioned Mr. Salisbury, "you have free leave to migrate to York, Bath, Jericho, or any other equally convenient resort for bores in general, and you in particular."

"Please, Mr. Digby," said the little boy, "will you just show me this?"

"Indeed I can't," said Frank; "I can't do my own, so in all reason you could not expect me to find brains for two exercises."

"Oh! please somebody show me—Dr. Wilkinson will be so angry if Mr. Norton sends me up again to-morrow."

"WILL YOU GO?" shouted Salisbury, with such deliberate energy of enunciation that Alfred shrunk back:

3

" what's the use of your exercises, if you're shown how to do them ?"

" Come here, Alfred," said Louis, softly. Alfred readily obeyed ; and Louis, taking his book, began to show him what to do.

" Louis, you must not tell him word for word," said Reginald : " Hamilton wouldn't like it—he never does himself."

" But I may help him to do it for himself, may I not ?" said Louis.

" Yes ; but, Louis, you have not time—and he is so stupid," replied Reginald ; " you won't have time to do your own."

But Louis thought he should have time for both, and, putting his arm round Alfred, he kindly and patiently set him in the way of doing his lesson properly, and then resumed his own disturbed studies.

Hardly, however, was he settled than he found himself listening to Frank, who remarked, as Alfred left the room, " We shall be sure to have ' Oars ' in soon !"

" Who do you mean by Oars ?" asked Louis.

" Churchill," said Reginald, laughing.

" What an extraordinary name !" said Louis.

" I say, Digby," cried a boy from the opposite side of the table, " they give you the credit of that cognomen— but we are all in the dark as to its origin."

" Like the origin of all truly great," answered Frank, " it was very simple : Churchill came one day to me with his usual ' Do tell us a bit, that's a good fellow,' and after he had badgered me some minutes, I asked him if he had not the smallest idea of his lesson—so, after looking at it

another minute, he begins thus, ' *Omnes*, all.' 'Bravo!'
replied I. ' *Conticuere*—What's that, Frank?' 'Were
silent,' I answered : 'Go on.' After deep cogitation, and
sundry hints, he discovered that *tenebant* must have some
remote relationship to a verb signifying to hold fast, and
forthwith a bright thought strikes him, and on we go:
' *Intentique ora tenebant*—and intently they hold their oars,'
he said, exultingly. 'Very well,' quoth I, approvingly,
and continued for him, ' *Inde toro pater*—the waters flowed
glibly farther on, *ab alto*—to the music of the spheres;
the inseparable Castor and Pollux looking down benignantly
on their namesake below.' Here I was stopped by the
innocent youth's remark, that I certainly was quizzing, for
he knew that Castor and Pollux were the same in Latin as
in English. Whereupon, I demanded, with profound gravity, whether *gemini* did not mean twins, and if the twins
were not Castor and Pollux—and if he knew (who knew
so much better than I) whether or no there might not be
some word in the Latin language, besides *gemini*, signifying
twins ; and that if it was his opinion that I was quizzing,
he had better do his lesson himself. He looked hard, and,
thinking I was offended, begged pardon ; and believing that
jubes was Castor and Pollux, we got on quite famously—
and he was quite reassured when we turned from the de-
scriptive to the historical, beginning with *Æneas sic orsus
infandum*—Æneas was such a horrid bear.''

" Didn't you tell him of his mistake ?" asked Louis, who
could not help laughing.

" What ! spoil the fun and the lesson I meant to give
him ?—not I."

" Well, what then, Frank ?" said Reginald.

"Why, imagine old Whitworth's surprise, when, confident in the free translation of a first-class man, Oars flowed
on as glibly as the waters; Whitworth heard him to the
end in his old dry way, and then asked him where he got
that farrago of nonsense;—I think he was promoted to the
society of dunces instanter, and learns either Delectus or
Eutropius now. Of course, he never applied again to me."

Louis did not express his opinion that Frank was ill-
natured, though he thought so, in spite of the hearty laugh
with which his story was greeted. When he turned again
to his lesson, he found his book had been abstracted.

"I tell you what," cried Reginald, fiercely, "I won't
have Louis tormented—who has taken his book? It's
you, Ferrers, I am sure."

"I! did you ever!" replied that young gentleman. "I
appeal to you, Digby—did you see me touch his book?"

"I did not, certainly," said Frank.

"Give me the book," exclaimed Reginald, jumping upon
the table, "give me the book, and let's have no more such
foolery."

"Get down, Mortimer, you're not transparent," cried
several voices.

Reginald, however, paid no attention to the command, but
pouncing upon Ferrers at a vantage, threw him backwards
off the form, tumbling over his prostrate foe, and in his descent bringing down books, inkstand, papers, and one of
the candles, in glorious confusion.

"What's the row!" exclaimed Salisbury, adding an expression more forcible than elegant; and, starting from his
seat, he pulled Reginald by main force from his adversary,
with whom he was now struggling on the floor, and at the

same instant the remaining candle was extinguished. Louis was almost stunned by the noise that ensued: some taking his brother's part, and some that of Ferrers, while, in the dark, friend struggled and quarrelled with friend as much as foe, no one attempting to quell the tumult, until the door was suddenly burst open, and Hamilton with Trevannion and two or three from the school-room entered. Hamilton stood still for a moment, astonished by the unlooked-for obscurity. His entrance checked the combatants, who at first imagined that one of their masters had made his appearance, if that could be said to appear which was hardly discernible in the dim light which came through the half-open door. Hamilton begged one of the boys with him to fetch a light, and taking advantage of the momentary lull, he called out, "Is this Bedlam, gentlemen? You ought to be ashamed of yourselves! What's the matter, Mortimer?"

"Oh!" replied Ferrers, "they've been teasing his little brother, and he can't abide it."

"I only mean to say, that Louis shan't be plagued in this manner," cried Reginald, passionately; "and you know if the others were not here you wouldn't dare to do it, you bully!"

"For shame, Mortimer," said Hamilton, decidedly; and coming up to Reginald he drew him a little aside, not without a little resistance on Reginald's part—"What's the matter, Mortimer?"

"Matter! why that they are doing all they can to hinder Louis from knowing his lessons to-morrow. I won't stand it. He has borne enough of it, and patiently too."

"But is that any reason you should forget that you are a gentleman?" said Hamilton.

"My book is here, dear Reginald," said Louis, touching his brother's shoulder.

Reginald darted a fierce glance at Ferrers, but not being able to substantiate an accusation against him, remained silent, and, under the eye of Hamilton and his friend Trevannion, the remainder of the evening passed in a way more befitting the high places in the school which the young gentlemen held ; but Louis had been so much interrupted, and was so much excited and unsettled by the noise and unwonted scenes, that when Dr. Wilkinson came at nine to read prayers, he had hardly prepared one of his lessons for the next day.

CHAPTER II.

LOUIS soon made himself a universal favorite among his school-fellows; and, though he was pronounced by some to be a "softy," and by others honored by the equally comprehensive and euphonious titles of "spooney" and "muff," there were few who were not won by his gentle good-nature, and the uniform good temper, and even playfulness, with which he bore the immoderate quizzing that fell to his lot, as a new boarder arrived in the middle of the half-year. If there were an errand to be run among the seniors, it was, "Louis Mortimer, will you get me this or that?" if a dunce wanted helping, Louis was sure to be applied to, with the certainty in both cases that the requests would be complied with, though they might, as was too often the case, interfere with his duties; but Louis had not courage to say *no.*

In proportion, however, as our hero grew in the good graces of his school-fellows, he fell out of those of his masters, for lessons were brought only half-learned, and exercises only half-written, or blotted and scrawled so as to be nearly unintelligible; and after he had been a fortnight at school, he seemed much more likely to descend to a lower class than to mount a step in his own. Day after day saw Louis kept in the school-room during play-hours, to learn lessons which ought to have been done the night before, or to write out some long imposition as a punishment for some neglected duty that had given place to the desire of assisting another.

Louis always seemed in a hurry, and never did any thing well. His mind was unsettled, and, like every thing else belonging to him at present, in a state of undesirable confusion.

There was one resource which Louis had which would have set all to rights, but his weakness of disposition often prevented him from taking advantage of even the short intervals for prayer allowed by the rules of the school, and he was often urged at night into telling stories till he dropped asleep, and hurried down by the morning bell, before he could summon up courage to brave the remarks of his school-fellows as to his being so very *religious*, &c., and sometimes did not feel sorry that there was some cause to prevent these solemn and precious duties. I need not say he was not happy. He enjoyed nothing thoroughly; he felt he was not steadily in earnest. Every day he came with a beating heart to his class, never certain that he could get through a single lesson.

One morning he was endeavoring to stammer through a few lines of some Greek play, and at last paused, unable to proceed.

" Well, sir," said his master quietly,—" as usual, I suppose—I shall give you only a few days' longer trial, and then, if you cannot do better, you must go down."

" Who is that, Mr. Danby ?" said a voice behind Louis, that startled him, and turning his blanched face round, he saw Dr. Wilkinson standing near. " Who is that, Mr. Danby ?" he repeated, in a deep stern voice.

"Louis Mortimer, sir," replied Mr. Danby. "Either he is totally unfit for this class, or he is very idle; I can make nothing of him."

Dr. Wilkinson fixed his eyes searchingly on Louis, and replied, in a tone of much displeasure:

"If you have the same fault to find the next two days, send him into a lower class. It is the most disgraceful idleness, Louis."

Louis' heart swelled with sorrow and shame as the doctor walked away. He stood with downcast eyes and quivering lids, hardly able to restrain his tears, until the class was dismissed, and he was desired to stay in and learn his unsaid lesson.

Reginald followed his brother into the study, where Louis took his books to learn more quietly than he could do in the school-room.

"My dear Louis," he said, "you must try; the doctor will be so displeased if you go into a lower class; and just think what a disgrace it will be."

"I know," said Louis, wiping his eyes: "I can't tell how it is, every thing seems to go wrong with me—I am not at all happy, and I am sure I wish to please everybody."

"A great deal too much, dear Louis," said Reginald. "You are always teaching everybody else, and you know you have scarcely any time for yourself. You must tell them you *won't* do it; I can't be always at your elbow; I've quarrelled more with the boys than ever I did, since you came, on your account."

"Oh dear! I am sorry I came," sighed Louis, "I do so long to be a little quiet. Reginald, dear, I am so sorry I should give you any trouble. Oh, I have lost all my happy thoughts, and I know every thing is sure to go wrong."

Louis remained sadly silent for a few minutes, and then, raising his tearful eyes to his brother, who was sitting with his chin on his hands, watching him, he begged him to leave him, declaring he should not learn any thing while Reginald was with him.

Thus urged, Reginald took his departure, though, with his customary unselfish affection, he would rather have stayed and helped him.

When he was gone, Louis began slowly to turn over the leaves of his Lexicon, in order to prepare his lesson. He had not been long thus employed, when he was interrupted by the irruption of the greatest dunce in the school, introduced to the reader in the former chapter as Churchill, *alias* Oars, a youth of fifteen, who had constant recourse to Louis for information. He now laid his dog's-eared Eutropius before Louis, and opened his business with his usual " Come now, tell us, Louis—help us a bit, Louis."

" Indeed, Harry, it is impossible," said Louis sorrowfully. " I have all my own to do, and if I do not get done before dinner I shall go into the third class—no one helps me, you know."

" It won't take you a minute," said Churchill.

" It does take much more. You know I was an hour last night writing your theme; and, Churchill, I do not think it is right."

" Oh stuff! who's been putting that nonsense into your head ?" replied Churchill. " It's all right and good, and like your own self, you're such a good-natured fellow."

"And a very foolish one, sometimes," said Louis. "Can't you get somebody else to show you?"

"Goodness gracious!" cried Churchill, "who do you think would do it now? and no one does it so well as you. Come, I say—come now—that's a good fellow,—now do."

"But how is it that you want to learn your lesson now," asked Louis? "Won't the evening do?"

"No; Dr. Wilkinson has given me leave to go out with my uncle this afternoon, if I learn this and say it to old Norton before I go; and I am sure I shan't get it done if you don't help me."

"I cannot," said poor Louis.

"Now I know you're too good-natured to let me lose this afternoon's fun. Come, you might have told me half."

And against his better judgment, Louis spent half an hour in hearing this idle youth a lesson, which, with a little extra trouble he might easily have mastered himself in three quarters of an hour.

"Thank you, Louis, you're a capital fellow; I know it now, don't I?"

"I think so," replied Louis; "and now you must not talk to me."

"What are you doing?" said Churchill, looking at his book; oh, 'Kenrick's Greek Exercises.' If I can't tell you, I can help you to something that will. Here's a key." As he spoke, he took down the identical book taken from Harrison on the day of Louis' arrival, and threw it on the table before him.

"Is that a key?" asked Louis, opening the book; "put it back, Harry, I cannot use it."

"Why not?"

"It would not be right. Oh no! I will not, Churchill; put it up."

"How precise you are!" said Churchill; "it's quite a common thing for those who can get them—Thompson and Harcourt always use one."

"Thompson ought to be ashamed of himself," cried Louis, "to be trying for a prize, and use a key."

"Well, so he ought, but you won't get a prize if you begin now, and try till breaking-up day; so you hurt nobody, and get yourself out of a scrape. Don't be a donkey, Louis."

When Churchill left him alone Louis looked at the title-page, and felt for an instant strongly tempted to avail himself of the assistance of the book; but something checked him, and he laid his arms suddenly on the table, and buried his face on them. A heavy hand laid on his shoulder roused him from this attitude; and looking up, with his eyes full of tears, he found Hamilton and Trevannion standing beside him.

"What's the matter, Louis?" said the former.

"I have so much to do;—I—I've been very careless and idle," stammered Louis.

"I can readily believe that," said Hamilton.

"A candid confession, at any rate," remarked Trevannion.

"And do you imagine that your brains will be edified by coming in contact with these books?" asked Hamilton. "What have you to do?"

"I have this exercise to re-write, and my Greek to learn,—and—and—twenty lines of Homer to write out. I can't do all now—I shall have to stay in this afternoon."

"I should think that more than probable," said Trevannion.

"What have we here?" said Hamilton, taking up the key. "Hey! what! Louis! Is this the way you are going to cheat your masters?"

"Pray don't think it?" said Louis, eagerly.

"If you use keys, I have done with you."

"Indeed I did not,—I never do,—I wasn't going. One of the boys left it here. I am sure I did not mean to do so," cried Louis in great confusion.

"Put it back," said Hamilton, gravely, "and then I will go over your lessons with you, and see if I can make you understand them better."

"Thank you, thank you,—how kind you are!" said poor Louis, who hastily put the dangerous book away, and then sat down.

Hamilton smiled, and remarked, "It is but fair that one should be assisted who loses his character in playing knight errant for all those who need, or fancy they need, his good services: but, Louis, you are very wrong to give up so much of your time to others; your time does not belong to yourself; your father did not send you here to assist Dr. Wilkinson—or, rather, I should say, to save a set of idle boys the trouble of doing their own work. There is a vast difference between weakness and good-nature; but now to business."

Trevannion withdrew with a book to the window, and Hamilton sat down by Louis, and took great pains to make him give his mind to his business; and so thoroughly did he succeed with his docile pupil, that, although he had come in rather late, all, with the exception of the imposi-

tion, was ready for Mr. Danby by the time the dinner-bell
rang.

Louis overwhelmed Hamilton with the expression of his
gratitude, and again and again laid his little hand on that
of his self-instituted tutor.   Hamilton did not withdraw his
hand, though he never returned the pressure, nor made
any reply to Louis' thanks, further than an abrupt admonition from time to time to "mind what he was about,"
and to "go on."

Several inquiries were made at the open window after
Louis, but all were answered by Trevannion, and our hero
was left undisturbed to his studies.

That evening Louis had the satisfaction of being seated
near his friend Hamilton, who, with a good-natured air of
authority, kept him steadily at work until his business was
properly concluded.   Unhappily for Louis, Hamilton was
not unfrequently with the doctor in the evenings, or he
might generally have relied on his protection and assistance :
however, for the next two or three days, Louis steadily resisted all allurements to leave his own lesson until learned ;
and, in consequence, was able to report to Hamilton the
desirable circumstance of his having gained two places in
his class.

CHAPTER III.

FOR some time before Louis' arrival at Ashfield House, preparations had been making in the doctor's domestic *ménage* for the approaching marriage of Miss Wilkinson, the doctor's only daughter. The young gentlemen had, likewise, their preparations for the auspicious event, the result of which was a Latin Epithalamium, composed by the seniors, and three magnificent triumphal arches, erected on the way from the house-door to the gate of the grounds. Much was the day talked of, and eagerly were plans laid, both by masters and pupils, for the proper enjoyment of the whole holiday that had been promised on the occasion, and which, by the way—whatever young gentlemen generally may think of their masters' extreme partiality for teaching—was now a greater boon to the wearied and over-fagged ushers, than to the party for whose enjoyment it was principally designed.

The bridal day came.—No need to descant on the weather. The sun shone as brightly as could be desired, and as the interesting procession passed under the green bowers, cheer after cheer rose on the air, handfuls of flowers were trodden under the horses' feet, and hats, by common consent, performd various somersaults some yards above their owners' heads.

There was a long watch till the carriages returned, and the same scene was enacted and repeated, when the single vehicle rolled away from the door; and the last mark of honor having been paid, the party dispersed over the large playground, each one in search of his own amusement. Louis wandered away by himself, and enjoyed a quiet hour unmolested, and tried, with the help of his little hymn-book, and thinking over old times, to bring back some of his former happy thoughts. There were more than ordinary temptations around him, and he felt less able to resist them; and this little rest from noise and hurry was to him very grateful. When, at length, a little party found out his retreat and begged him to join in a game of "hocky," he complied with a light and merry heart, freer from that restless anxiety to which he had been lately so much subject.

In the afternoon, determining to let nothing interfere with the learning of his lessons, Louis sat down in the school-room to business. There were but two persons besides himself in the room, one of whom was an usher, who was writing a letter, and the other, his school-fellow Ferrers. The latter was sitting on the opposite side of the same range of desks Louis had chosen, very intently engaged in the same work which had brought Louis there.

Louis felt very happy in the consciousness that he was foregoing the pleasure of the merry playground for the stern business that his duty had imposed on him; and the noise of his companions' voices, and the soft breezes that came in through the open door leading into the playground, only spurred him on to finish his work as quickly as possible.

Ferrers and his younger *vis-à-vis* pursued their work in silence, apparently unconscious of the presence of each other, until the former, raising his head, asked Louis to fetch him an atlas out of the study.

"With pleasure," said Louis, jumping up and running into the study; he returned almost immediately with a large atlas, and laid it down on Ferrers' books. He had once more given his close attention to his difficult exercises, when a movement from his companion attracted his notice.

"Did you speak?" he said.

"Will you—oh, never mind, I'll do it myself," muttered Ferrers, rising and going into the class-room himself.

Louis had become again so intent upon his study, that he was hardly aware of the return of his school-fellow, nor did he notice the precipitation with which he hurried into his place, and half hid the book he had brought with him, a book that he imagined to be a key to his exercises, but which, in fact, was a counterpart to that taken away from Harrison, though bound exactly like the one Ferrers had gone for, and so nearly the same size as easily to be mistaken for it in the confusion attendant on the abstraction of it.

Just at this moment, Hamilton, Trevannion, and Salisbury, with one or two more of the first class, entered from the playground, and walked directly across to Ferrers.

Alive to all the disgrace of being found by his class fellows in possession of a key, and unable to return it unobserved, Ferrers, in the first moment of alarm, tried to push it into the desk at which he was writing, but finding it locked, he stood up with as much self-possession as he could assume, and pretending to be looking among his books and papers, managed, unobserved, to pass the obnoxious volume over to Louis' heap of books, laying it half under one of them. Louis was wholly unconscious of the danger so near him, and did not raise his head from his absorbing occupation when the fresh comers approached the desk.

"Ferrers," said Salisbury, as they came up, "we want your advice on a small matter ; come with us into the class-room."

Accordingly Ferrers obeyed, glad to leave the dangerous spot, and Louis was left in undisturbed possession of the apartment for more than half an hour, at the end of which time the party returned from the inner room laughing, and all walked out of doors. Just as they passed out, Mr. Witworth, the usher, approached Louis, and asked him if he could lend him a pencil. Louis laid his pen down, and began to search his pockets for a pencil he knew should be there, when he was startled by the ejaculation of the master :

"Hey !—what !—This is it, is it ?   So I have found you out, sir."

Louis looked up in alarm.   "Found me out, sir ?" he said, in a terrified tone : "what have I done ?"

"Done !" exclaimed Mr. Witworth,—"done, indeed : what are you doing there ?"

"My exercise, sir."

"To be sure, to be sure.   What's the meaning of this, sir ?" and he held up the key.   "What have you done, indeed !—you hoped that it was nicely concealed, I dare say.   I wonder how you can be so artful."

"I am sure I don't know any thing about that book," said Louis, in great agitation.

"Admirably acted," said Mr. Witworth.   "It would'nt walk here, however, Master Mortimer : some one must have brought it."

" I am sure I don't know who did—I don't indeed," said poor Louis, despairingly.

" Perhaps you'll try to make me believe you don't know what it is, and that you never saw the book before," remarked Mr. Witworth, scornfully.

" I do know what it is, but I never used it, I do assure you, sir, and I did not bring it here. Will you not believe me ?"

" It is very likely that I should believe you, is it not ? Well, sir, this book goes up with you to-morrow to Dr. Wilkinson, and we shall see how much he will believe of your story. This accounts for your apparent industry lately." So saying, Mr. Witworth walked off with the book in his hand, leaving Louis in the greatest distress.

" And all my pains are quite lost !" he exclaimed, as he burst into tears. " The doctor is sure not to believe me, and there will be—oh, who could have left it there ?"

" Louis, are you coming out this afternoon ; what's the matter ?" exclaimed the welcome voice of his brother.

" What, Lady Louisa in tears ! Here's the ink bottle ; do let me catch the crystal drops," said Frank Digby, who accompanied Reginald in search of his brother.

" Oh, Reginald !" exclaimed Louis, regardless of Frank's nonsense, " some one has left a key to my exercises on my books, and Mr. Witworth has just found it. What shall I do ?"

" *Some one has left*," ejaculated Frank. That's a good story, Louis ; only one can't quite swallow it, you know. Who would leave it, eh ?"

" How ? where, Louis ?" said Reginald.

" It was just here it was found. I am sure I cannot think who put it there."

" Well of all the"—began Frank; "my astonishment positively chokes me. Louis, are you not ashamed of yourself ?"

" Oh, Frank! I am speaking the truth; I am, indeed, I am—Reginald, I am, you know I am."

" It is very strange," remarked Reginald, who was standing with a clouded, unsatisfied brow, and did not exhibit that enthusiasm respecting his innocence which Louis expected from him. Reginald knew too much, and dared not yet be certain when appearances were so sadly against him.

" Reginald, dear Reginald, tell me," cried Louis, almost frantically; "surely you believe me ?"

" Believe you !" echoed Frank, scornfully; " he knows you too well, and so do I. Remember last year, Louis: you'd better have thought of it sooner."

Reginald cast a threatening glance on his cousin, who undauntedly replied to it.

" You can't gainsay that, at any rate, Reginald."

" Reginald, dear Reginald," cried Louis, with streaming eyes, "you know I always spoke the truth to you; I declare solemnly that I am speaking only the truth now."

Reginald looked gloomily at his brother.

" Indeed it is. If you will not believe me, who will ?"

" Who, indeed ?" said Frank.

" I do believe you, Louis," said Reginald, quickly, " I do believe you; but this matter must be sifted. It is very strange, but I will make all the inquiries I can. Who sat with you?"

"Ferrers was sitting there," replied Louis.

"Any one else?"

"No," replied Louis.

"I'll answer for it, it was Ferrers," said Reginald.

"A likely story," said Frank.

"I think it very likely," said Reginald, firmly, "and woe be to him if he has."

As he finished speaking, Reginald ran off in search of Ferrers, whom he found in a group of the head boys, into the midst of which he burst without the smallest ceremony.

"Manners!" exclaimed Hamilton; "I beg your pardon, Mr. Mortimer, for standing in your way."

"I am very sorry," said Reginald, bluntly, "but I can't stand upon ceremony. Ferrers, what have you been doing with Kenrick's Exercises—I mean the key to it?"

"I!" cried Ferrers, reddening violently; "what—what do you mean, Mortimer?"

"You have left the key on Louis' desk, to get him into a scrape—you know you have."

"Upon my word, Mortimer! what next!" exclaimed Salisbury. "Who do you think would fash themselves about such a little hop-o'-my-thumb?"

"Will you let Ferrers answer!" cried Reginald, imperiously.

Unconscious of the mistake he had made, Ferrers felt exceedingly uncomfortable in his present position, and, assuming an air of contemptuous indignation, he turned his back on Reginald, saying as he did so, "Such impertinence merits nothing but silent contempt."

"You did it, you coward!" cried Reginald, enraged

almost beyond control. "I know you did, and *you* know you did. Will you answer me?"

"Answer him, Ferrers, answer him at once, and let us have an end of his impertinence," cried several voices: "he's like a wild-cat."

"Well then, I did not," said Ferrers, turning round with a violent effort; "will that satisfy you?"

Reginald glared angrily and doubtfully on the changing countenance of the speaker, and then burst out vehemently,

"I don't believe a word you say: you did it either to spite him, or you mistook your aim. Do you never use keys, Mr. Ferrers?"

"Really, Mortimer!" exclaimed Trevannion, "your language is very intemperate and ungentlemanly. I have no doubt your brother knows how to help himself; and now, for your comfort, know that I saw him the other day with that same book, and here is Hamilton, who can corroborate my statement."

"Where? when?" asked Reginald, in a subdued tone.

"In the class-room alone, when he was writing his exercise. Hamilton, am I not right?"

Hamilton nodded.

"Dr. Wilkinson will do justice to-morrow," said Reginald, as after a moment's painful silence he looked up with assumed confidence, and turned proudly away from Ferrers' reassured look of exultation, though the latter hardly dared exult, for he thought Reginald had mistaken the book, and feared the suspicions that might rest on himself when it should be discovered that it was not a second-class key. "And now, Mortimer, let's have no more of this violent language," said Hamilton. "If the matter is to come before the doctor, he will do all justice; let him be sole arbitrator; but I would not bring it before him were I in your place. Make an apology to Ferrers, and say nothing more. You will do your brother more harm than good."

"*Make an apology,*" said Reginald, ironically; "I haven't changed my mind yet. It must come before the doctor. Mr. Witworth found the book, and has carried it by this time, or certainly will carry it, to head-quarters."

"Come along with me, and tell me the whole affair," said Hamilton.

While Reginald was unfolding the matter to Hamilton, the party they had left was reinforced by Frank Digby, who warmly took Ferrers' part, and enlightened the company as to many particulars of his cousin's former character: and so much was said about the injury Reginald had done to Ferrers by his suspicions, that when that youth discovered the certainty of the mistake he had made, he was so far involved as to render it impossible to him to acknowledge that even out of a spirit of teasing he had placed the book near Louis; and his anxiety was so great to free himself from any suspicion, that he was selfishly and ungenerously insensible to the trouble entailed upon Louis, whom he disliked on account of his superiority to himself, but on whom he had not seriously contemplated inflicting so great an injury—so imperceptibly does one fault lead to another, so unable are we to decide where the effects of one false step, one dishonest thought, shall end.

The story was soon spread among Louis' immediate companions, who were anxious to learn the cause of his swollen eyes and sad demeanor, and Louis had to endure many sneers, and, what was still harder to bear, much silent contempt from those whose high sense of honor made them despise any approach to the meanness of which he was supposed guilty. Hamilton, though in the study the whole evening, took no notice of him, and when his eyes met Louis', they bore no more consciousness of his presence than if he had been a piece of stone. Frank Digby did not tease Louis, but he let fall many insinuations, and a few remarks so bitter in their sarcasm, that Reginald more than once looked up with a glance so threatening in its fierceness, that it checked even that audacious speaker. Even little Alfred was not allowed to sit with Louis; though Hamilton made no remark, nor even alluded to the subject to his brother, he called him immediately to himself, and only allowed him to leave him at bed-time.

As the elder boys went up stairs to bed, Frank continued his aggravating allusions to Louis' weakness, but in so covert a manner, that no one but those acquainted with Louis' former history could have understood their import. For some time Reginald pretended not to hear them; there was a strong struggle within him, for his high spirit rose indignantly at his cousin's unkindness, yet was for some time checked by a better feeling within; but, at length, on Frank's making some peculiarly insulting remark in a low tone, his pent-up ire boiled forth, and, in the madness of his fury, he seized on his cousin with a strength that passion rendered irresistible. "You've tried to provoke me to this all the evening—you *will* have it, you dastardly coward! you WILL have it, will you?"

These exclamations were poured forth in a shout, and

Reginald, after striking his cousin several violent blows, threw him from him with such force that his head struck against the door-post, and he fell motionless to the ground, the blood streaming from a wound in his forehead.

There was an awful silence for a minute. The boys, horror-struck, stood as if paralyzed, gazing on the inanimate form of their school-fellow. Reginald's passion subsided in an instant; his face turned pale, the color fled from his lips, and clasping his hands in terror, he muttered, "Oh! what have I done!" and then there was a shout, "Oh, Frank Digby's killed! Digby's killed—he's dead!"

Hamilton at length pushed forward and raised Frank's head, and at this moment Mr. Norton and Dr. Wilkinson, with two or three of the servants, came from different directions. The crowd round Frank made way for the doctor, who hurriedly approached, and assisted Hamilton to raise Frank and carry him to his bed.

"He's dead, he's dead!" cried the boys all round.

"How did this happen?" asked the doctor, and without waiting for an answer he tore open the handkerchief and collar of the insensible youth, and dispatched some one immediately for a medical man. One was sent for a smelling-bottle, another for some water, and Mrs. Wilkinson soon made her appearance with a fan, and other apparatus for restoring a fainting person. But it was long before there were any signs of returning life. It was a terrible time for Reginald. It was agony to look on the motionless form, and blood-streaked countenance before him——to watch the cloud of anxiety that seemed to deepen on his master's face as each new restorative failed its accustomed virtue,—to listen to the subdued murmurs and fearful whispers, and to

5

note the blanched faces of his school-fellows. He stood with clasped hands, and there was a prayer in his heart that he might not be called to suffer so very deeply for this sinful expression of his temper. What if he should have sent his cousin unprepared into eternity? Oh, what would he give to see one motion; what, that he had been able to restrain his ungovernable fury! There was almost despair in his wild thoughts, when at last Frank sighed faintly, and then opened his eyes. He closed them immediately, and just then the surgeon arriving, more potent remedies were used, and he was at length restored to consciousness, though unable to speak aloud. Doctor Wilkinson had him removed to another room, and after seeing him comfortably arranged, returned to Reginald's bedroom.

" Now, how did this happen?" he said.

No one spoke, and the silence was only broken by the sound of sobs from the further end of the room.

" Who did this?" asked the doctor again.

" I did, sir," said Reginald, in a broken voice.

" Come forward. Who is·it that speaks?" said Doctor Wilkinson. " Mortimer! is this some passion of yours that has so nearly caused the death of your cousin? I am deeply grieved to find that your temper is still so ungovernable. What was the matter?"

Reginald was incapable of answering, and none of his companions understood the quarrel; so Doctor Wilkinson left the room, determined to make a strict investigation the next morning.

Poor Reginald was almost overwhelmed: he knelt with his brother after their candle was extinguished, by their bedside, and both wept bitterly, though quite silently. Distress at his own fault, and his brother's new trouble, and deep thankfulness that his cousin was alive, and not dangerously hurt, filled Reginald's mind, and kept him awake long after all besides in the room were asleep.

CHAPTER IV.

THE next morning, after the early school-hours, Doctor Wilkinson kept Reginald back as he was following the stream to breakfast, and led the way into the class-room, where, after closing the door, he seated himself, and motioning Reginald to draw closer to him, thus opened his inquiry.

"I wish to know, Mortimer, how this affair began last night : it appears, from all I can make out, to have been a most unprovoked attack on your part, but as there is often more than appears on the surface, I shall be glad to hear what you have to allege in extenuation of your savage conduct."

Reginald colored very deeply, and dropping his eyes under the piercing gaze of his master, remained silent.

"Am I to conclude from your silence that you have no excuse to make ?" asked the doctor in a tone of mixed sorrow and indignation ; "and am I to believe that from some petty insult you have allowed your temper such uncontrolled sway as nearly to have cost your cousin his life ?"

"I had very great provocation," said Reginald, sullenly.

"And what might that be ?" asked his master. "If the wrong be on Digby's side, you can have no hesitation in telling me what the wrong was."

Reginald made no answer, and, after a pause, Dr. Wilkinson continued : "Unless you can give me some reason, I must come to the conclusion that you have again given way to your violent passions without even the smallest excuse of injury from another. The assertion that you have been 'provoked' will not avail you much : I know that Digby is teasing and provoking, and is therefore very wrong, but if you cannot bear a little teasing, how are you to get on in the world? You are not a baby now, though you have acted more like a wild beast than a reasonable creature. I am willing and desirous to believe that something more than usual has been the cause of this ebullition of temper, for I hoped lately that you were endeavoring to overcome this sad propensity of yours."

"I assure you, sir," said Reginald, raising his open countenance to his master's, "I tried very much to bear with Frank, and I think I should if he had not said so much about—about—"

Here Reginald's voice failed; a sensation of choking anger prevented him from finishing his sentence.

"About what?" said the doctor, steadily.

"About my brother," said Reginald, abruptly.

"And what did he say about your brother that chafed you so much?"

Reginald changed color, and his eyes lighted up with passion. He did not reply at first, but as his master seemed quietly awaiting his answer, he at length burst out,—

"He had been going on all the afternoon about Louis : he tried to put me in a passion; he said all he could— every thing that was unkind and provoking, and it was more than a fellow could stand. I bore it as long as I could—"

"You are giving me a proof of your gentle endurance now, I suppose," said the doctor.

"I beg your pardon, sir, but I can't help it,—I feel so angry when I think of it, that I am afraid I should knock him down again if he were to repeat it."

"For shame, sir!" said the doctor, sternly; "I should have thought that you had already had a lesson you would not easily have forgotten. What did he say of your brother that irritated you? I insist upon knowing."

"He said Louis was—that Louis did not speak the truth, sir. He said that I believed it—that *I* believed it"—and Reginald's passionate sobs choked his utterance.

"Belived what?" asked the doctor.

"Something that happened yesterday," said Reginald; "he said that—he was a hypocrite, and he went on taunt-ing me about last summer."

"*About last summer!*" repeated the doctor.

"Yes, sir—about a mistake. Nobody makes allowances for Louis. I could have borne it all if he had not said that *I* knew Louis was a liar. I'd knock any one down that I was able who should say so! Indeed," continued Reginald, fiercely, "I begged him to leave off, and not provoke me, but he would have it, and he knew what I was."

"Enough—enough—hush," said Dr. Wilkinson: "I beg I may hear no more of knocking down. Don't add to your fault by working yourself into a passion with me. Some provocation you certainly have had, but nothing can justify such unrestrained fury. Consider what would have been your condition at present, if your rage had been fatal to your cousin ; it would have availed you little to have pleaded the aggravation ; your whole life would have been embittered by the indulgence of your vengeful feelings—one moment have destroyed the enjoyment of years. Thank God, Mortimer, that you have been spared so terrible a punishment. But you will always be in danger of this unless you learn to put a curb on your hasty temper. The same feelings which urge you into a quarrel as a boy, will hurry you into the duel as a man. It is a false spirit of honor and manliness that makes you so ready to resent every little insult. In the life of the only perfect Man that ever lived, our great Example and Master, we do not see this impatience of contradiction : 'When He was reviled, He reviled not again ;' and if He, the Lord of all, could condescend to endure such contradiction of sinners against Himself, shall it be too much for us to bear a little with the contradiction of our fellow-creatures ? My boy, if we do not strive to bear a little of the burden and heat of the day, we are not worthy to bear the noble name of Christians."

"I am very sorry, sir," said Reginald, quite softened by the earnest manner of his master ; "I am very sorry I have been so hasty and wrong. I dare not make any promises for the future, for I know I cannot certainly keep them, but, with God's help, I hope to remember what you have so kindly said to me."

"With His help we may do all things," said Dr. Wilkinson ; "you may by this help overcome the stumbling-stone of your violent passions, which otherwise may become an effectual barrier in the way of your attaining the prize of eternal life ; and remember that 'he that is slow to anger is better than the mighty; and he that ruleth his spirit than he that taketh a city.' "

There was a minute's silence, which Reginald broke by asking if he might attend on Frank until he was well.

" Can I hope that you will be gentle," said the doctor; " that you will remember he is an invalid—one of your making, Mortimer; and that if he is impatient and fretful, you are the cause ?"

" I will try, sir, to make amends to him," said Reginald, looking down; " I hope I may be able to be patient."

" I will give orders that you may go to him," said the doctor; and after a pause, he added, "another offence of this kind I shall visit with the heaviest displeasure. I am in hopes that the anxiety you have undergone, and the present state of your cousin, may be a lesson to you; but if I find this ineffectual, I shall cease to consider you a reasonable creature, and shall treat you accordingly."

Dr. Wilkinson then rose and left the room. Reginald lingered a few minutes to compose himself before joining his school-fellows; his heart was very full, and he felt an earnest desire to abide by his master's counsel, as well as grateful for the leniency and kindness with which he had been treated, which made him feel his fault much more deeply than the severest punishment.

The breakfast time was very unpleasant for Louis that morning; he was full of anxiety as to the result of Mr. Witworth s discovery, and his sickness of heart entirely deprived him of appetite. When the meal was dispatched, Reginald went off to Frank, whom he found in a darkened room, very restless and impatient. He had passed a very bad night, and was suffering considerable pain. Reginald had to endure much ill-nature and peevishness; all of which he endeavored to bear with gentleness, and during the time Frank was ill, he gave up all his play-hours to wait on him and to amuse him as he grew better; and the exercise of patience which this office entailed was greatly beneficial to his hasty and proud spirit.

Mr. Danby was in the midst of the second-class lessons that morning, when one of the first class brought him a little slip of paper. Mr. Danby glanced at the few words written thereon, and when the class had finished he desired Louis to go to Dr. Wilkinson. All remnant of color fled from Louis' cheek, though he obeyed without making any reply, and with a very sinking heart entered the room where the doctor was engaged with the first class. The keen eye of his master detected him the instant he made his appearance, but he took no notice of him until he had finished his business; then, while his pupils were putting up their books he turned to Louis, and pointing to a little table by his side, said, " *There* is a volume, Louis Mortimer, with which I suspect you have some acquaintance."

Louis advanced to the table, and beheld the Key to Kenrick's Greek Exercises.

" You know it ?" said the doctor.

" Yes, sir, but I did not use it," said Louis.

" You will not deny that it was found among your books in the school-room," said the doctor.

" I know, sir, Mr. Witworth found it, but I assure you I did not put it there," replied Louis, very gently.

" Have you never used it at all?" asked Dr. Wilkinson.

" Never, sir," replied Louis, firmly.

At this moment, he met the eye of Hamilton, who was

standing near Dr. Wilkinson, and who looked very scorn-fully and incredulously at him as he paused to hear the re-sult of the inquiry. Louis remembered that Hamilton had seen the key Churchill had left, and he hastily exclaimed, " I assure you, Mr. Hamilton, I did not."

" What is this, Hamilton?" said Dr. Wilkinson, turning round. " Do you know any thing of this matter?"

" I would much rather not answer," said Hamilton, abruptly, " if you will excuse me, sir."

" I must, however, beg that you will, if you please," re-plied the doctor.

" I really know nothing positively, I can say nothing cer-tainly. You would not wish, sir, that any imagination of mine should prejudice you to Louis Mortimer's disadvan-tage ; I am not able to say any thing," and Hamilton turned away in some confusion, vexed that he should have been appealed to.

Dr. Wilkinson looked half perplexed—he paused a mo-ment and fixed his eyes on the table. Louis ventured to say, " Mr. Hamilton saw a book once before with my lesson books, but I never used it."

" What do you mean by *saw a book?*" asked the doctor. " What book did Mr. Hamilton see ? How came it there, and why was it there?'

" It was ' Kenrick's Greek Exercises,' sir."

" You mean the ' Key,' I suppose ?"

Louis answered in the affirmative.

" Whose was it?" asked the doctor, with a countenance more ominous in its expression.

" It was the one you took from Harrison, sir," replied Louis.

"Humph! I thought I took it away. Bring it here."
Louis obeyed, and the doctor having looked at it, continued,
"Well, you had this *with your lesson books*, you say. How
did it come there?"

"One of the boys gave it to me, sir," replied Louis.

"And why did you not put it away?"

"I was going, sir;" and the color rushed into Louis'
pale face. "I did not use it—and I hope I should not."

"Who left the book?" asked Dr. Wilkinson.

"Churchill, sir."

"Call Churchill, Salisbury."

Salisbury obeyed; and during his absence a profound
silence reigned in the room, for all the first class were
watching the proceedings in deep interest. Dr. Wilkinson
seemed lost in thought; and Louis, in painful anxiety,
scanned the strongly marked countenance of his master,
now wearing its most unpleasing mask, and those of Hamilton and Trevannion, alternately. Hamilton did not look
at him, but bent over a table at a book, the leaves of which
he nervously turned. Trevannion eyed him haughtily as
he leaned in his most graceful attitude against the wall behind the doctor's chair; and poor Louis read his condemnation in his eyes, as well as in the faces of most present.

Salisbury at length returned with Churchill, who was
the more awe-struck at the unwonted summons, as he was
so low in the school as seldom to have any business with
the principal.

"Churchill," said the doctor, gravely, "I have sent for
you to hear what is said of you. Now, Louis Mortimer,
who gave you this book on the day Mr. Hamilton discovered it in your possession?"

"Churchill, sir," replied Louis, in great agitation ; "you did, Churchill, did you not? Oh! do say you did."

"Hush," said the doctor. "What have you to say against this, Churchill?"

"Nothing, sir—I did—I gave it to Louis Mortimer," stammered Churchill, looking from Louis to the doctor, and back again.

"And how came you to give it to him?"

Churchill did not reply until the question was repeated, when he reluctantly said, he had given it to Louis to assist him in his exercise.

"Did Mortimer ask you for it?"

"No, sir."

"Did he wish for it?"

"No, sir, not that I know of."

"You know, Harry, that I asked you to put it away—did I not?" cried Louis.

"I don't know—yes—I think you did," said Churchill, growing very hot.

"Why did you not put it away?" asked Dr. Wilkinson.

"Because I thought he wanted it, please sir."

"But I did not, Harry! I told you I did not," said Louis, eagerly.

Dr. Wilkinson desired Louis to be silent, and continued his questions—

"Did you try to persuade him to use it?"

Again Churchill paused, and again confessed, most unwillingly, that he had done so—and received a severe reprimand for his conduct on the occasion, and a long task to write out which would keep him employed during the play-hours of that day.

He was then dismissed, and Dr. Wilkinson again addressed himself to Louis: "I am glad to find that part of your story is correct; but I now wish you to explain how my key found its way into the school-room yesterday, when discovered by Mr. Witworth. The book must have been deliberately taken out of this room into the school-room. You appear to have been alone, or nearly so, in the school-room the greater part of yesterday afternoon, and Mr. Witworth found the book half concealed by your lesson books while you were writing your exercises."

"I assure you, sir, I did not take it," said Louis.

"Unhappily," replied Dr. Wilkinson, "I cannot take a mere assurance in the present instance. Had not the case been so palpable, I should have been bound to believe you until I had had reason to mistrust your word—but with these facts I *cannot*, Louis;" and he added, in a very low tone, so as to be heard only by Louis, who was much nearer to him than the others, "Your honor has not always been sacred—beware."

His school-fellows wondered what made the red flush mount so furiously in Louis' forehead, and the tears spring to his eyes. The painful feelings called forth by his master's speech prevented him from speaking for a few minutes. He was roused by Dr. Wilkinson saying—

"The discovery of this Key in your possession would involve your immediate dismissal from the second class, a sufficient disgrace, but the matter assumes a far more serious aspect from these assertions of innocence. If you had not used the book when discovered, it must have been taken either by you, or another, for use. The question is now, who took it?"

"I did not, sir," said Louis, in great alarm.

"Who did, then?   Were any of your class with you?"

"No, sir."

"Was any one with you?"

Louis paused.   A sudden thought flashed across him—a sudden recollection of seeing that book passed over and slipped among his books; an action he had taken no notice of at the time, and which had never struck him till this moment.   He now glanced eagerly at Ferrers, and then, in a tremulous voice, said, "I remember now, Ferrers put it there—I am almost sure."

"Ferrers!" exclaimed the young men, with one voice.

"What humbugging nonsense!" said Salisbury, in a low tone.

"Do you hear, Mr. Ferrers?" said the doctor: "how came you to put that Key among Louis Mortimer's books?"

"I, sir—I never," stammered Ferrers.   "What should I want with it?   What good could I get by it?   Is it likely?"

"I am not arguing on the possibility of such an event, I simply wish to know if you did it?" said the doctor.

"I, sir—no," exclaimed Ferrers, with an air of injured innocence.   "If I had done it, why did he not accuse me at once, instead of remembering it all of a sudden?"

"Because I only just remembered that I saw you moving something towards me, and I am *almost* sure it was that book now—I think so," replied Louis.

"You'd better be quite sure," said Ferrers.

Dr. Wilkinson looked from one to the other, and his look might have made a less unprincipled youth fear to persist in so horrible a falsehood.

" Were you learning your lessons in the school-room yesterday afternoon, Mr. Ferrers, at the same time with Louis
Mortimer?" Ferrers acknowledging this, Dr. Wilkinson
sent for Mr. Witworth, and asked him if he had observed
either Ferrers or Louis go into the study during the afternoon, and if he knew what each brought out with him.
Mr. Witworth replied that both went in, but he did not
know what for.

" I went in to get an atlas for Ferrers," cried Louis, in
great agitation.

" I got the atlas myself, Mortimer, you know," said
Ferrers.

Louis was quite overcome. He covered his face with
his hands, and burst into tears.

" This is a sad business," said Dr. Wilkinson, very
gravely; " much worse than I expected—one of you must
be giving utterance to the most frightful untruths. Which
of you is it?"

" What would Ferrers want with the Key to the Greek
Exercises, sir?" suggested Trevannion, " unless he wished
to do an ill turn to Mortimer, which you cannot suppose."

" I have hitherto trusted Mr. Ferrers," replied Dr. Wilkinson; " and am not disposed to withdraw that confidence
without sufficient cause. Mr. Ferrers, on your word of
honor, am I to believe your statement?"

Ferrers turned pale, but the doctor's steady gaze was
upon him, and all his class-fellows awaited his reply—visions
of disgrace, contempt, and scorn were before him, and there
was no restraining power from within to check him, as he
hastily replied, " On my word of honor, sir."

" I must believe you, then, as I can imagine no motive

which could induce you to act dishonorably by this boy;
were I to discover that any one in my school had acted so,
his immediate expulsion should be the consequence."

The dead silence that followed the doctor's words struck
coldly on the heart of the guilty coward.

"Now, Louis Mortimer," said the doctor, sternly, "I
wish to give you another chance of confessing your fault."

Louis' thick convulsive sobs only replied to this. After
waiting a few minutes, Dr. Wilkinson said, "Go now to
the little study joining my dining-room, and wait there till
I come: I shall give you half an hour to consider."

Louis left the room, and repaired to the study, where he
threw himself on a chair in a paroxysm of grief, which,
for the first quarter of an hour, admitted of no alleviation :
" He had no character. The doctor had heard all before.
All believed him guilty—and how *could* Ferrers act so ?
How could it ever be found out ? And, oh! his dear
father and mother, and his grandfather, would believe it."

By degrees the violence of his distress subsided, and he
sent up his tearful petitions to his heavenly Father, till his
overloaded heart felt lightened of some of its sorrow. As
he grew calmer, remembrances of old faults came before
him, and he thought of a similar sin of his own, and how
nearly an innocent person had suffered for it—and this he
felt was much easier to bear than the consciousness of having committed the fault himself ; and he remembered the
sweet verses in the first Epistle of St. Peter : " What glory
is it if, when ye be buffeted for your faults, ye take it
patiently ; but if when ye do well and suffer for it, ye take
it patiently, this is acceptable with God. For even here-
unto ye were called, because Christ also suffered for us,

leaving us an example that we should follow His steps:
who did no sin, neither was guile found in His mouth; who,
when He was reviled, reviled not again ; when He suffered,
He threatened not; but committed Himself to Him that
judgeth righteously,"—and the feeling of indignation
against Ferrers was gradually changed into almost pity for
him, for Louis knew by experience the pain of a loaded
conscience.   While his thoughts thus ran over the past and
present, he heard the firm step of Dr. Wilkinson crossing
the hall, and nearly at the same moment that gentleman
entered the room.   There was no pity in his countenance—
the dark lines in his face seemed fixed in their most iron
mould ; and briefly announcing to his trembling pupil that
the time allowed him for consideration had expired, he asked
whether he were prepared to acknowledge his fault.   Louis
meekly persisted in his denial, which had only the effect of
making the doctor consider him a more hardened offender;
and after a few words, expressing the strongest reprehension of his wickedness and cowardice, he gave him a severe
caning, and sent him immediately to bed, although it was
but the middle of the day.   In spite of the better feelings
which urged poor Louis to acknowledge the justice, under
the circumstances, of his master's proceedings, he could
not help thinking that he had been very hardly treated.
He hurried up stairs, glad to indulge his grief in silence.
How many times, in the affliction of the next few hours,
did he repeat a little hymn he had learned at home :

> " Thy lambs, dear Shepherd, that are weak,
>   Are thy peculiar care ;
> 'Tis Thine in judgment to afflict,
>   And Thine in love to spare.

"Though young in years, yet, oh! how oft
    Have I a rebel been;
My punishment, O Lord, is mild,
    Nor equals all my sin.

"Since all the chastisements I feel
    Are from Thy love alone,
Let not one murmuring thought arise,
    But may Thy will be done.

"Then let me blush with holy shame,
    And mourn before my Lord,
That I have lived to Thee no more,
    No more obeyed Thy word."*

At last he fell asleep, and oh! to wake from that sleep! It was surely good to be afflicted, and in the happiness of his mind Louis forgot his trouble. But he had yet to endure much more, and the bitterest part of his punishment came the next morning, when, according to his master's orders, he repaired to the study with his books. He had been desired to remain in this room out of school-hours, and was forbidden to speak to any of his school-fellows without leave. While he was sitting there the first morning after the inquiry related in this chapter, Dr. Wilkinson entered with a letter, and sat down at the table where Louis was reading. As he opened his desk, he said, "I have a painful task to perform. This is a letter from your father, Louis Mortimer, and he particularly requests that I should give him an account of your conduct and your brother's; you know what an account I can give of you both."

Louis had listened very attentively to his master's speech, and when it was concluded he gave way to such a burst of

* "Hymns for Sunday-Schools."

sorrow as quite touched the doctor. For some minutes he wept almost frantically, and then clasping his hands, he implored Dr. Wilkinson not to tell his father what had happened : "It will break mamma's heart, it will break mamma's heart, sir—do not tell my father."

"Confess your fault, Louis, and I may then speak of amendment," said the doctor.

"I cannot, indeed—indeed I cannot. It will all come out by and bye : you will see, sir—oh ! you will see, sir," sobbed Louis, deprecating the gathering of the angry cloud on the doctor's face. "Oh ! do not tell mamma, for it is not true."

"I do not wish to hear any more, sir," said the doctor, sternly.

"Oh ! what shall I do—what shall I do !" cried Louis ; and he pushed his chair quickly from the table, and, throwing himself on his knees by Dr. Wilkinson, seized the hand that was beginning to date the dreaded letter—"I assure you I did not, sir—I am speaking the truth."

"As you always do, doubtless," said the doctor, drawing his hand roughly away. "Get up, sir ; kneel to Him you have so deeply offended, but not to me."

Louis rose, but stood still in the same place. "Will you hear only this one thing, sir ? I will not say any thing more about my innocence—just hear me, if you please, sir."

Dr. Wilkinson turned his head coldly towards him.

Louis dried his tears, and spoke with tolerable calmness : "I have one thing to ask, sir—will you allow me still to remain in the second class, and to do my lessons always in this room ? You will then see if I can do without keys, or having any help."

"I know you can if you choose," replied Dr. Wilkinson, coldly, "or I should not have placed you in that class."

"But, if you please, sir, I know all,"—Louis paused, he had promised to say no more on that subject.

There was a little silence, during which Dr. Wilkinson looked earnestly at Louis. At last he said, "You may stay in the class; but, remember, you are forbidden to speak to any of your school-fellows for the next week without express permission."

"Not to my brother, sir?"

"No; now go."

"May I write to mamma?"

"Yes, if you wish it."

After timidly thanking the doctor, Louis returned to his seat, and Dr. Wilkinson continued his letter, which went off by the same post that took Louis' to his mother.

CHAPTER V.

"Now no chastening for the present seemeth to be joyous, but gr.ev-
ous; nevertheless, afterward it yieldeth the peaceable fruit of
righteousness unto them which are exercised thereby."—*Heb.* xii. 11.
"Before I was afflicted I went astray, but now have I kept Thy
word."—*Psalm* cxix. 67.

PERHAPS there is no state more dangerous to a Christian's
peace of mind than one of continual prosperity. In adversity even the worldly man will sometimes talk of resigna-
tion, and feel that it is a good thing to be acquainted and
at peace with God, and that when all human help is cut
off, it is a sweet thing to have a sure refuge in an almighty
Saviour. But in prosperity the ungodly never look to
Him; and His own children, carrying about with them a
sinful nature, against which they must continually maintain
a warfare, are too apt to forget the Giver in his gifts, and
to imagine that all is well because nothing occurs to disturb
the regularity of their blessings.

Our little Louis, though the trial he now underwent was
a bitter one, and though at times it seemed almost too hard
to be endured, learned by degrees to feel that it was good
for him. He had been in too high favor, he had trusted
too much in the good word of his school-fellows, and had

suffered the fear of man to deter him from his duty to God ;
and now, isolated and looked upon as an unworthy member
of the little society to which he belonged, he learned to find
his sole happiness in that sweet communion which he had
now solitary leisure to enjoy.   His very troubles carried him
to a throne of grace ; his desolate condition made him feel
that there was only One who never changed nor forsook
His people ; only One who could understand and feel for
the infirmities and sorrows of a human creature ; and though
to the ungodly it is a terror to know that there is "nothing
that is not manifest in God's sight," to the true child of
God it is an unspeakable comfort to feel that his thoughts
and actions are "known long before" by his unwearied
Guardian.

The effects of Louis' lonely communings were soon visible in his daily conduct, and after his term of punishment
had expired, the meekness of his bearing, and the gentle
lowliness of his demeanor, often disarmed the most severe
and unpitying of his youthful judges.   There was no ser-
vility in his manner, for he neither courted nor shunned ob-
servation ; nor, though he was as willing as ever to do a
kind action for any one, did he allow himself to be persuaded to give up all his time to his idler school-fellows.
There seemed more firmness and decision in his naturally
yielding disposition, and those who knew not the power of
assisting grace, looked and wondered at the firmness the
sweet but weak boy could at times assume.   He would have
told them it was not his own.   He was very quiet, and spoke
little, even to his brother, of what was passing in his mind,
and sometimes his thoughts were so quietly happy that he
did not like to be spoken to.   To Ferrers, Louis was as gen-

tle and courteous as to the rest of his companions, and, indeed, he had now little other feeling towards him than that
of sorrow and pity.

There had been an unusual noise in the study one evening, while Louis was absent, and when he entered it, he
found the confusion attendant on a grand uproar. Very
little was doing, and tokens of the late skirmish lay about
the floor in torn and scattered books, and overthrown forms.
Among others, Ferrers was hunting for a missing book, but
to discover it in such a chaos was a difficult task, especially
as no one would now allow the candles to be used in the
search.

With many expressions, so unfitted for refined ears that
I do not choose to present them to my reader, Ferrers continued his search, now and then attempting to snatch a candle from the table, in which he was regularly foiled by
those sitting there.

"Well, at least have the civility to move and let me see
if it is under the table," he said at length.

"You have hindered us long enough," said Salisbury;
"Smith, Jones, and I have done nothing to-night. If you
will have rows, you must e'en take the consequences."

"Can't you get under the form?" asked Smith, de-
risively.

Ferrers was going to make some angry reply, when
Louis dived between the table and the form, with some
trouble, and, at the expense of receiving a few uncere-
monious kicks, recovered the book and gave it to Ferrers, who hardly thanked him, but leaning his head on
his hand, seemed almost incapable of doing any thing.
Presently he looked up, and asked in a tone of mingled

anger and weariness, what had become of the inkstand
he had brought.

> " Loosing's seeking,
> Finding's keeping,"

said Salisbury.   " Which is yours ?   Perhaps it's under the
table too."

" Hold your nonsense," cried Ferrers, angrily.   " It's very
shabby of you to hinder me in this manner."

Louis quietly slipped an inkstand near him, an action of
which Ferrers was quite aware, and though he pretended
not to notice it, he availed himself presently of the convenience.   A racking headache, however, almost disabled
him from thinking, and though he was really unwell, there
was only the boy he had so cruelly injured who felt any
sympathy for his suffering.

Louis carefully avoided any direct manifestation of his
anxiety to return good for evil, for he felt, though he hardly
knew why, that his actions would be misconstrued, but
whenever any little opportunity occurred in which he could
really render any service, he was always as ready to do it
for Ferrers as for another; and now, when from his class-
mates Ferrers met with nothing but jokes on his " beautiful temper," and " placid state of mind," he could not help
feeling the gentleness of Louis' conduct, the absence of
pleasure in his annoyance, and the look of evident sympathy he met whenever he accidentally turned his eyes in
his direction.   For a few days after this he was obliged to
keep his bed, and during this time, though Louis only once
saw him, he thought of every little kind attention he could,
that might be grateful to the invalid.   Knowing that he
was not a favorite, and that few in the school would trouble

themselves about him, he borrowed books and sent them to him for his amusement, and empowered the old cake man to procure some grapes, which he sent up to him by a servant, with strict orders to say nothing of where they came from. The servant met Hamilton at the door of the room, and he relieved her of her charge, and as she did not consider herself under promise of secrecy towards him, she mentioned it, desiring him at the same time to say nothing to Ferrers.

Louis had now established a regular time for doing his own lessons, and kept to it with great perseverance to the end of the half-year, with one exception, when he had been acting prisoner in a trial performed in the school-room, by half his own class and the third, and let the evening slip by without remembering how late it grew. His class-fellows were in the same predicament as himself, and as they had barely time to write a necessary exercise, they agreed among themselves to learn each his own piece of the lesson they had to repeat. Louis did not seriously consider the deceit they were practising, and adopted the same plan. One of the number, not trusting to his memory, hit upon the singular expedient of writing the whole of his piece and the next on a piece of paper, and wafering it to the instep of his shoe when he went up to his class. Unhappily for his scheme, he was so placed that he dared not expose his foot so as to allow him to avail himself of this delectable assistance, and consequently, after much looking on the floor for inspiration, and much incoherent muttering, was passed over, and the order of things being thereby disturbed, of course no one could say the missing lines until the head boy was applied to, and the lower half of the class was turned down, with the exception of Louis, who, standing on this occasion just above the gentleman of shoe memory, had been able to say his share.

As they were breaking up, Mr. Danby said to Louis, "You have been very industrious lately, Louis Mortimer: I am glad you have been so correct to-day."

Louis blushed from a consciousness of undeserved praise; but though his natural fear of offending and losing favor sprung up directly, a higher principle faced it, and bearing down all obstacles, forced him to acknowledge his unworthiness of the present encomium.

"I ought to learn mine, sir,—I learned my piece to-day."

"What do you mean?" asked Mr. Danby.

"I learned my part of the lesson, as well as Harris, Williams, Sutton, and Charles Salisbury. We forgot our lessons last night, but it is quite an accident that I have said mine to-day."

"I am glad you have had the honor to say so," said Mr. Danby. "Of course you must learn yours, but let me have no more learning pieces, if you please."

CHAPTER VI.

" Blessed are they that dwell in Thy house, they will be still prais-
ing Thee.   For a day in Thy courts is better than a thousand.
I had rather be a door-keeper in the house of my God, than to
dwell in the tents of wickedness."—*Psalm* lxxxiv. 4, 10.

DR. WILKINSON's school was too large to be entirely
accommodated with sittings in the nearest church—and,
consequently, was divided into two bodies on Sunday, one
of which regularly attended one of the churches in Bristol,
where Mr. Wilkinson, the doctor's son, occasionally did
duty.   It fell to Louis' lot, generally, to be of the Bristol
party, and unless the day was rainy he was not ill-pleased
with his destiny, for the walk was very pleasant, and there
was something in the chorus of bells in that many-churched
city, and the sight of the gray towers and spires, very con-
genial to his feelings.   It happened that the Sunday after
Louis had received permission to mix as usual with his
school-fellows was one of those peculiarly sunny days that
seem to call upon God's people especially to rejoice and be
glad in the works of His hand.   Louis' mind was in a more
than usually peaceful state, and his heart overflowed with
quiet happiness as he looked down from the height of
Brandon Hill upon the city below.   He and his companion

had walked on rather faster than the rest of their school-
fellows, and now stood waiting till they came up.

" A penny for your thoughts, Mortimer," said his companion, a pleasant-looking boy of fifteen or sixteen years of
age; "you are very silent to-day—what may be the subject of your profound meditations?"

Louis hardly seemed to hear the question, for he suddenly turned his bright face to his interrogator, and exclaimed, "What a beautiful sight it is to see so many
churches together, Meredith! I think our churches make
us such a happy country."

"Upon my word," replied Meredith, "you are endowing
those piles of stone with considerable potency.   What becomes of commerce and—"

"I mean, of course," interrupted Louis, "that it is religion that makes us a happier country than others.   I love
so to look at the churches; the sight of one sometimes,
when all is fair and quiet, brings the tears into my eyes."

"Hey-dey! quite sentimental!   You'd better be a par-
son, I think."

" I hope I shall be a clergyman—I wish very much to
be one—there is not such another happy life.   I was just
thinking, Meredith, when you spoke to me, of a verse we
read yesterday morning, which quite expresses my feelings :
'One thing have I desired of the Lord which I will seek
after, that I may dwell in the house of the Lord all the
days of my life, to behold the fair beauty of the Lord, and
to inquire in His temple.' "

Meredith looked with some surprise at Louis, and as
they moved on he said carelessly, "I suppose somebody
will have the gratification of beholding me in a long gown

some day, holding forth for the edification of my devoted flock."

"Are you going to be a clergyman ?" asked Louis.

"Yes, I suppose I must. Don't you think I shall be a most useful character ?"

"Oh ! surely you wish it, do you not ?"

"Well, I don't much mind," replied Meredith, snatching a handful of leaves from the hedge near him ; " I shall have a nice fat living, and it's a respectable kind of thing."

Louis was horror-struck—he had not imagined such an idea—he almost gasped out, "Oh! Meredith, I can hardly understand you. Surely that is not your only wish about it : that cannot be a reason—not a right one."

"Why, what's the harm ?" said Meredith, laughing. " I only say outright what hundreds think. If I could choose, perhaps I might like the army best, but my father has a comfortable provision in the church for me, and so I, like a dutiful son, don't demur, especially as, if I follow the ex-ample of my predecessor, it will be vastly more easy than a soldier's life."

"Meredith, Meredith, this is too solemn a thing to laugh about. I have often wondered how it is there are clergy-men who can take their duties so easily as some do ; but if they only undertake them for your reasons, I cannot feel so much surprised that they should be so careless. How can you expect any happiness from such a life ! I should be afraid to talk so."

Meredith stared contemptuously. " You are a Methodist, Louis," he said ; " I have no doubt I shall preach as good sermons as you : just put on a grave face, and use a set of tender phrases, and wear a brilliant on your little finger,

and a curly head, and there you are a fashionable preacher
at once—and if you use your white pocket-handkerchief
occasionally, throw your arms about a little, look as if you
intended to tumble over the pulpit and embrace the con-
gregation, and dose your audience with a little pathos, you
may draw crowds—the ladies will idolize you."

"I should not think that such popularity would be very
good," replied Louis, "supposing you could do as you say;
but it seems to me quite shocking to speak in such a slight-
ing manner of so holy a thing.   Were you ever at an ordination, Meredith?"

"Not I," said Meredith.

"I should think if you had been you would be afraid to
think of going to answer the solemn questions you will be
asked when you are ordained.   I was once with papa at
an ordination at Norwich cathedral, and I shall never forget how solemnly that beautiful service came upon me.   I
could not help thinking how dreadful it must be to come
there carelessly, and I wondered how the gentlemen felt
who were kneeling there—and the hymn was so magnificent, Meredith.   I think if you were there with your present feelings, you would be afraid to stay.   It would seem
like mocking God to come to answer all those solemn questions, and not mean what you said.   I think it is wicked."

Louis spoke rapidly, and with great emotion.

Meredith looked angry, struggling with a feeling of shame,
and a wish to laugh it off.   "You are exclusively precise,"
he said; "others are not, and have as much right to their
opinion as you to yours.   Trevannion, for instance—he's
going into the church because it is so genteel."

"I hope you are mistaken," said Louis, quickly.

"Not I; I heard him say the same thing myself."

"I am *very* sorry," said Louis, sadly. "Oh! I would rather be a laborer than go into the church with such a wish—and yet, I had rather be a very poor curate than a rich duke: it is such a happy, holy life." The last part of Louis' speech was nearly inaudible, and no more was said until the afternoon.

It was Dr. Wilkinson's wish that the Sabbath should be passed as blamelessly as he had the power of ordering it in his household; but to make it a day of reverence and delight among so large a number of boys, with different dispositions and habits of life, was an arduous task. Mr. James Wilkinson was with the boys the whole afternoon, as well as his father, to whose utmost endeavors he joined his own, that the day might not be wholly unprofitable. In spite, however, of all diligence, it could not fail of often being grossly misspent with many of the pupils; for it is not possible for human power effectually to influence the heart, and, until that is done, any thing else can be but an outward form.

This afternoon the boys were scattered over the large playground. In one corner was the doctor, with twenty or thirty boys around him, and in other directions, the different ushers hearing Catechisms and other lessons. Some of the parties were very dull, for no effort was made by the instructor to impart a real delight in the Word of God to his pupils; and religion was made merely a matter of question and answer, to remain engraved in such heartless form on the repugnant mind of the learner. And, alas! how can it be otherwise, where the teacher himself does not know that religion is a real and happy thing, and not to be learned as we teach our boys the outlines of heathen mythology ?

Sitting on the ground, lolling against one of the benches under a tree, sat Hastings Meredith and Reginald and Louis Mortimer ; and one or two more were standing or sitting near ; all of whom had just finished answering all the questions in the Church Catechism to Mr. Danby, and had said a Psalm.

Louis was sitting on the bench, looking flushed, thinking of holidays, and, of course, of home,—home Sabbaths, those brightest days of home life,—when Trevannion came up with his usual air of cool, easy confidence. Trevannion was the most gentlemanly young man in the school ; he never was in a hurry ; was particularly alive to any thing " vulgar," or " snobbish," and would have thought it especially unbecoming in him to exhibit the smallest degree of annoyance at any untoward event. It took a good deal to put him out of countenance, and he esteemed it rather plebeian to go his own errands, or, indeed, to take any unnecessary trouble.

" Were you in Bristol this morning, Meredith ?" he said.

" Yes, sure, your highness," replied Meredith, yawning.

" Tired apparently," said Trevannion ironically, glancing at the recumbent attitude of the speaker.

" Worried to death with that old bore Danby, who's been going backwards and forwards for the last hour, with ' What is your name ?' and ' My good child,' &c. I'm as tired as—as—oh help me for as imile ! as a pair of worn-out shoes."

" A poetical simile at last," remarked Reginald, laughing.

" You would have a nice walk," said Trevannion.

" Very! and a sermon gratis to boot," replied Meredith.
" It would have done you good, Trevannion, to have heard
what shocking things you have done in being so *very
genteel.*"

" What do you mean ?" said Trevannion, coolly.

" Louis Mortimer was giving me a taste of his Methodis-
tical mind on the duties of clergymen generally, and your
humble servant especially."

" I presume you do not include yourself in the fraternity
yet ?" said Trevannion.

" Not exactly ; but having informed him of my prospects,
the good child began to upbraid me with my hypocrisy,
and, bless you, such a thundering sermon,—positively quite
eloquent."

" Perhaps I may be allowed to profit by the second part
of it," said Trevannion, turning to Louis ; " will you be
kind enough to edify me ?"

Louis did not reply, and Trevannion's lips curled slightly
as he remarked, " There is an old proverb about those who
live in glass houses—'Physician, cure thyself.' "

Poor Louis turned away, and Meredith, stretching himself and yawning terrifically, continued, " You must know,
Trevannion, that it is very wicked to be any thing but a
Methodist, very wicked for a clergyman to be genteel, or to
wish to make himself comfortable."

" Hastings, I did not say so," said Louis, turning his head.

" And so," continued Meredith, without noticing Louis,
" if we dare to follow up our own or our fathers' wishes,
we must listen to Louis Mortimer, and he will tell us what
to do."

"Much obliged to him, I am sure," said Trevannion.

"Yes, so am I," rejoined Meredith, "though I forgot to tender my thanks before; and hereby give notice, that when I am in orders, I will not hunt more than convenient, nor play cards on Good Friday, nor go to dancing parties on Saturday evening."

"Pshaw, Meredith," said Trevannion: "it is very unbecoming to talk in this manner of so sacred a profession. A hunting and card-playing clergyman ought to be stripped of his gown without hesitation. Any right-minded person would recoil with horror at such a character. It is a great disgrace to the profession; no clergyman ought to enter into any kind of improper dissipation. Your ideas are very light and indelicate."

"Will you be kind enough to define that term, *improper dissipation*," said Meredith, carelessly. "I presume you have no objection to a quiet dance now and then, only they must not call it a ball."

"A clergyman ought not to dance," replied Trevannion, in precisely the same cool, dictatorial manner.

"He may look on them, may he not?" said Meredith.

"A clergyman has many serious duties to perform, and he should be very careful that he does not degrade his office," replied Trevannion. "He has to uphold the dignity of the church, and should take care that his conduct is such that no reproach can fall on that church from his inconsistency."

"Well, for my part," said Meredith, lightly, "I think the church too important to miss the weight of my example. I mean to have a most exemplary curate."

Near these speakers sat Mr. James Wilkinson, with a few

little boys, whom at this moment he hastily dismissed, for
the sound of the light conversation reached him, and he
arose quickly and introduced himself to the little côterie
just as Reginald exclaimed, "For shame, Meredith!"

"Ay, for shame," said Mr. James: "I have heard a
little of what has been going on among you, and am really
very sorry to hear such expressions on a subject so solemn
and important. Meredith, you cannot be aware of what
you are saying. I should like to have a little talk about
this matter; and, Mr. Trevannion, if you will give me your
attention for a few minutes, I shall be obliged to you."

Trevannion seated himself on the bench, and folding his
arms, remained in an attitude of passive attention.

"Lend me your prayer-book, Mortimer," said Mr. James,
and he quickly turned to the service for the ordering of
deacons. "The first question here put to the candidate for
holy orders is, 'Do you trust that you are inwardly moved
by the Holy Ghost, to take upon you this office and minis-
tration, to serve God for the promoting of His glory and
the edifying of His people?' Now, Meredith, I ask you
to think, whether, with such sentiments as you have just
expressed, you can dare to answer, '*I trust so?*'"

"I never thought very seriously about it," said Meredith,
rather abruptly.

"But you know these things must be thought of seriously and prayerfully. It is required of a man in every
station of life, that he be faithful and diligent, serving the
Lord, and whoever does not remember this, must answer
for his neglect of such duty to his Maker. It will not do
to say that our individual example can be of no importance;
the command, 'Occupy till I come,' is laid upon each one

of us; but what must be said of him who, in a careless, light frame of mind, takes these holy vows upon him, knowing in his own mind that he intends to break them; that his sole desire to be put into the priest's office is to eat a morsel of bread? What shall be said of him who goes into the house of God, and in the presence of His people declares that it is his intention, ' to search gladly and willingly for the sick and poor of his parish, to relieve their necessities; to frame his own life and the lives of his family according to the doctrine of Christ; to be diligent in prayers and in reading of the Holy Scriptures, laying aside the study of the world and the flesh,' and yet knows that he intends to enjoy himself in the things of this world—a very hireling who forgets that his master's eye is upon him. It is a fearful thing. It is coming before the Almighty with a lie. Nay, hear me a little longer. The clergyman's is a glorious and exalted path, the happiest I know of on earth. It is his especially to bear the message of salvation from a tender Saviour. It is his to go forth with the balm of heavenly comfort, to bind up the wounds sin and grief have made. It is his indeed pre-eminently to dwell in the house of his God, to be hid away from the world and its many allurements; but as every great blessing brings with it a great responsibility, so the responsibility of the minister of Christ is very great, and if he turn from the commandment delivered to him, his condemnation is fearful. I should be much obliged to you, Meredith, if you would read me these verses."

Meredith took the open Bible from Mr. Wilkinson's hand, and read aloud the first ten verses of the 34th of Ezekiel.

"In this holy word, which must be the standard for all our conduct, we do not find that the Almighty looks upon this office as a light thing. In the thirty-third chapter there is so solemn a warning to the careless watchman, that I wonder any one who does not steadfastly intend to give himself to his sacred duties, can read it and not tremble. 'If the watchman see the sword come, and blow not the trumpet, and the people be not warned; if the sword come, and take away any person from among them, he is taken away in his iniquity; but HIS BLOOD WILL I REQUIRE AT THE WATCHMAN'S HAND. So thou, O son of man, I have set thee a watchman unto the house of Israel; therefore thou shalt hear the word at my mouth, and warn them from me. When I say unto the wicked, Oh wicked man, thou shalt surely die; if thou dost not speak to warn the wicked from his way, that wicked man shall die in his iniquity; but his blood will I require at thine hand.' This is the second solemn warning to the same purport given to Ezekiel; for, in the third chapter, we find the same thing; and these are awful truths engraved in God's everlasting word, by which we are to be judged at the last day. You must excuse me," continued Mr. Wilkinson, and his eyes glistened with emotion; "but I am a watchman, and I must warn you of the fearful sin you are contemplating."

Meredith was silent. He was impressed with the earnestness displayed by Mr. Wilkinson, and the solemn truths he had brought before him—truths it would be well if all those who are looking forward to entering the sacred ministry would seriously and prayerfully consider.

The tea bell ringing at this moment, the conversation was necessarily concluded; but that evening after prayers,

Mr. Wilkinson put into Meredith's hand a piece of paper, on which were written the following references: Num. xvi. 9; Isaiah lii. 7, 8; lxii. 6, 7; Jer. xxiii. 1—4; Ezek. iii. 17—21; xxxiii. 1—9; xxxiv. 1—10; John xxi. 15—17; 1 Cor. ix. 16, 17, 19; and both the Epistles to Timothy; and underneath the references was the Apostle's injunction, "Meditate upon these things; give thyself wholly to them, that thy profiting may appear unto all."

When Louis was fairly in bed that night, he was called on for a story.

"Tell us the end of the princess Rosetta, Louis," cried Frank; "I want to know how the fair animal got out of her watery bedroom, and whether the green dog ever got his nose nipped by the oysters he was so fond of snapping up."

"Yes, Rosetta!" cried several voices. "Did she ever get to the king of the peacocks, Louis?"

"No, no," cried Reginald; "it is not fit for Sunday."

"I am sure we have been doing heaps of good things to-day," replied Frank, lightly; "come, Louis."

"I must not," said Louis, gently. "I do not like telling stories at night at all, because I think we ought not to fill our heads with such things when we are going to sleep; but I must not tell you Rosetta to-night, Frank."

"Get along," said Frank, contemptuously; "you are not worth the snap of a finger. All you are ever worth is to tell stories, and now you must needs set up for a good, pious boy—you, forsooth, of all others!"

"Indeed, Frank, you will not understand me."

"If you dare to say any more to Louis," cried Reginald, "I'll make you—"

Louis' hand was upon Reginald's mouth.

Frank replied, tauntingly, "Ay, finish your work this time, that's right. Come boys, never mind, I'll tell you a wonderful tale."

"I think we'd better not have one to-night," said one; "perhaps Mortimer's right."

"Don't have one, don't!" said Louis, starting up; "do not let us forget that all this day is God's day, and that we must not even speak our own words."

"None of your cant," cried one.

"Well, I propose that we go to sleep, and then we shan't hear what he says," said Meredith. "They talk of his not having pluck enough to speak, but he can do it when he pleases," he remarked in a low tone to his next companion, Frank Digby, who rejoined,

"More shame for him, the little hypocrite. I like real religious people, but I can't bear cant."

What Frank's idea of real religion was, may be rather a difficult matter to settle. Probably it was an obscure idea to himself,—an idea of certain sentiment and no vitality.

CHAPTER VII.

THE next Saturday afternoon proving unusually fine, the community at Ashfield House sallied forth to enjoy their half-holiday on the downs. A few of the seniors had received permission to pay a visit to Bristol, and not a small party was arranged for a good game of cricket. Among the latter was Reginald Mortimer, whose strong arm and swift foot were deemed almost indispensable on such occasions. As he rushed out of the playground gates, bat in hand, accompanied by Meredith, he overtook his brother, who had discovered a poem unknown to him in *Coleridge's Ancient Mariner*, and was anticipating a pleasant mental feast in its perusal.

"Louis, you lazy fellow," cried Reginald, good-temperedly, "you shan't read this fine afternoon—come, join us."

"I don't play cricket, I have not learned," replied Louis.

"And you never will," rejoined Reginald, "if you don't make a beginning: I'll teach you—now put away that stupid book."

"*Stupid!*" said Louis. "It's Coleridge, that mamma promised to read to us."

"I hate poetry," exclaimed Reginald; "I wonder how anybody can read such stuff. Give me the book, Louis, and come along."

"No, thank you, I'd rather not."

"What a donkey you are!" said Meredith: "why don't you learn?"

"Perhaps my reputation may be the safer for not divulging my reasons," said Louis, archly: "it is sufficient for present purposes that I had rather not."

"*Rather not—rather not,*" echoed Meredith: "like one of your sensible reasons."

"He has refused to give them, so you cannot call that his reason, Meredith," remarked Reginald; "but let us be off, as Louis won't come."

Away they ran, and after looking at them for a minute, Louis turned off his own way, but it was destined that he should not read the *Ancient Mariner* that day, for he was presently interrupted by little Alfred Hamilton, who pounced upon him full of joy.

"Louis," he cried, "I am so glad to speak to you! I don't know how it is that I have not been able to speak to you lately: I half thought Edward did not like it, but he asked me to-day why I did not come to you now."

"Did he?" exclaimed Louis, with joyful surprise; "I am very glad you are come. I think we shall have a beautiful walk."

"I can't think how it is, Louis, that everybody is either so grave or rude when I speak of you. What is the matter?"

"A mistake; and a sad one for me," said Louis, gravely. "But don't say any thing about it, Alfred; they think I have been doing something very wrong; but all will come out some day."

"I hope so," replied little Alfred; "I cannot think what

you can have done wrong, Louis, you always seem so good."

The child looked wistfully up in Louis' face as he spoke, and seemed to wait some explanation.

"That is because you do not know much about me, Alfred," replied Louis; "but in this one case I have not done wrong, I assure you."

Alfred asked no more questions, though he looked more than once in the now sorrowful young face by him, as they sauntered along the wide downs.

"Here come Edward and Mr. Trevannion," said Alfred, turning round; "and there is Frank Digby, and Mr. Ferrers, too. I think Edward is going to Bristol this afternoon."

This intimation of the august approach of his majesty and court was hardly given when the young gentlemen passed Louis. Hamilton, with Trevannion, as usual, leaning on his arm, and Frank Digby walking backwards before them, vainly endeavoring to support a failing argument with a flood of nonsense, a common custom with this young gentleman; and, by the way, we might recommend it as remarkably convenient at such times, to prevent the pain of a total discomfiture, it being more pleasant to slip quietly and unseen from your pedestal to some perfectly remote topic, than to allow yourself to be hurled roughly there from by the rude hand of a more sound and successful disputant.

"Enough, enough, Frank!" exclaimed Hamilton, laughing. "I see through your flimsy veil. We won't say any more: you either argue in a circle, or try to blind us."

Louis looked up as Hamilton passed, in hopes that that

magnate might give him a favorable glance, in which he was not mistaken, for Edward the Great had been watching him from some distance, and was perfectly aware of his near approach to him.

He certainly did not seem displeased, though the grave countenance bore no marks of particular satisfaction at the rencontre. He spoke carelessly to his brother, and then, addressing Louis, said, "You must look after him, Louis, if you wish for his company; if not, dismiss him at once."

"I do wish for him," said Louis, with a bright look of gratitude; "I promise to take care of him. Mr. Hamilton, I am getting up in my class—I am fifth now."

The latter communication was made doubtfully, in a tone indicating mixed pleasure and timidity.

"I am glad to hear it," was Hamilton's laconic reply. He did not quicken his pace. "What have you there?" he asked, noticing his book.

"Coleridge's *Ancient Mariner*; I was going to read it," replied Louis; "but now Alfred has come we shall talk. shall we not, Alfred?"

This was accompanied by another look of grateful pleasure at Alfred's brother.

What was passing in Hamilton's mind was not to be gathered from his countenance, which exhibited no emotion of any kind. He turned to Trevannion, as their party was strengthened by Churchill, remarking, "Here comes the sucking fish."

"It's *uncommon* hot," said Churchill, taking off his hat, and fanning himself with his handkerchief.

"*Dreadful* warm," said Frank Digby, in exactly the same tone.

" And there is not a breath of wind on the horrid downs," continued the sapient youth, perfectly unconscious of Frank's mimicry.

" What will the fair Louisa do ?" cried Frank: " O that a zephyr would have pity on that delicate form !"

Across their path lay a wagon, from which the horses had been detached, and which now offered a tempting though homely shelter to those among the pedestrians who might choose to sit on the shady side, or to avail themselves of the accommodation afforded by the awning over the interior. Ferrers threw himself full length inside the cart: and Louis, drawing Alfred to the shady side, seated himself by him on the grass. His example was followed by Churchill, who exclaimed rapturously as he did so, " How nice! This puts me in mind of a Latin sentence ; I forget the Latin, but I remember the English—' Oh, 'tis pleasant to sit in the shade !' "

" Of a wagon," said Frank, laughing. " Remarkably romantic! It is so sweet to hear the birds chirp, and the distant hum of human voices—but language fails ! As for Lady Louisa, she is in the Elysium of ecstasy. It's *so* romantic."

" Are you going to Bristol, Frank, for I'm off ?" said Hamilton.

" Coming," replied Frank. " We'll leave these romantic mortals to their sequestered glen. There ain't nothing like imagination, my good sirs."

As he joined his companions, Trevannion remarked to Hamilton, " Little Mortimer is so much the gentleman, you never know him do or say any thing vulgar or awkward. It is a pity one can't depend upon him."

"I am not quite sure that you cannot," replied Hamilton.

"How!" said Trevannion, in astonishment.

"Are you going to turn Paladin for her ladyship?" asked Frank.

"I have been watching Louis very carefully, and the more I see, the more I doubt his guilt," replied Hamilton.

"After what you saw yourself? After all that was seen by others? Impossible, my dear Hamilton!" exclaimed Trevannion. "You cannot exonerate him without criminating others."

"We shall see," replied Hamilton; "and more than that, Trevannion, I am certain that Dr. Wilkinson has his doubts now, too."

"But does Fudge know any thing about his old pranks?" asked Frank, incredulously.

"I cannot say," replied Hamilton; "but I think that he probably does; for what is so well known now among ourselves, is likely enough to reach his quick ears."

"But knowing all you do, my dear Hamilton," said Trevannion, expostulatingly, "you must be strongly prejudiced in your protegé's favor to admit a doubt in this case. Has Dr. Wilkinson told you that he has any doubts?"

"No," replied Hamilton; "you know the doctor would not reveal his mind unless he were confident, but I have noticed some little things, and am sure that though he seems generally so indifferent to Louis' presence and concerns, and so distant and cold towards him, he is nevertheless watching him very narrowly; and I, for my part, expect to see things take a new turn before long."

"The boy seems quite to have won your heart," said Trevannion.

"Poor fellow," replied Hamilton, smiling. "He is a sweet-tempered, gentle boy; a little too anxious to be well thought of, and has, perhaps, too little *moral courage*. I own he has interested me. His very timidity and his numerous scrapes called forth pity in the first instance, and then I saw more. I should not have been surprised at his telling a lie in the first place, but I do not think he would persist in it."

"I'm afraid wisdom's at fault," said Frank, shaking nis head: "you would not say that Ferrers helped him?—I mean took the key to get him into a scrape."

"I accused no one, Digby," replied Hamilton, in a reserved tone; "nor am I going to wrong any one by uttering unformed suspicions."

"Enough has been said," remarked Trevannion; "let us drop the subject, and talk of something more interesting to all parties."

While these young gentlemen pursue their walk, we will retrace our steps to the wagon, where Louis and his little friend have taken shelter.

Churchill, finding neither seemed very much inclined to encourage his conversational powers, took himself off, after remaining in the shade long enough to cool himself. After his departure Louis and Alfred talked lazily on of their own pleasant thoughts and schemes, both delighted at being once more in each other's society. They were within sight of the masters out on the downs, and who had forbidden them to wander beyond certain limits, but still so far from their school-fellows as to be able to enjoy their own private conversation unmolested, and in the feeling of seclusion.

At length, after a pause, Louis made an original remark on the beauty of the weather, which was immediately responded to by his companion, who added that he had not known such a fine day since Miss Wilkinson's wedding.

"Don't you think so?" said Louis; "I think we had one or two Sundays quite as fine."

"Perhaps I thought that day so very fine, because I wanted to go out," said Alfred.

"What do you mean?" asked Louis: "we had a holiday then."

"Yes, I know, but I was not allowed to go out because I had been idle, and had spoken improperly to Mr. Norton. I remember it was so sad. I assure you, Louis, I cried nearly all day; for I was shut up in your class-room, and I heard all the boys so merry outside. The very thought makes me quite sorrowful now."

A thought flashed across Louis' mind, and he asked quickly—

"Were you shut up in our class-room that holiday, Alfred? I never saw you when I went in."

"But I saw you once," said Alfred, "when you came in for an atlas; and I saw Mr. Ferrers, and afterwards Edward and Mr. Salisbury and Mr. Trevannion come in; but I was ashamed, and I did not want any one to see me, so I hid myself between the book-case and the wall."

"Did your brother know you were there?" asked Louis.

"Not *there*," replied Alfred. "He thought I was to go into Dr. Wilkinson's study; but I could not go there, and I didn't want him to speak to me."

"Did Ferrers come to fetch any thing, Alfred?"

Alfred laughed. "It won't be telling tales out of school

to tell you, Louis. He came for a key to the first-class exercise book."

"How do you know it was a first-class exercise book, Alfred?" asked Louis, with a glowing face and beating heart.

"I know Edward does Kenrick's Latin Exercises, and I know the key because it's just like the book, and I have seen Mr. Ferrers with it before. I remember once on a half-holiday he did his lessons in the school-room at my desk, and he had it open in the desk, and as I wanted something out, I saw it, though he did not think I did."

"Oh Alfred, Alfred!" cried Louis, clasping him very tightly. "Oh Alfred! *dear* Alfred!"

The child looked up in astonishment, but Louis was so wild with excitement that he could not say any more.

Just at that moment there was an abrupt movement in the wagon, and Ferrers' head was put over the side.

Alfred uttered an exclamation of fear. "Oh, there's Mr. Ferrers!"

"What rubbish have you been talking, you little impostor?" cried Ferrers. "How dare you talk in such a manner? I've a great mind to kick you from Land's End to John o' Groat's house."

"Ferrers, you know it's all true," said Louis.

Ferrers' face was white with passion and anxiety. "Get along with you, Alfred, you'd better not let me hear any more of your lies, I can tell you."

"If you had not been listening you would not have heard," replied Alfred, taking care to stand out of Ferrers' reach. "Listeners never hear any good of themselves, Mr.

Ferrers begins to be found out.   Page 96.

Ferrers: you know it's all true, and if I'd told Edward, you wouldn't have liked it."

"Alfred dear, don't say so much," said Louis.

Alfred here set off running, as Ferrers had dismounted in a very threatening attitude, but instead of giving chase to the daring fugitive, the conscience-stricken youth drew near Louis, who was standing in a state of such delight that he must be excused a little if no thought of his school-fellow's disgrace marred it at present. A glance at the changed and terror-stricken countenance of that school-fellow checked the exuberance of Louis' joy, for he was too sympathizing not to feel for him, and he said in a gentle tone,

"I am very sorry for you, Ferrers,—you have heard all that Alfred has said."

"Louis Mortimer!" exclaimed Ferrers, in agony; and Louis was half alarmed by the wild despair of his manner, and the vehemence with which he seized his arm. "Louis Mortimer—it is all true—but what shall I do?"

Louis was so startled that he could not answer at first: at last he replied,

"Go and tell the doctor yourself—that will be much the best way."

"Listen to me a moment—just listen a moment—as soon as Dr. Wilkinson knows it, I shall be expelled, and I shall be ruined for life. What I have suffered, Louis! Oh—you see how it was; I dared not tell about it—how can I hope you can forgive me?"

"I think you must have seen that I forgave you long ago," replied Louis; "I wish I could do any thing for you, Ferrers, but you cannot expect me to bear the blame of this any longer. I think if you tell it to the doctor yourself, he will, perhaps, overlook it, and I will beg for you."

"Oh, Louis!" said Ferrers, seizing the passive hand, and speaking more vehemently; "you heard what the doctor said, and he will do it—and for one fault to lose all my prospects in life! I shall leave at the holidays, and then I will tell Dr. Wilkinson; will you—can you—to save a fellow from such disgrace, spare me a little longer? There are only four weeks—oh, Louis! I shall be eternally obliged—but if you could tell—I have a father—just think how yours would feel. Louis, will you, can you do this very great favor for me? I don't deserve any mercy from you, I know; but you are better than I am."

All the bright visions of acknowledged innocence fled, and a blank seemed to come over poor Louis' soul. The sacrifice seemed far too great, and he felt as if he were not called to make it; and yet—a glance at Ferrers' face—his distress, but not his meanness, struck him. A minute before, he had indulged in bright dreams of more than restoration to favor—of his brother's delight—of his father's and mother's approbation—of his grandfather's satisfaction—and Hamilton's friendly congratulations. And to give up this! it was surely too much to expect.

During his silence, Ferrers kept squeezing, and even kissing, his now cold hand, and repeating,

"Dear Louis—be merciful—will you pity me?—think of all—I don't deserve it, I know." And though the meanness and cowardliness were apparent, Louis looked at little else than the extreme agony of the suppliant.

"Don't kiss my hand, Ferrers—I can't bear it," he said at length, drawing his hand quickly away; and there was something akin to disgust mingled with the sorrowful look he gave to his companion.

"But Louis, will you?"

"Oh Ferrers! it is a hard thing to ask of me," said Louis, bitterly.

"Just for a little longer," implored Ferrers, "to save me from a lasting disgrace."

Louis turned his head away—it was a hard, hard struggle: "I will try to bear it if God will help me," he said; "I will not mention it at present."

"Oh! how can I thank you! how can I! how shall I ever be able!" cried Ferrers: "but will Alfred tell?"

"He does not know," replied Louis, in a low tone.

"But will he not mention what has passed?"

"I will warn him then," said Louis.

Ferrers then in broken sentences renewed his thanks, and Louis, after hearing a few in silence, as if he heard nothing, turned his full moist eyes on him with a sorrowful beseeching look,

"You have done a very wicked thing, Ferrers. Oh do pray to God to forgive you."

"I will try to do any thing you wish," replied Ferrers.

"A prayer because *I* wished, could do you no good. You must feel you have sinned against God. Do try to think of this. If it should make you do so, I *think* I could cheerfully bear this disgrace a little longer for you, though what it is to bear I cannot tell you."

"You are almost an angel, Louis!" exclaimed Ferrers.

"Oh don't say such things to me, Ferrers," said Louis, "pray don't. I am not more so than I was before this—I am but a sinful creature like yourself, and it is the remembrance of this that makes me pity you. Now do leave me alone ; I cannot bear to hear you flatter me now."

Ferrers lingered yet, though Louis moved from him with a shuddering abhorrence of the fawning, creeping manner of his school-fellow. Seeing that Ferrers still loitered near him, he asked if there were any thing more to say.

" Will your brother know this ?"

" Reginald ?" replied Louis. " Of course—no—*I* shall not tell him."

" A thousand thousand times I thank you,—oh Louis, Louis, you are too good !"

" Will you be kind enough to let me alone," said Louis gently, but very decidedly.

This time the request was complied with, and Louis resumed his former seat, and fixing his eyes vacantly on the sweet prospect before him, ruminated with a full heart on the recent discovery ; and, strange to say, though he had voluntarily promised to screen Ferrers a little longer from his justly merited disgrace, he felt as if it had been only a compulsory sense of duty and not benevolence which had led him to do so, and was inclined to murmur at his hard lot. For some time he sat in a kind of sullen apathy, without being able to send up a prayer, even though he felt he needed help to feel rightly. At length the kindly tears burst forth, and covering his face with his hands he wept softly. " I am very wrong—very ungrateful to God for His love to me. He has borne so much for me, and I am so unwilling to bear a little for poor Ferrers. Oh what sinful feelings I have ! My heavenly Father, teach me to feel pity for him, for he has no one to help him ; help him, teach him, Thyself."

Such, and many more, were the deep heart-breathings of the dear boy, and who ever sought for guidance and grace, and was rejected ? and how unspeakably comfortable is the assurance, that for each of us there is with Christ the very grace we need.

The sullen fit was gone, and Louis was his own happy self again, when little Alfred came to tell him that Mr. Witworth had given the order to return home,—" And I came to tell you, dear Louis, for I wanted to walk home with you. What a beast that Ferrers is! see if I won't tell Edward of him."

" Hush, Alfred!" said Louis, putting his finger on the little boy's mouth. " Do you know that God is very angry when we call each other bad names, and surely you do not wish to revenge yourself? I will tell you a very sweet verse which our Saviour said: ' *Love your enemies, bless them that curse you, and pray for them that despitefully use you and persecute you, that ye may be the children of your Father who is in heaven.'* " As the little monitor spoke, the soft consciousness of the comfort of those sweet words rushed over his own mind, " *children of your Father who is in heaven.*"

" And am I a child—His child indeed! I will try to glorify my Saviour who has given me that great name."

That is a sure promise that " they who water shall be watered," and who is there that has endeavored to lead another heavenward, that has not felt, at one time or another, a double share of that living water refreshing his own soul ?

With one arm round his little friend's neck, Louis wandered home, and, during the walk, easily persuaded Alfred

9*

not to say a word of what had passed ; and as for Louis—
oh, his eye was brighter, his step more buoyant, his heart
full of gladness !

A little word, and I will close this long chapter.   It is
good for us to consider how unable we are to think and to
do rightly ourselves : we must do so if we would be saved
by Christ.   When we have done all, we are unprofitable
servants ; but oh, how gracious—how incomprehensible is
that love that puts into our minds good desires, brings the
same to good effect, and rewards us for those things which
He Himself has enabled us to do !

CHAPTER VIII.

"Charity suffereth long, and is kind."—1 *Cor*. xiii. 4.

LOUIS entered the class-room sooner than usual one evening, and sitting down by his brother, spread before him a few strawberries and some sweet-cakes, inviting him and one of Salisbury's brothers who was on the other side of him to partake of them.

"What beauties they are!" exclaimed John Salisbury; "have you had a box, Louis? How *did* you get them?"

"Guess," said Louis.

"Nay, I can't guess. Strawberries like these don't come at this time of the year in boxes."

"I guess," said Frank Digby from the opposite side of the table, in a tone as if he had been speaking to some one behind him. "Fudge has a dinner party to-night, hasn't he?"

"Yes," said Louis, laughing; "how did you know that?"

"Oh, I have the little green bird that tells every thing," replied Frank.

"What's that, Frank?" cried Salisbury; "Fudge a dinner party? How snug he's kept it!"

"Why you don't suppose that he's obliged to inform us

all when he has some idea of doing the genteel," remarked
one of the first class.

"Are Hamilton and Trevannion invited?" asked Salisbury.

"In good troth! thou art a bat of the most blind species,"
said Frank; "didn't you see them both just now in all
their best toggery? Trevannion went up to his room just
after school, and has, I believe, at last adorned his beaute-
ous person to his mind—all graces and delicious odors.—
Faugh! he puts me in mind of a hair-dresser's shop."

"He declares that his new perfumes are something ex-
pressly superior," said another. "*He* wouldn't touch your
vulgar scents."

"His *millefleurs* is at all events uncommonly like a musk-
rat," said Salisbury.

"And," remarked Frank, "as that erudite youth, Oars,
would say, 'puts me in mind of some poet, but I've forgotten his name.' However, two lines borrowed from him,
which my sister quotes to me when I am genteel, will do as
well as his name:

> "'I cannot talk with civet in the room—
> A fine puss gentleman, that's all perfume.'"

Reginald laughed. "I often think of the overrun flower-
pots in the cottages at Dashwood, when Trevannion has
been adorning himself. I once mortally offended him by
the same quotation."

"Had you the amazing audacity! the intolerable pre-
sumption!" cried Frank, pretending to start. "I perceive
his magnificent scorn didn't quite annihilate you; I think,
though, he was three hours embellishing himself to-night."

"Frank, that's impossible!" cried Louis, laughing, "for it was four o'clock when he went, and it's only half-past six now."

"Cease your speech, and eat your booty : I dare say it is sweet enough ; sweetness is the usual concomitant of goods so obtained."

"What do you mean, Frank?" asked Louis.

"Sweet little innocent ; of course he don't know—no, in course he don't—how should he? they came into his hand by accident," said Frank, mockingly ; "I wish such fortunate accidents would happen to me."

"They were given to me, Frank," said Louis, quietly. "Mrs. Wilkinson gave them to me when she told me I must not stay in the study."

"What a kind person Mrs. Wilkinson is!—oh! Louis, Louis, *Tanta est depravitas humani generis !*"

"FRANK!" shouted Reginald, "at your peril!"

"Well, my dear—what, is my life in peril from you again? I must take care then."

"Come, Frank, have done," cried one of his class-fellows, "can't you leave Louis Mortimer alone—it doesn't signify to you."

"I only meant to admonish him by a gentle hint, that he must not presume to contradict gentlemen whose honor and veracity may at least be on a par with his own."

"Frank," said Louis, "I cannot think how you can suppose me guilty of such meanness."

"The least said, the soonest mended," remarked Salisbury. "We must have large powers of credence where you are concerned. Clear off your old scores, and then we will begin a new one with you."

Reginald started to his feet. "You shall rue this, Salisbury."

"Two can play at your game," rejoined Salisbury, rising.

Reginald was springing forward, but was checked by Louis, who threw himself on him. "Do not fight, dear Reginald—do not, pray."

"I will—unhand me, Louis! I tell you I WILL—let me go."

"Dear Reginald, not for me—wait a minute."

At this moment the form behind them fell with a heavy bang, and in struggling to release himself, Reginald fell over it, dragging Louis with him. Louis was a little hurt, but he did not let go his hold. "Reginald," he said, "ask Mrs. Wilkinson to say so herself; they will believe her, I suppose."

The fall had a little checked his rage, and Reginald sat brooding in sullen anger on the ground. At last he started up and left the room, saying to Louis, "It's all your fault, then—you've no spirit, and you don't want me to have any."

Louis mechanically assisted in raising the form, and stood silently by the table. He looked quickly round, and pushing the little share of his untasted fruit from him, went into the school-room. He did not recover his spirits again that evening, even when Reginald apologized to him for his roughness, pleading in excuse the extreme trouble it gave him to prevent himself from fighting with Salisbury.

As they went up stairs that night, in spite of the cautions given by the usher to be quiet, a sham scuffle ensued on purpose between Salisbury and Frank Digby, during which the former let his candle fall over the bannisters, and they were left in darkness ; though, happily for the comfort of the doctor's dinner party, the second hall and back staircase arrangement effectually prevented the noise that ensued from reaching the drawing-room.

"Halloa there—you fellows! Mortimer, ahoa!" cried one of Salisbury's party ; "bring your light."

"You may come and fetch it if you want it," shouted Reginald from his room.

"We're in the dark," was the reply.

"So much the better," said Reginald : "perhaps you will behave a little better now ; if you want a light you may come and light your candle here."

"Our candle's on the hall floor," said another voice, amidst suppressed laughter.

"Pick it up, then."

"We're desperately afraid of hobgoblins," cried Frank, rushing into his room and blowing their candle out.

"What did you do that for, Frank?" asked several indignant voices.

"Because Salisbury and his myrmidons were coming to carry it off by a *coup de main*—he-he-he—" giggled Frank.

"And so you've given your own head a blow to punish your tooth! well done," exclaimed another voice at the door.

"Peters, is that you?"

"What's to be done now?"

"How shall we get a light?"

"If you will give me the candle I will get one," said Louis.

Accordingly, the extinguished candle was delivered into

his hands, and he felt his way to the kitchen door, where he obtained a light, and then, picking up the fallen candle, tried to arrange its shattered form, and replace it. While thus employed, Ferrers joined him, and offered his aid, and on Louis' accepting it, said in a low tone,—

"Louis, I am a wretch, I am so very miserable. I can't think how you can bear so much from one who has never done you any thing but harm."

Louis raised his head from his work in astonishment, and saw that Ferrers looked as he said, very miserable, and was deadly pale.

"I do so despise myself—to see you bearing all so sweetly, Louis. I should have been different, perhaps, if I had known you before—I love, I admire you, as much as I hate myself."

"Are you coming with the candle there?" cried a voice from above: "Louis Mortimer and William Ferrers in deep confabulation—wonders will never cease."

Ferrers jumped up and ran up stairs with his candle, and Louis followed more leisurely to his own room, nor could any thing induce him that night to tell a story. How long and earnest was his prayer for one who had injured him so cruelly, but towards whom he now, instead of resentment, felt only pity and interest!

Ferrers, after tossing from side to side, and trying all schemes for several hours, in vain, to drown his remorse in sleep, at last, at daybreak, sank into an uneasy slumber. The image of Louis, and his mute expression of patient sorrow that evening, haunted him, and he felt an indefinable longing to be like him, and a horror of himself in comparison with him. He remembered Louis' words, "Pray to

God;" and one murmured petition was whispered in the stillness of the night, "Lord have mercy on a great sinner."

Since his disgrace, Louis generally had his brother for a
companion during their walks; but the next morning Ferrers joined him, and asked Louis to walk with him to the
downs. They were both naturally silent for the beginning
of the walk; but on Louis making some remark, Ferrers
said, "I can't think of any thing just now, Louis; I have
done every thing wrong to-day. My only satisfaction is in
telling you how much I feel your goodness. I can't think
how you can endure me."

"Oh, Ferrers!" said Louis, "what am I that I should
not bear you? and if you are really sorry, and wish to be
better, I think I may some day love you."

"*That* you can never do, Louis,—you must hate and
despise me."

"No, I do not," said Louis, kindly; "I am very sorry
for you."

"You must have felt very angry."

"I did feel very unkind and shocked at first," replied
Louis; "but by God's grace I learned afterwards to feel
very differently, and you can't think how often I have pitied you since."

"Pitied *me!*" said Ferrers.

"Oh yes," replied Louis, sweetly; "because I am sure
you must have been very unhappy with the knowledge of
sin in your heart—I don't think there is any thing so hard as
remorse to bear."

"I did not feel much sorrow till you were so kind to me,"
said Ferrers. "What a wretch you must think me!"

"I have sinned too greatly myself to judge very hardly

10

of you; and when I think of all the love shown to me, I feel anxious to show some love to others; and I should be afraid, if I thought too hardly of you, I should soon be left to find out what I am."

Ferrers did not reply; he did not understand the motives which induced Louis' forbearance and gentleness, for he was an entire stranger to religion, and never having met with any one resembling Louis, could not comprehend, though he did not fail to admire, his character, now its beauty was so conspicuously before him. He felt there was an immeasurable distance between them—for the first time he found himself wanting. Mentally putting himself in Louis' place, he acknowledged that no persuasion could have induced him to act so generously and disinterestedly; and knowing the keen sensitiveness of Louis to disgrace, he wondered how one so alive to the opinion of others, and naturally so yielding and wavering, could steadily and un-complainingly persevere in his benevolent purpose; for not by word or sign did Louis even hint the truth to Reginald —the usual depository of his cares and secrets.

Louis, imagining the silence of his companion to proceed from shame and distress, proceeded after a few minutes to reassure him.

"You must not think that I am miserable, Ferrers, for lately I have been much happier than even when I was in favor, for now I do not care so much what the boys will think or say of me, and that thought was always coming in the way of every thing; and there are many things which make me very happy, often."

"What things, Louis?"

"I do not think you would understand me," replied

Louis, timidly ; " the things and thoughts that make me happy are so different from what we hear generally here."

" But tell me, Louis. I want to know how it is you are so much better than any one else here. I want to be better myself."

" Oh, dear Ferrers," said Louis, gazing earnestly in Ferrers' face, " if you *do* want to be better, come to our Saviour, and He will make you all you want to be. It is the feeling of His goodness, and the happy hope of being God's children, and having all their sins forgiven, that make all God's people so happy ; and you may have this happiness too, if you will. I do not think we think enough of our great name of Christian."

" You read your Bible a great deal, Louis, don't you ?"

" Not so much as I ought," replied Louis, blushing, " but I love it very much."

" It always seems to me such a dull book, I am always very glad when our daily reading's over."

" I remember when I thought something in the same way," said Louis : " only mamma used always to explain things so pleasantly, that even then I used to like to hear her read it to us. Papa once said to me that the Bible is like a garden of flowers, through which a careless person may walk, and notice nothing, but that one who is really anxious to find flowers or herbs to cure his disease, will look carefully till he finds what he wants, and that some happy and eager seekers will find pleasure in all.'"

" Louis, you are very happy," said Ferrers, " though very strange. I would give a world, were it mine, to lay this heavy burden of mine down somewhere, and be as light in disgrace as you are."

Ferrers sighed deeply, and Louis said softly, " ' Come unto Him all ye that are heavy laden, and He will give you rest. His yoke is easy and His burden is light.' "

Here they parted. The last whispers of the Saviour's gracious invitation, those " comfortable words," lingered in Ferrers' ears as he entered the house, and returned at night ; but he did not throw himself and his burden at the Saviour's feet. And what hindered him ? It was pride, pride—though forced to feel himself a sinner, pride still retained its hold, more feebly than before, but still as a giant.

CHAPTER IX.

THE holidays were fast approaching. Ten days of the three weeks' examination had passed, and every energy was exerted, and every feeling of emulation called out, among those who had any hope of obtaining the honors held out to the successful candidates. It was surprising to see what could be, and what was, done. Even idle boys who had let their fair amount of talent lie dormant during the half year, now came forth, and, straining every nerve, were seen late and early at work which should have been gradually mastered during the last five months; denying themselves both recreation and sleep, with an energy, which, had it been earlier exerted in only half the degree, would have been highly laudable. Some of the latter, who possessed great talent, were successful, but generally the prizes fell to the lot of those who had throughout been uniformly steady, and who had gained an amount of thorough information which the eager study of a few weeks could not attain. Now there were beating hearts and anxious faces, and noisy summing up of the day's successes or losses, when the daily close of school proclaimed a truce to the emulous combatants. A few there were who appeared totally indifferent as to the issue of the contest, and who hailed the term of examination as entailing no set tasks to

10*

be said the ensuing day under certain penalties, and, revelling in extended play-hours, cared nothing for disgrace, having no character to lose.

Reginald bid fair to carry off all, or nearly all, the second-class honors; still, there were in his class several whose determined efforts and talents gave him considerable work in winning the battle.

Amongst all this spirited warfare, it is not to be supposed that Louis was tranquil; for, though naturally of an indolent temperament, there was in him a fund of latent emulation, which only wanted a stimulus such as the present to rouse him to action. Louis was a boy of no mean ability, and now, fired with the hope of distinguishing himself, and gaining a little honor that might efface the remembrance of past idleness, and give some pleasure to his dear parents, he applied himself so diligently and unremittingly to his studies during the last month, as to astonish his masters.

I do not mean to particularize the subjects for examination given by Dr. Wilkinson to the two upper classes, for this simple reason, that my classical and mathematical ignorance might cause mistakes more amusing to the erudite reader than pleasant to the author. It shall be sufficient to say, that whatever these subjects had been, the day's examination had gone through in a manner equally creditable to masters and pupils; and after a few turns in the fresh air when tea was over, a knot, comprising the greater part of the above-mentioned classes, assembled round their head man to congratulate him on his undoubted successes, and to talk over the events of the day elsewhere. Reginald and Louis could spare little time for talking, and were walking up and down the playground, questioning and answering each other with the most untiring diligence, though both of them had been up since four o'clock that morning. There were a few who had risen still earlier, and who now lay fast asleep on forms in the school-room, or endeavored to keep their eyes open by following the example of our hero and his brother.

"John's fast asleep," said Salisbury, laughing; "he has a capital way of gaining time—by getting up at half-past three, and falling asleep at seven."

"How does he stand for the prizes?" asked Smith.

"I'm sure I can't tell you; I suppose Mortimer's sure of the first classics and history—and he ought, for he's coming to us next half. John's next to him."

"I hear little Mortimer's winning laurels," remarked Trevannion.

"Oh! for *him*," said Harris, a second-class boy, "because he's been such a dunce before;—I suspect Ferrers helps him."

"Ferrers!" cried all at once, and there was a laugh— "Do you hear, Ferrers?"

"Of course I do," replied Ferrers.

"He's not good-natured enough," remarked another.

"He needs no help," said Ferrers.

"You're sure of the mathematical prize, Ferrers; and Hamilton, of course, gets that for Latin composition."

Ferrers did not reply—his thoughts had flown to Louis, from whom they were now seldom absent; and, though he had been generally successful, yet the settled gloom and anxiety of his manner led many to suppose that he entertained fears for the issue of his examination. There were others who imagined that there was some deeper cause of anxiety preying on his mind, or that he was suffering from illness and fatigue—and one or two made mysterious remarks on his intimacy with Louis, and wondered what all foreboded.

"I wonder who'll get the medal," said one.

"Hamilton, of course," replied Smith.

"You're out there," said Frank Digby. "My magic has discovered that either the Lady Louisa or myself will obtain it. I admire your selfishness, young gentlemen—you assign to yourselves every thing, and leave us out of the question. If I can't be a genius, I mean to be a good boy."

Many bitter remarks were then made on Louis' late good behavior, and a few upon his manner towards Ferrers, which, by some, was styled meanness of the highest degree.

Ferrers could not endure it—he left the circle and walked about the playground alone, full of remorse, thinking over every plan he had formed for making amends to Louis for all. He looked up once or twice with a gasping effort, and, oh! in the wrinkled and contracted forehead what trouble might be read. "Oh! that it were a dream," he at last uttered, "that I could wake and find it a warning."

There was a soft, warm hand in his, and Louis' gentle voice replied, "Do not grieve now about me, Ferrers, it will soon be over."

Ferrers started and drew his hand away.

"You are not angry with me, are you?" said Louis; "I saw you alone, and I was afraid you wanted comfort—I did not like to come before, for fear the boys should make remarks, Reginald especially."

Ferrers looked at Louis a minute without speaking, and then, pushing him off, walked quickly to the house, and did not show himself any more that evening.

Breakfast had long been finished, and the school was once more assembled ; the second class was waiting impatiently on the raised end of the school-room for the doctor's entrance, or for a summons to his presence ; and near, at their several desks, busily writing answers to a number of printed questions, sat the first class. It was nearly an hour past the time, and impatient eyes were directed to the clock over the folding-doors, which steadily marked the flying minutes.

" Where can the doctor be ?" had been asked many times already, but no one could answer.

" We shall have no time—we shall not get done before night," muttered several malcontents. " What can keep the doctor ?"

At this moment the folding-doors were quickly flung open, and Dr. Wilkinson entered, and rapidly made his way towards the upper end of the school-room, but in such a state of unwonted agitation that the boys were by common consent hushed into silence, and every occupation was suspended to watch their master's movements. " How strange he looks !" whispered one ; " something's the matter." Dr. Wilkinson took no notice of the open eyes and mouths of his awe-struck pupils—all his aim seemed to be to reach his seat with the greatest speed.

" What's the row ?" muttered Salisbury, in an undertone to Hamilton, having some idea that the latter could afford a clue to the clearing up of the mystery. " Do you know of any thing, Hamilton?" Hamilton shook his head, and fairly stood up to see what was going on.

Dr. Wilkinson at length reached his place, and there stood a few minutes to collect himself. He then looked around, and asked, in a quick, low tone, for Louis Mortimer. Louis was almost behind him, and in some terror presented himself; though he was unconscious of any misdemeanor, he did not know what new suspicion might have attached to him. His gentle "Here, sir," was distinctly heard in every part of the large room, in the breathless silence which now ruled. Dr. Wilkinson looked on him, but there was no anger in his gaze—his eyes glistened, and though there might be indignation mixed with the many emotions struggling for expression in his countenance, Louis felt, as he raised his timid eyes, that there was nothing now to fear. The doctor seemed incapable of speaking; after one or two vain efforts he placed both hands on Louis' head, and uttered a deep " God bless you !"

It would be impossible to describe the flood of rapture which this action poured upon poor Louis. The endurance of the last few weeks was amply repaid by the consciousness that somehow—and he did not consider how—his innocence was established, and now, in the presence of his school-fellows, publicly acknowledged.

For another minute Dr. Wilkinson stood with both hands resting on the head of his gentle pupil, then, removing one, he placed it under Louis' chin, and turned the glowing face up to himself and smiled—such a smile none remembered ever to have seen on that stern face.

" Have you found all out, sir?" cried Reginald, starting forward.

Dr. Wilkinson proclaims Louis innocent.   Page 118.

The doctor's hand motioned him back, and turning Louis round, so as to face the school, he said in a distinct, yet excited manner,

"Young gentlemen, we have been doing a wrong unconsciously, and I, as one of the first, am anxious to make to the subject of it the only reparation in my power, by declaring to you all that Louis Mortimer is entirely innocent of the offence with which he was charged; and I am sure I may say in the name of you all, as well as of myself, that we are very sorry that he should have suffered so much on account of it."

There was a hum all around, and many of the lower school who knew nothing of the matter, began whispering among themselves. But all was hushed directly the doctor resumed his speech.

"There are some among you who are not aware, I believe, to what I allude; but those who do know, can bear testimony to the gentle endurance of false accusation that Louis Mortimer has exhibited during the whole time he has been made to suffer so severely for the fault of another. I cannot express my admiration of his conduct—conduct which I am sure has had for its foundation the fear and love of God. Stay, gentlemen," said the doctor, stilling with a motion of his hand the rising murmur of approbation, "all is not yet told. This patient endurance might be lauded as an unusual occurrence, were there nothing more—but there is more. Louis Mortimer might have produced proofs of his innocence and cleared himself in the eyes of us all."

"Louis!" exclaimed Reginald, involuntarily.

Louis' head was down as far as his master's hand would

allow it, and deep crimson blushes passed quickly over the nearly tearful face—and now the remembrance of Ferrers, poor Ferrers, who had surely told all.   Louis felt very sorry for him, and almost ashamed on his own account.   He wished he could get behind his master, but that was impossible, and he stood still, as the doctor continued, "Three weeks ago Louis discovered that a little boy was in the study on the day when Kenrick's Key was abstracted, who could, of course, bring the desired information—the information which would have righted him in all our eyes ; but mark—you who are ready to revenge injuries—because this would have involved the expulsion of one who had deeply injured him, he has never, by sign or word, made known to any one the existence of such information, persuading the little boy also to keep the secret ; and this, which from him I should never have learned, I have just heard from the guilty person, who, unable to bear the remorse of his own mind, has voluntarily confessed his sin and Louis' estimable conduct.   Young gentlemen, I would say to all of you, 'Go and do likewise.' "

During this speech, Reginald had hardly been able to control himself, especially when he found that Louis had never mentioned his knowledge to himself ; and now he sprang forward, unchecked by the doctor, and, seizing his brother, who was immediately released, asked, "Why did you not tell me, Louis ?   How was it I never guessed ?"

While he spoke, there was a buz of inquiry at the lower end of the school, and those who knew the story crowded eagerly up to the dais to speak to Louis.   Alfred's voice was very distinct, for he had worked himself up to his brother :

"Edward, tell me all about it. I'm sure if I'd known I'd have told. I didn't know why Louis was so joyful."

Edward could answer nothing: his heart was as full as the doctor's, and with almost overflowing eyes and a trembling step, he pushed his way to Louis, who had thrown himself on Reginald and was sobbing violently.

"Louis, I'm very sorry," said one. "Louis, you'll forgive me—I'm sure I beg pardon," said other voices; and others added, "How good you are!—I shouldn't have done it."

Louis raised his head from that dear shoulder, so often the place where it had rested in his troubles, and said, amidst his sobs,

"Oh! don't praise me. I was very unwilling to do it."

"Let him alone," said the doctor. "Reginald, take him up stairs. Gentlemen, I can do nothing more, nor you neither, I think, to-day. I shall give you a holiday for the remainder of it."

There was a lull in the noise as Dr. Wilkinson spoke, but just as Louis was going out, there arose a deafening cheer, three times repeated, and then the boys picked up their books and hurried out of doors.

Louis' heart was ful of gratitude, but at the same time it was sobered by the recollection of what Ferrers must now suffer, and the doubt he felt respecting his fate; and as soon as he had recovered himself, he sought the doctor to beg pardon for him.

"As he has voluntarily confessed his fault, I shall not expel him," replied the doctor; "but I intend that he shall beg your pardon before the school."

Louis, however, pleaded so earnestly that he had already

11

suffered enough, and begged as a favor that nothing more might be said, that at length Dr. Wilkinson gave way.

The sensation that this event had caused in the school was very great: those who had been loudest in condemning Louis, were now the loudest in his praise, and most anxious to load him with every honor; and when he made his appearance among them with Reginald, whose manly face beamed with satisfaction and brotherly pride, he was seized by a party, and against his will, chaired round the playground, everywhere greeted by loud cheers, with now and then "A groan for Ferrers!"

"Louis, my man, you look sorrowful," said Hamilton, as he was landed at last on the threshold of the school-room door.

"No, no," said Salisbury, who had been foremost in the rioting; "cheer up, Louis—what's the matter?"

"I am afraid," said Louis, turning away.

"Afraid! of what old boy?" said Salisbury. "Come, out with it."

"I am afraid you will make me think too much of what ought not to be thought of at all—you are all very kind, but—"

"Nonsense!" exclaimed Salisbury; "we're all so vexed that we have been such bears, and we want to make it up."

"I am sure I do not think any thing about it now," said Louis, holding out both his hands and shaking all by turns; "I am very happy. Will you let me ask one thing of you?"

"A hundred," was the reply; "and we'll fly on Mercury's pennons to do your bidding."

"Put a girdle round the earth in forty minutes," said Frank Digby.

"When poor Ferrers comes among us, for my sake, do not take any notice of what has happened."

There was a dark cloud on the faces before Louis, and Hamilton's lip trembled with scorn. No reply was made.

"I am the only one who has any thing to forgive; please promise me to leave him alone."

"Then," said Salisbury, abruptly, "whenever he comes in, I walk out, for I can't sit in the same room and be civil."

"I shan't be particularly inclined to favor him with my discourse," said Frank; "so I promise to leave him alone."

"Will you try to be the same as you were before? Do!" said Louis.

"That's impossible!" they all cried; "we *cannot*, Louis."

"If you only knew how unhappy he has been, you would pity him very much," said Louis, sorrowfully. "He has been so very sad—and do not talk of this to other people, please. I should be so much more happy if you would try to be the same to him."

"All we can promise, is not to notice it, Louis," said Hamilton; "and now, don't be sad any longer."

Yet Louis was sad and anxious; though now and then a thought that all was clear, darted like a sunbeam across his mind, and called forth a grateful emotion. He longed for the holidays to come,—the favor he was in was almost painful.

Ferrers was invisible till the next evening, when he joined his class-fellows at prayers. In spite of the half-promise Louis had obtained from them, a studied unconsciousness of his presence, and a chilling coldness, greeted him.   Louis alone stood by him, and looked in the deadly white countenance by him with heartfelt sympathy and compassion; and glanced at several of his companions to remind them of his wish.   Ferrers seemed hardly the same; the proud, bullying air of arrogance had given place to a saddened, subdued despair; and yet his expression was far more pleasing in its humility than the natural one.

One or two, noticing Louis' anxiety, addressed him civilly, and even wished him " Good-night !" which he did not return by more than an inclination of the head.   He expected no pity, and had nerved himself to bear the scorn he had brought on himself; but any attention was a matter of surprise to him.

CHAPTER X.

WEARILY and joylessly had the last week of the examination passed away for Ferrers ; although in one branch he
had borne away the palm from all competitors.   His confession had, in some measure, atoned for his great fault, in
the eyes of his judicious master ; for, however much it
called for the severest reprehension, the fact of the mind
not being hardened to all sense of shame and right feeling,
made the doctor anxious to improve his better feelings ;
and, instead of driving them all away by ill-timed severity,
considering how lamentably the early training of Ferrers
had been neglected, he endeavored, after the first emotion
of indignation had passed away, to rouse the fallen youth
to a sense of honor and Christian responsibility ; and sought
to excite, as far as he was able, some feeling of compassion
for him among his school-fellows.

There were, however, few among them who had learned
the Christian duty of bearing one another's burdens ; few
among them, who, because circumstances over which they
had had no control, had placed them out of the temptations that had overcome their penitent school-fellow, did
not esteem themselves better than he, and look scornfully
upon him, as though they would say with the proud Phari-
see of old, " Stand by, for I am holier than thou !"   And

is it not the case around us generally? Alas! how apt we are all to condemn our fellow-creatures; forgetting that, had we been throughout similarly situated, our course might have been the same, or even worse. "Who is it that has made us to differ from another?"

Louis, as I have mentioned, felt very deeply for Ferrers; for, besides their late close connection, had he not known what it was to suffer for sin? He knew what it was to carry about a heavy heart, and to wake in the morning as if life had no joy to give; and he knew, too, what it was to lay his sins at a Saviour's feet, and to take the light yoke upon him. How anxious was he to lead his fellow-sinner there! Though his simple efforts seemed impotent at the time, years after, when his school-fellow had grown a steady and useful Christian, he dated his first serious impressions to this time of disgrace; and the remembrance of Louis' sweet conduct was often before him.

Louis' mind had been so chastened by his previous adversity that his present prosperity was meekly though thankfully borne. It came like sunshine after showers, cheering and refreshing his path, but not too powerful; for he was gradually learning more and more, to fear any thing that had a tendency to draw his mind to rest complacently on himself.

But the prize-day came—the joyful breaking-up-day—the day that was to bring his dear parents; and of all the bounding hearts, there were none more so than those of the two brothers. Mr. and Mrs. Mortimer had given their boys reason to expect them in the afternoon of that day, and they were to go from Clifton to Heronhurst before returning home.

Although Dr. Wilkinson's breaking-up-day was not ostensibly a public day, yet so many of the pupils' friends claimed admittance to the hall on the occasion, that it became so in fact, and was usually very respectably attended. Many of the doctor's old pupils came, to recall their old feelings, by a sight of this most memorable exhibition. And on this day, Vernon Digby was present with a younger brother, not to witness Frank's triumph, for that young gentleman had none to boast of, but to look on the theatre of his former fame, and to see how his place was now filled.

Dr. Wilkinson's high desk had been removed from the dais, and in its place stood a long table covered with a red cloth, on which were arranged a number of handsomely bound books of different sizes ; and in front of the dais, in a semicircular form, were placed the rows of seats for the boys. On each side of this semicircle, and behind and parallel with Dr. Wilkinson's seat, was accommodation for the spectators. The room was in the most inviting order, and had been hung with garlands of flowers by the boys. At eleven o'clock the pupils assembled, and under the inspection of two of the under masters, seated themselves in the places assigned them, the little boys being placed in the front row.

As the exact fate of each was unknown, though tolerably accurately guessed, there was much anxiety. Some of the youths were quite silent and pale, others endeavored to hide their agitation by laughing and talking quietly, and some affected to consider their nearest companion as more sure than themselves. Even Hamilton was not free from a little nervousness, and though he talked away to Vernon Digby, who was sitting by him, he cast more than one fidgety glance at the red-covered table, and perceptibly changed color when the class-room door opened to allow the long train of ladies and gentlemen to enter, and closed after Dr. Wilkinson, and a few of his particular friends, among whom were two great scholars who had assisted in the examination of the past week.

When every one was comfortably settled, Dr. Wilkinson leaned forward over the table, and drew a paper towards him. His preliminary "hem" was the signal for many fidgety motions on the forms in front of him, and every eye was riveted on him as he prefaced his distribution of the prizes by a short statement of his general satisfaction, and a slight notice of those particular points in which he could desire improvement. He then spoke of his pleasure at the report his friends had made of the proficiency of the upper classes, and particularly alluding to the first class, stopped and mentioned by name those who had especially distinguished themselves. Among these, as a matter of course, Hamilton stood foremost, and carried away the prize for Latin composition, as well as another. Ferrers gained that for mathematics—and two other prizes were awarded to the next in order. Dr. Wilkinson mentioned Frank Digby as having taken so high a place during the examination, as to induce one of the gentlemen who assisted him to consider him entitled to one of the classical prizes; but the doctor added that Frank Digby's indifference and idleness during the term had made him so unwilling that he should, by mere force of natural ability, deprive his more industrious class-fellows of a hard-earned honor, that he had not felt himself justified in listening to the recommendation, but hoped that his talents would, the following term, be exerted from the beginning, in which case, he should have pleasure in awarding to him the meed of successful application.

Frank colored, half angrily, but said, *sotto voce,*

" I don't care—I just like to see whether I can't do as well as any one else without fagging."

Vernon was half provoked and half amused at his brother's discomfiture.

Then came Reginald's turn, and he carried off three out of the four prizes of his class, leaving one for John Salisbury.

As each one was called up to receive his reward, an immense clapping and stamping took place, and Louis, all exuberance, stamped most vigorously when his brother and his particular friends went up. There were very slight manifestations when poor Ferrers was summoned, but Louis exerted himself so manfully in the applauding department, that the contagion spread a little before the despised recipient was seated.

The other classes were taken in order ; and when all was finished, Dr. Wilkinson took up a little morocco case, and, after clearing his throat once or twice, began anew :

" There remains now but one reward to be assigned, but it is the greatest of all, though undoubtedly that one which it is the most difficult to adjudge rightly. It is the medal for good conduct. Hitherto it has been my practice never to give it to any one who has not been with me the whole term, but on the present occasion I am inclined to depart from my custom in favor of a young gentleman whose conduct has been most praiseworthy, though he has only been with me since Easter. Before adjudging it. I will, however

appeal to the young gentlemen themselves, and ask them
who they think among them is the most deserving of this
honor?"

Dr. Wilkinson paused, and immediately a shout, led by
Hamilton, arose, of " Louis Mortimer."

" I expected it," said the doctor, with a smile: " Louis
Mortimer has been placed, perhaps, in a situation in the
school a little beyond him, and has, therefore, made no great
figure in the examination, but of his conduct I can speak in
the highest terms, and believe that his sense of duty is so
strong that he only wants the conviction that it is his duty
to exert himself a little more, to make him for the future as
habitually industrious as he has been during the last six
weeks.—Louis Mortimer!"

Almost overcome with astonishment and delight, Louis
hardly understood the summons, but Reginald whispered,
" Go, Louis, the doctor calls you," and all made way for
him with the most pleasant looks of sympathy and congrat-
ulation.   His modesty and elegance prepossessed the spectators greatly in his favor, as he passed timidly along the
ranks to the table.   Dr. Wilkinson smiled kindly on him
as he delivered the bright silver medal, in its claret-colored
case, saying as he did so,

" I have the greatest pleasure in giving this to you, and
trust that you will be encouraged, when you look on it,
to go on as you have begun."

Louis was covered with blushes—he bowed, and as he
turned away, the most deafening applause greeted him;
and, as the last prize was now given, the boys left their
seats and mingled among the company.   Louis was drawn
immediately into a little côterie, composed of Hamilton,

Reginald, his three cousins, and one or two others, all of whom congratulated him upon his distinction.

"And so, Louis, you are the hero," said Vernon; "and what is the drama in which you have been acting so much to your credit?"

"Too long a tale to tell now," replied Hamilton, smiling on Louis; "we will talk over it by and by. We have been treating him very ill, Digby, but next half-year we shall understand him better—shall we not, Louis?"

Louis was so full of delight that he could hardly speak—it was especially a happy moment to stand before his cousin Vernon with a bright fame and well-established character.

· "I said my magic knew who would gain the medal," said Frank.

"But your magic did not anticipate such magnificent honors for yourself, I imagine," said Vernon.

"I was a little out," said Frank, carelessly; "for it has proved that Lady Louisa has all the goodness, and I the genius. My head is quite overloaded with the laurels Fudge heaped on me: I shan't be able to hold it up these holidays."

"A good thing that something will press it down: it is generally high enough," remarked Hamilton.

"How delighted father and mother will be to hear of your industry!" said Vernon.

"I am sure," replied the incorrigible youth, "they ought to be proud of having a son too clever to win the prizes. Louis, it puts me in mind of the man in your tale, who had to bind his legs for fear he should outrun the hares. I am, however, heartily glad for you, and amazingly sorry we should have so misunderstood you."

"Louis Mortimer," cried a little boy, very smartly dressed, "mamma wants to look at your medal—will you come and show it to her?"

"And go off, Reginald, with him, and tell Lady Stanhope all the news," said Vernon, as Louis went away with little Stanhope; "I will come and pay my respects as soon as it is convenient for me to be aware of her ladyship's presence."

Louis' medal was examined and passed from hand to hand, and many compliments were made on the occasion. Lady Stanhope was very kind, and would hear the history, a command Reginald was by no manner of means unwilling to obey, though he suppressed the name of the guilty party. The doctor was in great request, for many of the ladies were very anxious to know more of "that lovely boy," but he was very guarded in his accounts of the matter, though bearing the strongest testimony to Louis' good conduct. He turned to Mr. Percy, who was present, and said, quietly, "That, sir, is the boy you mentioned to me at Easter; the son of Mr. Mortimer, of Dashwood."

The excitement was almost too much for Louis, tried as he had been lately by unusual fagging and early rising. He was glad to get away into the playground, and after watching one or two departures he ran wildly about, now and then laughing aloud in his delight, "Oh! papa and mamma, how glad they will be!" and then the well-spring of deep gladness seemed to overflow, and the excess of happiness and gratitude made him mute.. His heart swelled with emotions too great for any words; a deep sense of mercies and goodness of which he was unworthy, but for which he felt as if he could have poured out his being in praise. Oh the blessing of a thankful heart! How happy is he who sees his Father's hand in every thing that befalls him, and in whom each mercy calls forth a gush of gratitude!

> " Ten thousand thousand precious gifts
> My daily thanks employ ;
> Nor is the least a thankful heart.
> To taste those gifts with joy."
>
> ADDISON.

The playground was empty, for the boys were either engaged with their friends, or else departing; and Louis, from his little nook, saw many vehicles of different descriptions drive away from the door. When the dinner-bell rang he re-entered the house, but the dinner-table looked very empty—there was not half the usual party.

"Where have you been, Louis?" asked Reginald, as he entered; "I have been looking everywhere for you. Hamilton was quite vexed to go away without bidding you good-bye, and he begged me to do it for him."

"I am very sorry, indeed," said Louis; "I have been in the playground. Reginald, does it not make you feel very pleasant to see the heap of boxes in the hall? I stood a long time looking at our directions."

"I am almost cracked," cried Reginald, joyously ;—

> " ' Midsummer's coming again, my boys,
> Jolly Midsummer and all its joys!' "

How far Reginald's reminiscences of his holiday song might have continued, I cannot pretend to say, had it not been interrupted by a desire from the presiding master, that " he would recollect himself, and where he was;" but order was out of the question, most of the party being in

Reginald's condition—and, after several useless appeals to
the sense of gentlemanly decorum proper to be observed
by the noisy party, Mr. Witworth found his best plan would
be to let every thing pass that did not absolutely interfere
with the business in hand, and, dinner being over, the ill-
mannered troop dispersed.   Several of them, among whom
were Reginald and Louis, stopped in the hall to feast their
eyes on the piles of trunks and portmanteaus ; and Reginald
discovered that a direction was wanting on one of theirs ;
" And I declare, Louis, see what Frank has been doing."

Louis laughed, as he perceived that one of the directions
on his luggage was altered to " Lady Louisa Mortimer," and
ran away to rectify it.   When he returned, the party in the
hall was considerably enlarged, and Ferrers came towards
him to wish him good-bye.   " Good-bye, Louis, I am coming back next half-year," he said, in a low tone ; " and you
must help me to regain my character."   Louis squeezed his
hand, and promised to write to him, though he hoped, he
said, that he should not come back himself ; and when Ferrers left the hall, the business of affixing the necessary directions went on very busily.   Reginald was in a state of
such overflowing delight, as to be quite boisterous, and now
and then burst out into snatches of noisy songs, rendered remarkably effective by an occasional squeak and grunt, which
proclaimed his voice to be rather unmanageable.

" Now, Louis, here's a piece of string, and my knife.

'Christmas is coming again, my boys !' "

" *Christmas*, Reginald—Midsummer !" cried Louis, laughing.

" Well then, ah, well ! tie it tight.

' Midsummer's coming again, my boys,
  Jolly Midsummer, and all its joys;
  And we're all of us cracked, so we'll kick up a noise.
Chorus. Ri-toorul-loor, rul-loor, rul-loor-rul. Hip, hip, hurrah!
  Hollo!' "

The sensible chorus was shouted at the utmost pitch of
the voices of the assembled youths, who waved hats, hands,
and handkerchiefs, during the process.

"Bravissimo!" exclaimed Reginald, quite red with his
exertions, and beaming with excitement. "But my beautiful voice is very unruly; the last few times I have tried to
sing, it has been quite disobedient. I think it must be
cracked, at last."

"Are you not pleased?" said Louis, archly.

"Not particularly," replied Reginald.

"You said you should be, last Christmas. Do you remember the ladies at grandpapa's?"

"Well, there is that comfort at any rate," said Reginald,
"we shan't have any more of their humbug; but think of
the dear old madrigals, and—it's no laughing matter, Mr.
Louis, for all your fun."

"Acknowledge, then, that you spoke rashly, when you
said you should be glad of it," said Louis, who was full of
merriment at his brother's misfortune.

And now Vernon, Arthur, and Frank Digby pressed forward, to bid good-bye.

As Vernon shook Louis' hand, he said, "I shall see you
at Heronhurst, I suppose."

"I suppose *I* mustn't dare to go," said Frank.

"And now I shall go and gather some of those white
roses by the wall, for mamma," said Louis. "I hope it

won't be very long, Reginald, they must be here soon—oh,
how delightful it will be !"

Louis ran off, and succeeded in finding a few half-blown
roses for his dear mother, and was engaged in carefully cutting off the thorns, when one of his school-fellows ran up
to him, and called out that his father and mother were
come.

" Papa and mamma !   Where's Reginald ?" he cried, and
flew over the playground without waiting for an answer.
" Where are papa and mamma ?   Where is Reginald ?" he
cried, as he ran into the hall.   His hurried question was as
quickly answered ; and Louis, jumping over the many pack-
ages, made his way to the drawing-room.   Here were his
dear father and mother, with Dr. Wilkinson.   Reginald had
been in the room several minutes ; and when Louis entered,
was standing by his mother, whose arm was round him,
and close behind him stood his father.

" My Louis !" was his mother's affectionate greeting, and
the next moment he was in her arms, his own being clasped
tightly round her neck, and he could only kiss her in
speechless joy, at first ; and then, when the kind arms that
strained him to her bosom were loosened, there was his dear
father, and then words came, and as he looked with flash-
ing eyes and crimsoned cheek, from one to the other, he
exclaimed, " Oh, mamma ! I have a medal—mamma, it
is all come out !   Papa, I am innocent ; I have a character
now !   Oh, dear mamma, I said it would—I am quite
cleared !"

His head sank on his father's shoulder ; a strange, dull
sound in his head overpowered him ; a slight faintness
seemed to blow over his face ; his eyes were fixed and

glassy, and he became unconscious.   Mr. Mortimer changed color, and hastily catching the falling boy, he carried him to the sofa.   Dr. Wilkinson sent Reginald immediately for some water, but before he could return, and almost before Mrs. Mortimer could raise her dear boy's head from the pillow to her shoulder, the color came again, and his eyes resumed their natural expression.

"What was the matter, my darling?" said his mother, kissing him.

"I don't know, mamma," replied Louis, sitting up.   "I only felt giddy, and something like a little wind in my face."

"I think he has been overwrought," said Dr. Wilkinson, kindly; "he has gone through a great deal lately.   We will take him up stairs and let him lie down; I think he wants a little quiet."

"I am quite well now," said Louis.

"I will sit by your side; you had better go up stairs, dear," said his mother.

Louis yielded, and Mr. Mortimer assisted him up stairs, despite his declarations that he was quite strong and well, and, being laid on a bed, Mrs. Mortimer stationed herself by his side.

All they said I have not time to relate, but long Louis lay with his mother's hand in both of his, telling her of the events of the last two months, and often she bent her head down and kissed his broad forehead and flushed cheek; and when she would not let him talk any more, he lay very passively, his eyes filling with grateful tears, and now and then in the overflowing of his heart, raising them to his mother, with "Mamma, thank God for me.   Oh, how very grateful I ought to be!"

At length he fell asleep, and his mother sat still, watching the quiet face, and the glittering tear-drop that trembled on his eyelash, and she too felt that her mercies were very great—she did thank God for him, and for herself.

CHAPTER XI.

"Keep thy heart with all diligence, for out of it are the issues of life."—*Prov.* iv. 23.

AFTER a long and tedious journey Mr. and Mrs. Mortimer, with their two boys, reached Heronhurst, where they met with the affectionate welcome usually given by Sir George and Lady Vernon to all so nearly related to them. The castle was full of visitors, amongst whom were Lady Digby and her two eldest daughters, and many young people—personages grandmamma never forgot in the holidays, however unimportant they may appear in the eyes of some. Children liked to come to Heronhurst, for there was always so much mirth and amusement, and Lady Vernon was so remarkably clever in arranging pleasant pic-nics and excursions. Vernon and Frank Digby arrived the same day as Mr. Mortimer, a few hours before him, and as Vernon had announced the fact of Louis' having gained the medal, every one was prepared to receive our hero with due honor.

It was with no little satisfaction that Louis felt in the hearty shake of the hand, and the kind tone, that he was now more than re-established in his grandfather's good opinion. Had it not been for the salutary effects of his former disgrace, and the long trial he had lately undergone, there would have been great danger now of his falling into some open fault, for he was praised so much by his kind relations, and flattered by the company, and his medal had so often to be exhibited, that it needed much that in himself he did not possess, to guard him from falling into the error of imagining himself to be already perfect.

It was settled that there was to be a fête on the 27th, which some of my readers may remember was Louis' birth-day; and Sir George, anxious to efface from his grandson's memory any painful reminiscences of the last, arranged the order of things much in the same manner, taking care that Louis' protegés, the school-children, should not be for-gotten.

This news had just been communicated to Louis by his grandfather, with many expressions of commendation, and he was in a state of complacent self-gratulation, that feel-ing which would have led him to say, " By the strength of my hand I have done this;" instead of, " My strength will I ascribe unto the Lord," when a kind, soft hand, glittering with rings, was laid upon his arm, and the pleasant voice of his old friend Mrs. Paget greeted him.

" So, Master Louis, we are to have a fête, I hear. Are you really fourteen on the 27th ?   Come and sit down and tell me all about your school.   I knew you would soon be a favorite.   What's all this long story that everybody talks of and nobody knows ?   I said I would ask you, the most proper person to know it ; and I know you will tell me the secret."

" It is no secret, ma'am," said Louis ; " I would rather not talk of it."

"Just like your own modest little self : and it might not be kind to tell every one all the story, perhaps ; but with an old friend like me, you know you are safe."

"But, ma'am, you might forget when every one is talking——"

Louis stopped and colored, for he thought it seemed rather conceited to imagine every one must be talking of him, and he corrected himself,

"At least, dear Mrs. Paget, I had much rather not, I mean."

"You are a dear, kind little boy," said the injudicious lady ; "I know very well you are afraid of committing that naughty school-fellow of yours. I can't understand about the *keys*—I heard your brother saying something about them—what keys ? Were they the keys of the boy's desks ?"

Louis could hardly help laughing—"No, ma'am, Kenrick's keys."

"And who is Kenrick—one of the masters ?"

"It is a book, ma'am—a key to the Greek exercises."

"Oh, I see—a sort of translation—well, he stole this from Dr. Wilkinson, and said you'd done it ?"

"No, not that," replied Louis. "He took it out of the study. Some of the boys were in the habit of using the keys when they could."

"Well, there was nothing so very terrible in it, poor fellows. I dare say the lessons are very hard. I think every boy ought to have an English translation of those frightful Latin and Greek books."

Louis opened his eyes and quietly said—

"We think it very dishonorable and unfair, ma'am."

"Well, if I understood all about it, I might too, I dare
say. I only see a little bit, but of course you know the
rules and all the rest,—well, was that all?"

"No, ma'am," said Louis, uneasily.

"He said you had taken it, I dare say?"

"Something like it," replied Louis. "He slipped it
among my books to hide it, ma'am, but not intending to do
me any harm; and when it was found he was afraid to
speak the truth."

"And so you bore the blame—and did you not try to
clear yourself?"

"To be sure, ma'am; but he was older and better known
than I was, and so he was believed."

"And you couldn't help yourself? I thought you bore
it out of kindness to him."

"Afterwards I found it out, ma'am. I found that Alfred
Hamilton knew something about it."

"Who is Alfred Hamilton?" asked Mrs. Paget.

"A little boy, ma'am, at school."

"And he found it out—and didn't he tell of it?"

"I did not wish him," replied Louis, with less reserve.
"It would have been very unkind to poor Ferrers; he
would have been expelled. Alfred was going to tell, but
you would not have wished him to do it, I am sure."

Ah Louis, Louis! anxiety for Ferrers' reputation was
quite lost in the selfish desire of admiration. Mrs. Paget
put her arm round him, and her kindly eyes nearly overflowed with affectionate emotion, for she, poor lady, could
only see the surface; the inward workings of the little
vain heart were hid from her, or she would have been surprised to find under the appearance of sweetness and

humility, Louis was only thinking of seeming lovely and amiable in her eyes.

"No, my darling, I know you could not do any thing unkind—you are a sweet, dear creature, and I am sure I love you; and so this Master Ferrers never spoke the truth, and you bore the blame?"

"He did at last, ma'am, at the end of the half-year: but it was not very long to bear it, only five weeks."

"*Only!* I wonder you could have done it for so long; Ferrers, that was the name, was it?"

"If you please, don't mention it," exclaimed Louis, with unaffected earnestness; "I did not mean to say his name. Please, dear Mrs. Paget, do not mention it. He is so very sorry, and confessed all so handsomely—I think you would like him if you knew all about him, for he is not so bad as others make him out to be."

Mrs. Paget had only time to give him a kind of half promise, when she was called away; and Louis, left to himself, became aware of the vanity his foolish heart had persuaded him was Christian kindness. His enjoyment was destroyed that evening, for he was full of anxiety lest Mrs. Paget should talk of the matter, and he wandered restlessly about the rooms, longing for an opportunity of speaking a kind word for Ferrers, wishing vainly that what he had said could be undone. He felt more than ever the necessity of keeping a watch over his heart and tongue, and almost inclined to despair of ever overcoming the many stumbling-blocks in the way of attaining to holiness. Thus, little by little, is the evil of our hearts disclosed to us, and the longer the true Christian lives, the less he finds to be satisfied with in himself; not that he is further removed from holiness, but he has more sight given him to know what he really is by nature—and the nearer he arrives to the perfect day, the greater is the light to disclose his own deformities, and the exceeding loveliness of the righteousness he possesses in Jesus his Lord.

Louis, in common with the young visitors at Heronhurst, thought often and expectantly of his birthday—and when the morning at last arrived, he awoke much earlier than usual, with a strong sensation of some great happiness. The light on the blind of his window was not bright, nor promising brightness—and when he jumped up and ran to examine the day, expressing to his brother his hope that the weather was propitious, he found to his dismay that the rain was pouring in torrents, and the dull unbroken clouds gave but little promise of a change in the prospect.

" Oh ! Reginald, it's raining, raining hard."

" How very provoking !" cried Reginald. " Let me see —there is not much hope neither—how exceedingly tiresome—there's an end to our fun—who'd have thought it—how VERY—"

" Hush !" said poor Louis, who was very much disappointed, " it is not right to say *tiresome* when it pleases God that the weather shall not suit us."

" I can't help it," said Reginald.

" I dare say we shall be very happy. I am most sorry about the school-children."

" I don't care a fig about them," said Reginald, impatiently ; " there's that cricket match, and all."

" What, not the poor little things, Reginald ? just think how they have been expecting this day—it is quite an event for them, and we have so many pleasures: I dare say you will have the cricket the first fine day."

Reginald felt rather ashamed, and yet unwilling to acknowledge himself in the wrong; therefore he satisfied himself with remarking, that Louis did not like cricket, and he didn't care about the children, and there was no difference.

Louis' attention was at that moment attracted by something on the table. "Oh! here is something for me, Reginald!—A beautiful new Bible from dear papa and mamma—and a church service from grandmamma, and what's this?—'*The Lady of the Manor*' from uncle and aunt Clarence; how kind, look Reginald! and here's another—a beautiful little red and gold book, '*Mrs. Rowe's Poems,*' the book I am so fond of—from you: oh! thank you, dear Reginald."

"And many happy returns of the day, dear Louis," said Reginald, who had by this time completely recovered his ordinary good-humor.

At the foot of the stairs, when he descended, Louis met some of the young party, who hardly waited to offer the compliments of the day before they loudly expressed the disappointment felt by each at the unfavorable weather. "Raining, raining—nothing but splashing and dark clouds—so tiresome, so disappointing—we shall be obliged to stay in-doors," sounded round him in different keys as they marched in close phalanx to the breakfast-room, where they found Bessie Vernon, a little girl of seven years old, kneeling on a chair at the window, singing, in the most doleful accents,

> " Rain, rain, go to Spain,
> And mind you don't come back again."

13

" Good morning, Bessie," said Louis

" Oh ! Louis, many happy returns.   I haven't got a
present for you, because I hadn't money enough."

" Never mind," said Louis ; " I would rather have your
love and kisses than any present."

" And I will give you many, many kisses," cried the
little girl, fulfilling her promise in good earnest.

" *My love and a kiss*," said her brother ; " that's what
Bessie always sends at the end of her letters : isn't it,
Bessie, *I send you my love and a kiss ?*"

" Well, I mean it," said Bessie, " and you needn't laugh.
I wonder what we shall do to-day—dear me—I think,
though, there's a little lighter bit of sky over the oak."

" Let me see—where are my spectacles ?" said Frank.

" Not much hope, I fear," said Sir George's hearty voice
behind her.   " Not much hope, Bessie.   What an array of
long faces.   How do you do ?   Good morning, ladies and
gentlemen, I hope I see you in health and spirits.   A happy
birthday, and many of them to you, my boy ; the rain does
not appear to have damped you so much as some of your
play-fellows—well, Miss Bessie ?"

" Grandpapa, grandpapa ! what shall we do ? you must
find some pleasure for us," cried Bessie, clinging round her
grandfather's knees, and looking up very beseechingly in
the kind face so far above her.

" Ah, well—we'll see, we'll see—now let me go to breakfast ; when that important business is dispatched, and
grandmamma makes her appearance, we will find something to do."

Fortified with this promise, an excellent breakfast was
eaten by the martyrs to disappointment, and then, after

some consultation, it was decided that the band should be
in attendance in the hall, and a messenger should be sent
forthwith to command the attendance of the school-children at a banquet in the same place, and Lady Vernon was
of opinion that with charades, a magic lantern, bagatelle,
tivoli, and dolls, a very merry morning might be spent.
The young people then dispersed in search of their own
peculiar amusements. Some of the young men went into
the billiard-room, and a few chess parties were formed.
Some began to act charades for the edification of such
among the elders as would choose to make an audience.
A still larger party adjourned to the school-room to play
at houses with their dolls, and two tables were soon spread
with ground plans of three magnificent establishments for
paper ladies and gentlemen, by three young ladies between
the ages of twelve and eight, assisted by Mr. Frank Digby.

At one o'clock they went to the hall, where the band
was playing a merry air. Here a long table was spread,
well covered with a nice plain dinner, and the school-children came two-and-two into the hall, just after the visitors
had arrived.

When all were seated, the girls at the upper, and the
boys at the lower end, Mr. Mortimer came forward and
said grace for them, and then the viands disappeared with
great rapidity. Some of the castle children, headed by
Louis, asked to be allowed to wait on them, and, the permission being given, they made themselves very busy,
though it must be confessed that they were sometimes
sadly in the servants' way. Sir George Vernon went round
the table very majestically, and now and then spoke a word
or two to one of the children—words which were treasured

up in their memories for many a long day, though they meant little or nothing ; but it is so easy to create a pleasant and grateful feeling.

Many of the spectators, including nearly all the gentlemen, had left the hall very soon after the commencement of the feast, and now a summons was given to the little ones of the castle to their own dinner. Louis, not being included in the little ones, went with the school-children into a large empty room, and with the help of his father and one or two others, exerted himself successfully for their entertainment, until his friends joined them, and, the room being darkened, the magic lantern was displayed. The humble little guests then, being supplied each with a cake and some fruit, returned to their homes, quite delighted with the pleasures of the day.

Frank and the three young ladies enjoyed an hour's amusement during the late dinner ; for the good-natured youth had yielded to the pressing invitation of the merry little party, and dined with them at two, to their great satisfaction, notwithstanding the declaration of some, that he was " a great tease."

The great dinner was much earlier than usual, to allow of the ball, which began at seven o'clock for the convenience of the younger ones, and was continued until eleven, at which time, though he had been very happy, Louis was very tired, and could not help thinking, that, after all, a whole day of pleasure-seeking in this manner, was very fatiguing and unsatisfying. He could hardly keep his eyes open, when Mrs. Paget seized him, and after a few compliments on his dancing, insisted upon hearing him sing " *Where the bee sucks.*"

Louis complied as well as he was able, and though his sleepiness robbed his song of some power, its sweetness not only satisfied the flattering lady, but a more unscrupulous auditor who stood behind him in the person of his grandfather.

" Your mother taught you to sing, Louis?" said he.

" Miss Spencer taught me," replied Louis.

" The mechanism, perhaps, but it's your mother's teaching. The taste, madam," said Sir George, turning to Mrs. Paget.

" Both Mr. and Mrs. Mortimer are first-rate amateurs," said Mrs. Paget.

" Mrs. Mortimer has great talent," replied Sir George; " and she has done something with this boy. I suppose you are very fond of music, Louis?"

Louis answered in the affirmative, and Sir George added—

" I shall give you a treat. You shall go on Sunday to A——, and hear the singing at the church there. The little boys sing very sweetly. Have you heard them ma'am?"

" No, I never have."

" Then I think it would be a wise step to pay a visit there during divine service next Sunday. The church is worth looking at,—a good specimen of the early English style of architecture. We can make up a little party to go, if you would like it."

Mrs. Paget expressed her entire approbation of the scheme, and Louis, too sleepy to think much of it, wished her and Sir George good night, and went to bed.

The next day, the rain continuing, in the morning Louis enjoyed *The Lady of the Manor* in his own room. He was still much excited by the yesterday's pleasure, and felt un-

settled, and disinclined to employ himself steadily with any
thing.   In the afternoon, as the weather was fine, his
mother insisted on his taking a walk, and Reginald and
Vernon Digby accompanied him.   They had a great scram-
ble through the hilly district that surrounded Heronhurst,
and merrily the talk (we will not dignify it by the name of
conversation) continued.   As they re-entered the grounds
it fell upon the scheme of visiting the church, and during
the light and common-place discussion that ensued, it struck
Louis that there might be something wrong in the plan.
He became very silent, and when he reached his room,
quietly thought over the matter, and came to the conclusion that, though they intended going to church, yet the
motives that induced their doing so were not to the glory
of God, and that to employ servants for such an end, on
God's holy day, was certainly wrong.   This was his first
impression; and when he next saw Reginald, he told him
what he had been thinking of.

" Well, but Louis, you know it won't make any difference
whether we go or not, and so *we* shan't engage the servants.
I don't see why, because you like nice singing, you should
go to the chapel where they screech so abominably."

Louis was silent, for he hardly liked to oppose his reasons
to Reginald's blunt speech, and Reginald, dismissing the
subject from his mind, began to talk of something else.
He ran on very volubly for a little while, without receiving
any interruption from his brother, and, looking at him, he
saw very plainly that Louis was not paying the slightest
attention to him.

" What is the matter, Louis ?   How dull you are !"

" Nothing," replied Louis.

"Nothing?" repeated Reginald; "*Something*, you ought to say. I know you are making yourself miserable about this church-going, and what need is there? We are going to church, and we can't prevent the carriage going. If it were on purpose for us it would be different."

"But there will be a great deal of nonsense, I know," said Louis, uneasily. "It seems very much like going to a show place. I hope I shall be able to ask mamma about it."

"As to nonsense," replied Reginald, "when do we have any thing else here?—you can't make Dashwood of Heron-hurst, and I think if you go to hear such beautiful singing, it is more likely to put good thoughts into your head than those lovely singers here; and then, Mr. Perrott is quite a famous man; everybody likes him better than Mr. Burton—you are too scrupulous, Louis. I think, sometimes, you are guilty of over-conscientiousness."

Before Louis could reply, some of their young friends entered the room, and one thing followed another so quickly that Louis had no time to think clearly on the subject till he went to bed; but when all was silent and nothing interfered with his thoughts, his anxious mind ran over all that had passed, and turn it which way he would, it still seemed wrong. What with this feeling, and the fear of making his grandfather angry, Louis felt very uncomfortable; and then came Reginald's sophistry, and Louis almost argued himself into the belief that his brother was right and he too scrupulous: and when he tried to pray for direction he did not feel sincere, for he was conscious of a wish to go to the church, and a great dread of offending his grandfather. After some hours' restless consideration, he dropped asleep, having made up his mind to con-sult his father and mother, and to abide by their counsel. The next day, however, he had no opportunity of speaking to them alone, and Saturday night found him as miserably undecided as before. " Oh dear, if there were any one I could ask !" There was One, and though aid was feebly asked, it was granted; and with much fear and anxiety, Louis declined accompanying the party to A—— church the next morning.

Vernon stared, and Reginald tried in vain to persuade him to alter his mind,—but he stood firm, and turning away from them, afraid to trust himself, stayed up stairs till the castle chapel bells began to ring, and then hastened down with a happy, free, and light heart, to join his mother.

" Hey-day, Louis !" exclaimed his grandfather ; " I thought you were off long ago. You're too late : the carriage has been gone this hour. What's the meaning of these late hours, sir ?"

" I was up quite early, grandfather," said Louis.

" Then how was it you let them go without you ?"

" Because I had rather not go, sir," said Louis, with a heightened color.

" And pray why could you not say so sooner ?—you are the most uncertain fellow ;—not the smallest dependence ever to be placed upon you. Do you know your own mind, Mr. Louis ?"

" Not always at first," replied Louis, in a low tone.

" Hold up your head and speak out. And pray why has your weather-cock mind changed ? What new wind has blown you round now, eh ?"

"It's Sunday, grandpapa," said Louis, looking up at his mother with a distressed face.

"Well! Is the boy moon-struck? '*It's Sunday, grandpapa.*' Don't you suppose I know that?"

"I didn't think it was quite right, sir, to go to A—— church when we had one so near us."

"Just as you please," said Sir George, contemptuously— "just as you please, Master Louis; only do not expect me to plan any thing for your pleasure again."

"I am very much obliged, grandpapa—you don't understand me."

"Oh, we understand each other very well, sir," said his grandfather, turning off very haughtily.

As he passed Mr. Mortimer he said,

"This comes of *molly-coddling* that boy at home; you'll make a Methodist of him."

What answer Mr. Mortimer made, Louis could not hear, and the next moment they all went into the chapel.

Many contemptuous smiles were exchanged among those of the visitors who heard the colloquy, but Louis was comforted by an approving smile from his parents, and from the sweet consciousness of having done what was right. The service was very sweet to him, and the lightness of his heart made even the inferior singing very pleasant, and he gained something from "tedious Mr. Burton's" sermon; so much depends on the frame of mind. Our Saviour has enjoined us to take heed *how* we hear.

Louis had a very pleasant stroll in the park with his father after service, and when he entered the house with a happy quiet mind, he contrasted his feelings with those he should have had, had he been one of the giddy party at that time returning from A——, and joyfully thanked his heavenly Father for keeping him from dishonoring His holy day in " seeking his own pleasure" on it.

The following Thursday evening Mr. Mortimer's carriage was seen coming along the road leading to Dashwood, and at each window was a very joyful face noting all the familiar objects around ; and as the horses dashed round a corner under a short grove of limes, the tongues belonging to the two began to move with astonishing rapidity.

" Here's Dashwood !" cried one.

" There's the river," exclaimed the other.

" The Priory chimneys," shouted the first.

" The Grange, Reginald," cried the second.

" And Bessie Gordon in the garden,—she sees us," cried Reginald, who had changed sides for a second. " Ann White's cottage, Louis—I saw the old picture of Lazarus large as ever—and the sheep—and I smell hay. Look, there's a hay-field, and Johnson with the hay-makers ! Hillo, Johnson ! He sees me."

" The bells, papa ! The bells, mamma !" exclaimed Louis—" Oh, it's home, dear, sweet home ! The bells are ringing because you are come home, papa ; and look, there are all the people coming out of the cottages—how glad they seem to be !"

" Louis, Louis, here we go !" shouted Reginald, as the carriage swept down a lane arched over with green boughs.

Presently they came to the lodge gate ; but not a moment had they to wait ; it was wide open, and they could scarcely exchange marks of recognition with the gatekeeper and family, when they were out of sight in the long winding carriage road that led through the park.

"Welcome, welcome—home! The dear, dear old Priory," said Louis, with increasing enthusiasm.

"Take care you are not out on the grass, Louis," said his mother, seizing his arm.

"Here we are!" cried Reginald. "And there's Mary, the little pussy, and sober Neville, looking out of his wits, for a wonder. Here we are!"

CHAPTER XII.

" Whatsoever thy hand findeth to do, do it with thy might."—
Eccles. ix. 10.

" Watch and pray."—*Matt.* xxvi. 41.

" The weapons of our warfare are not carnal, but mighty through
God to the pulling down of strongholds; casting down imaginations, and every high thing that exalteth itself against the *knowledge* of God."—2 *Cor.* x. 4, 5.

" Ah! Louis, *this* is home," exclaimed Reginald, as, after
the embraces in the hall, they entered the pleasant drawing-
room.   It *was* home, home with all its sweet associations
and dear beings; and, in a few minutes, Reginald and Louis
had run all over the house for the pleasure of seeing " the
dear old places;" had shaken hands with the old servants,
given nurse a kiss, and, having finished by wakening Freddy
from his first sleep, returned to the drawing-room, where tea
was ready.   It was a very pleasant tea that night.   Every
one had so much to say, and there was so much innocent
mirth—all agreed it was worth while going away from
home, for the pleasure of returning.   Gradually the broad
yellow light faded from the wall, table, carpet, and window;
and, the gray twilight usurping its place, little Mary was
obliged to leave her seat on her father's knee, and with
many kisses was marshalled up stairs by nurse and Neville.

When Neville returned, the happy party sat round the open window watching the bright stars in their trembling beauty, and the half-moon rise over the dark trees, whitening their tops, silvering the water, and casting the deep shadows into deeper darkness. There was something in the still beauty that hushed the speakers, and at last only a low remark was now and then made, until Louis asked his mother to walk out into the garden. Mrs. Mortimer at first pleaded the heavy dews as an excuse, but the request was so urgently pressed by Reginald and Neville, and a large shawl and pair of clogs being procured, they sallied forth, Neville and his father first, then Reginald and Miss Spencer, and lastly, to his great satisfaction, Louis and his mother.

"I am so fond of moonlight, mamma," said Louis.

"I think most people are," replied his mother.

"I wonder what is the reason that moonlight is so much sweeter than sunlight," said Louis.

"Do you like it better?" said his mother.

"I don't know that I like it *better*," replied Louis; "but it always seems so quiet and soothing. I always liked moonlight when I was a very little boy—but I thought very differently about it then."

"How so?" asked his mother.

"Oh! mamma, I thought it was very beautiful, and I felt a strange sort of feeling come into my mind—a sort of sad happiness: and sometimes I thought of fairies dancing in the moonlight; and when I grew older, I used to think a great deal of nonsense, or try to make poetry, and I called the moon 'Diana,' and 'queen of night'—and imagined a great deal that I hardly like to tell you, about lovers walking in moonlight."

"And your feelings are quite changed now?" asked his mother.

"Oh, yes! quite, mamma, it only seems more soothing, because I feel as if I were alone with God. Does it not seem to you, mamma, as if we see something of heaven in these lovely nights? I often wonder whether the bright stars are the many mansions our Saviour speaks of. Oh! mamma, what an immense thought it is to think of all these bright worlds constantly moving—either suns themselves with their planets revolving in ceaseless circles, or else themselves going round some bright sun!"

"And, perhaps," added his mother, "that bright sun carrying all its attendant worlds round some larger and brighter sun, whose distance is too great to be calculated. By the aid of powerful telescopes may be seen in the extremity of our firmament, appearances which those who have devoted themselves to this glorious science have decided are other firmaments, each one containing its countless systems. Oh! Louis, God is infinite—what if these wondrous creations have no limit, but circle beyond circle spread out to all eternity! We may see the infinity of our Maker in the smallest leaf. There is nothing lost. What we destroy does but change its form."

"Mamma, I once remember cutting a bit of paper into halves—that is to say, I first cut it into halves, and then cut one half into halves and so on, till my scissors would not divide the little bit. I was very idle that day, but I remember thinking that if I could get a pair of scissors small enough I could cut that speck up *forever*—and even if there only happened to be a grain left, I could not make that nothing."

Louis paused; he was lost in thoughts of wonders that human imagination cannot grasp: the immensity and mystery of the Almighty's works. Presently he added, "I cannot imagine it, mamma, my mind seems lost when I try to think of *forever*. But there is a little hymn you used to teach me that I cannot help thinking of——I often think of it—it was the first I ever learned :

> ' 'Twas God, my child, that made them all
> By His almighty skill;
> He keeps them that they do not fall,
> And rules them by His will.
> How very great that God must be !' "
>
> HYMNS FOR INFANT MINDS.

"Do you remember learning that hymn?" said his mother; "I should have thought it had been too long ago."

"Oh, no, mamma. I remember once very distinctly, you had drawn up the blind that I might look at the stars, and you leaned over my crib, and taught me that verse. Mamma, even when I did not love God, I used to like to hear *you* tell me Bible stories and hymns sometimes, but I did not think much of them after they were over; but now, almost every thing reminds me of something in the Bible; or seems a type or a figure of some of our heavenly Father's dealings with us."

"That is what the Apostle says," replied Mrs. Mortimer: "'The weapons of our warfare are not carnal, but mighty, through God, to the pulling down of strongholds; casting down imaginations, and every high thing that exalteth itself against the knowledge of God; and bringing into captivity every thought to the obedience of Christ.' Your imaginations before were not according to the will of God; you

never saw any thing lovely in Him, but now He has become
'altogether lovely' in your eyes; every imagination that is
contrary to His will is subdued, and all brought into obedience to Him.   And are you not far happier?"

"Indeed I am; oh, how much more happy!" said Louis:
"but, dear mamma, I do not wish you to think that I am
always so happy, because that would not be true.   Very
often, I seem almost to forget that I am a child of God,
and then, nothing awakens those happy feelings."

"I do not suppose you are always so happy, my dear
boy.   It is too often the case with Christians, that instead
of drawing their pleasures from the fountain of life, they
imagine that they can make cisterns of their own; they
look to the comforts around them, to the friends God has
given them, for satisfaction; and numberless other things
have a tendency to draw their minds from their heavenly
Father, which must inevitably destroy their peace of mind.
But how sad it should ever be so! we have only ourselves
to blame that we are not always happy.   A Christian
should be the most joyous creature that breathes."

"Dear mamma, how many pleasant conversations I have
had with you!" said Louis, affectionately kissing his mother's
hand, as it lay on his arm.   "They have been some of my
sweetest hours.   It makes me so happy to talk of God's
love to me."

"An inexhaustible subject," said his mother: "'Then they
that feared the Lord, spake often one to another; and the
Lord hearkened and heard it; and a book of remembrance
was written before Him, for them that feared the Lord,
and thought upon his name.   And they shall be mine, saith
the Lord of Hosts, in that day when I make up my jewels.'

"Our favorite poet has expressed your feelings very beautifully :

> 'Oh, days of heaven, and nights of equal praise,
> Serene and peaceful as those heavenly days
> When souls drawn upward, in communion sweet
> Enjoy the stillness of some close retreat;
> Discourse, as if released and safe at home,
> Of dangers past and wonders yet to come ;
> And spread the sacred treasures of the breast
> Upon the lap of covenanted rest.'"
>
> COWPER's "*Conversation.*"

"Come, I think I must order you in," said Mr. Mortimer, who came up with the others, just as these lines were finished. "These nocturnal perambulations will not improve your health, my love ; and it is past prayer-time already. What a sweet night !"

"I am afraid I have been a little imprudent, but it was a temptation when the dear boys pressed me so earnestly ; our first night at home too, after so long a separation."

"Mamma's very carefully wrapped up," said Neville.

"And it's so deliciously warm," said Reginald.

"Well, let us not increase the evil," said Mr. Mortimer. They presently re-entered the drawing-room, and the servants being summoned, Mr. Mortimer read prayers, and the boys went to bed.

The weather being generally wet for the next fortnight, all the in-door resources were drawn upon by the young people of the Priory, and time seldom hung heavily on their hands. I do not mean to say that there was never a moment wasted ; on the contrary, Louis had many lazy fits. It must be allowed that in holiday time, when no one is

expected to do much regularly, there are great temptations
to be idle, and boys are apt to forget that it is not particularly for parents and teachers' good that they are exhorted
to make the most of their time.

Louis' father and mother gave him many gentle reminders
of his failing, and many were the struggles which he had
with his dreamy indolence. Sometimes, when in accord-
ance with a plan laid down by his mother's advice, he sat
down to study for a stated time, he would open the book,
and, after leaning over it for half an hour, find that he had
built himself a nice little parsonage and school, and established himself a most laborious and useful minister in the
prettiest of villages. At other times he was a missionary,
or an eminent writer, and occasionally a member of Parlia-
ment.   Then, at other times, he must draw the plan of a
cottage or church, or put down a few verses ; and sometimes, when he heard the clock strike the hour that summoned him to his studies, he had some excessively interesting story to finish, or very much preferred some other
occupation.

"Now, Louis, my dear, there is ten o'clock."

"Yes, mamma, I will go directly."

"Directly," in some persons' vocabulary, being an am-
biguous term, another quarter of an hour saw Louis in the
same place, quite absorbed.

"Louis, Louis !"

"Yes, mamma."   And Louis got up, book and all, and
walked across the room, reading all the way.   After knocking his head against the door, and walking into the library
instead of into the school-room, he at last found himself
at the table where his writing-desk stood, without any fur-

ther excuse, but there he stood for a minute or two reading, and then, still continuing, felt for his key, and slipped it along the front of his desk for some time in the most absent and fruitless manner. Being obliged, at length, to lay aside the book, he unlocked the desk, and opening it, laid the dear volume thereon, and read while he carried his desk to another table. Then a few books were fetched in the same dawdling way, Louis all the while persuading himself—foolish boy—that he was merely occupying the time of walking across the room in reading. A few minutes more, and a chair was dragged along, and Louis seated. Then he reluctantly laid his book down open beside him and commenced. It would be tiresome to say how often when the dictionary or something else had to be referred to, a half page or more of the story was read, and to remark how equally Louis enjoyed his amusement and profited by his study. He was finally overwhelmed with confusion when his father, entering the room, came and looked over his shoulder, making some remark on the economy of time exhibited in thus ingeniously blending together his work and play without profiting by either.

"But indeed, papa, I don't know how it is; I made up my mind to be very industrious, and I was very steady yesterday."

"You put me in mind of a story of a man who made a vow to abstain from frequenting beer-shops, and who, on the first day of his resolution, passed several successively, until he came to the last that lay on his way home, when he stopped and exclaimed, 'Well done, Resolution! I'll treat you for this,' and walked in."

"Oh, papa!" exclaimed Louis, laughing.

" Don't you think this looks very much like treating resolution ?" said his father, taking up the open book.

" I can't tell how it is, papa," said Louis, looking ashamed. " I assure you I did not mean to waste time ; I cannot help being interested in stories, and unless I leave off reading them altogether, I don't know what to do."

" As reading stories is not a duty," said his father, " I would certainly advise your leaving off reading them if they interfere with what is so clearly one ; but do you not think there is any way of arranging your affairs so as to prevent a harmless recreation from doing this ?"

" I can't depend upon myself, papa. If it were Reginald, he could throw his book down directly, and do at once what he ought, and so would Neville, but it is quite a trouble to me sometimes even to bring my thoughts to bear upon dry studies, particularly mathematics, which I hate."

" I allow there is some difference of constitution ; Reginald is not so fond of reading as you are, and has naturally more power of turning his attention from one subject to another ; but this power may be acquired, and if you grow up with this inclination to attend only to those things for which you take fancies and fits, you will not be a very useful member of society ; for it must always be remembered that consistency is essential to a useful character, and that without it, though many may love, few will respect you."

" I wish I could be like Neville ; he is like a clock, and never lets any one thing interfere with another, and he always has time for all he wants to do, and is never in a hurry and flurry as I am ; I think he has nothing to struggle with."

"Indeed, my dear Louis, he has. Neville has as many faults as the generality of boys, but you must not forget how much longer he has begun the good fight than yourself; and the earlier we begin to struggle against the corruptions of our nature, the easier the task is; but, Louis, instead of wishing yourself like Neville, or any one else, think how you may approach most nearly to the high standard of excellence which is placed before us all."

"But, father, how can I? What must I do?" sighed Louis. "You cannot tell how difficult it is to keep good resolutions. I fear I shall never be any better."

"What is the grace of God, my boy?" said Mr. Mortimer, laying his hand on Louis' shoulder; "tell me, what is the grace of God?"

"God's favor and help," replied Louis.

"And to whom is this promised?"

"To all who will ask for it, father."

"And will you say you can do nothing? Oh, my dear son! God is a God of all grace, and can give to each of us what we need for every emergency. Without Him, we can, indeed, do *nothing*, but with *Him* we may do *all things;* and blessed be His name for this unspeakable gift by which He works in man a gradual restoration to more than his primeval condition. Called with a holy calling, my boy, seek to glorify God in every little affair of life; take your religion into these unpleasant studies, and you will find them pleasures."

"But, father, there is one thing I want to say. Often when I pray, I do not seem able to do things that I wish and ought."

"There may be two reasons for that," replied his father.

" The first, that you are not sufficiently in earnest in your petitions ; and next, that you imagine that your prayers are to do all, without any exertion on your part—that the mere fact of having asked the help of the Almighty will insure you a supernatural ease and delight in performing these duties, forgetting that, while we are in this world we have to fight, to run steadily forward, not to sit still and expect all to be smooth for us. We must show diligence unto the end—we must watch as well as pray. You remember the parable of the withered hand ?"

" Yes, father."

" And you remember that our Lord commanded the man to stretch forth his hand. He might have pleaded that it was powerless ; but no, the Lord had given him power at the moment he desired him to exert it ; and just so to every Christian, God is a God of all grace, and will give to each of us the peculiar grace we need ; but we must not lock it up, and imagine it to be efficacious without exertion on our part."

Louis was silent for some minutes. At length he turned his face up to his father, and said—

" What would you advise me to do ?"

" What do you think yourself would be best ?" said his father. " Think always *after* earnest prayer for divine guidance, what seems right to do, what the Bible says, and how it will be to the glory of your Saviour ; then, when you have made up your mind as to the rectitude of any plan of action, let your movements be prompt and decided, and do not leave the silly heart any room to suggest its excuses and modifications. Your judgment may sometimes err, but it is better for the judgment than the conscience to be in fault. Be assured that if you thus acknowledge God in all your ways, He will direct your paths."

Louis paused another moment, and said—

"Will you take that book, father, and not let me have it any more to-day, as it has interfered so much with my study; and I will try to be more industrious. I will finish my Prometheus and Euclid, and the projection of my map, and then, perhaps, I shall be ready for the reading."

Mr. Mortimer shook his head as he held up his watch before his son's eyes—

"Too late, Louis. The time is lost, and something must be missed to-day."

"Then, papa, I will do my Greek, and go to the reading, and then, instead of amusing myself after lunch, I will do the other things—and please take that book away with you."

"I had rather leave it," said Mr. Mortimer. "You must learn to act for yourself and by yourself. You do not expect to be always a boy, and if these weaknesses are not checked now, you will grow up a weak man, sadly dependent upon external influences and circumstances. Put the book out of your way by all means, but let it be your own act. And now I will leave you to do your work, for I see you have done very little, and that little very ill."

When his father had left the room, Louis put the book on a shelf, and, turning his back to it, set himself to work with earnest determination. He rewrote what he had done so badly, took great pains with the new edition, and had the satisfaction of receiving his father's approval of his work in the evening. After lunch his disagreeable Euclid was completed, and the map finished, and Louis refrained steadily from looking at the book for the rest of the day; nor did he, though sorely inclined, open it the next day until he could do so with a safe conscience.

For the remainder of the holidays Louis adhered to his resolution; but I do not mean to say he trusted on his own resolution: that he had found, by painful experience, to be a broken reed. In dependence upon an Almighty helper, he steadily endeavored from day to day to perform what was required of him in his station and circumstances, and found his reward in peace of mind and consciousness of growing in grace.

CHAPTER XIII.

It seems, by common consent, established among school-boys, that school and school-masters are necessary evils, only endurable because incurable, and that, as a matter of course, the return to school must be looked on as a species of martyrdom, the victims of which are unanimously opposed to the usual persuasives that school-days are the happiest, and that they will wish themselves back again before they have left it long. We will not attempt to account for this perversity of opinion in the minds of the individuals alluded to, nor have we any intention of instituting an inquiry as to the probability of the origin of this repugnance to scholastic life being in the natural opposition of man's mind to discipline or order, and the tendency therein to dislike all that is especially arranged and placed before him plainly for his benefit; but I am sure that most of those among my readers who either have been, or are school-boys at this moment, will agree with me in declaring that, returning to school, after the vacation, is a dismal affair, and that, during the first week or fortnight, certain rebellious feelings are prominent, which it would be treason to breathe.

The close of the holidays had arrived, and it was decided that Louis should return to school with his brother, not-

15

withstanding his great wish to the contrary; but now his principles were firmer, his father was of opinion that mixing with a large party of boys was more calculated to supply what was wanting in his character than staying at home with his mother and sister, and, consequently, a day or two after the reopening of Ashfield House, Reginald and Louis were placed by their father safely in a coach that started from Norwich, and, in a rather sorrowful mood, began their long journey.

I have no adventures to mention; romantic incidents are rarely met with in a school-boy's life; nor was there any thing remarkable to relate in the day and a half's travel, beyond the stoppage for meals, and the changes of vehicle. Louis and his brother generally patronized the top of the coach, but as they drew near Bristol, Louis grew so sleepy and tired, from the length of the journey, as well as the imperfect slumber obtained inside the preceding night, that he preferred changing his quarters, to the risk of falling from his perch above. It so happened that the coach was empty inside, and Louis indulged himself by stretching at full length on one of the seats, and soon lost the recollection of his troubles in sleep. How long he had slept he could not tell, when the stopping of the coach disturbed him, and rising lazily, he looked out to see where they were. Instead, however, of the "White Lion," in Bristol, or the "Roadside Inn," with the four waiting horses, there was opposite the window a pretty house, standing in a moderately sized garden, gay with countless flowers, green grass, and waving trees. It was such a house as Louis with his romance loved; low and old-fashioned, with a broad glass door in the centre, on one side of which was a long casement-win-

dow, and on the other, two thick sashes.   The house, ex-
tending to some length, displayed among the evergreen
shrubs, delicate roses and honey-suckles, a variety of odd
windows, from the elegant French to the deep old-fashioned
bay ; and over the front, almost entirely concealing the
rough gray stucco, was a vine, the young grapes of which
fell gracefully over the little bedroom windows, suggesting
the idea, how very pleasant it would be, when the fruit
was ripe, to obtain it at so little trouble.   Louis especially
noticed the sheltering trees, that grew to a great height
close behind the house, and the long shadows thrown by
the evening sun across the smooth green lawn.

While he was admiring the little prospect before him, a
maid-servant, assisted by the guard of the coach, appeared
at the door, carrying a black trunk, and behind followed
another elderly servant, with a carpet-bag and basket.   It
was very evident that another passenger might be expected,
and a few seconds more threw considerable light on the
doubt enveloping the expected personage.   The glass door
before mentioned, opened into a low square hall, and at the
further end, just as the carpet-bag reached the garden gate,
appeared a group, of which, till it arrived at the door, little
could be discerned but some white frocks.   Presently, however, a pleasant middle-aged gentleman came out, holding
by the hand a tearful-looking little boy, seemingly about
nine or ten years old.   The shade of his cap was pulled
down very far over his forehead, but enough of his face
was visible to betray some very showery inclinations.   Two
little girls, one older and the other younger, clung round
him ; the little one was weeping bitterly.   When they
reached the gate, the gentleman shook the boy's hand, and

gave him in charge of the guard, to see him safely into a
coach to convey him to Ashfield House.

"No fear of that, sir," replied the guard, opening the
coach door, and putting in the bag and basket. "I dare
say these young gentlemen would let him ride with them:
they are for Dr. Wilkinson's."

"Indeed," said the gentleman, looking at Reginald, and
then following the jerk of the guard's thumb at Louis;
"perhaps you will share your fly with my son?" Reginald replied that they would be most happy. The gentleman thanked him, and turning to his little boy, who was
hugging his youngest sister at the moment, said cheerfully,
"Well, Charles, this is pleasant; here are some school-
fellows already. You will have time to make friends before you reach the doctor's. Come, my boy."

Charles had burst into a torrent of fresh tears, and sobbing his "Good-byes," got into the coach very quickly.

"Come, come, you mustn't be a baby," said his father,
squeezing both his hands; and he shut the coach door
himself.

"Good-bye, Charlie," said the little girls.

"Good-bye, master Charles," said the servants.

"I shall be so glad when Christmas comes," sobbed the
little one.

The coach rolled away, amid the adieus and blessings
poured on the disconsolate boy, who watched his home
eagerly as long as he could see it. There they were all—
father, sisters, and servants, watching at the gate till the
coach was out of sight. For some time, Louis did not
attempt to console his new companion, who threw himself
into the opposite corner, and burying his face in his hand-

kerchief, sobbed passionately, without any effort at self-control. At length, the violence of his grief abating, Louis gently spoke to him, asking if he had ever been away from home before. At first, Charles was very reserved, and only answered Louis' questions; but by degrees his sobs decreased, and from declaring that he could not see the reason of his being sent away from home, he at last talked freely to Louis of his father, sisters, and home; and asked Louis of his. Louis was ready enough to enlarge on these topics, and entered into an enthusiastic description of home and its pleasures, and before they had reached their journey's end, they had become very good friends.

Charles had informed Louis that his father was a clergyman, and that his home was the parsonage house; and enlarged very much on the pleasure of being taught by his father. There was something in his manner of expressing himself that often surprised Louis, and made him think that he must be older than he appeared. Before they reached Bristol, they had agreed to be "great friends," and to help each other as much as possible. Charles had evidently been very carefully brought up, and Louis found that they had many things in common. They decided to be companions on Sunday, and to be together whenever they could.

Between seven and eight o'clock, the coach stopped in Bristol, where Reginald joined his brother; and after a few minutes spent in taking a hasty tea, the three boys were consigned to a suitable conveyance, and drove on to Dr. Wilkinson's.

Reginald had a mortal aversion to tears in any boy but Louis, and had consequently taken an antipathy to his new

school-fellow, besides caring very little about so small a boy.
He was just civil to him, and his manner bringing out all
Charles's shyness, he became very silent, and scarcely any
thing was said during the ride from Bristol to Ashfield
House.

It would be of little use describing the interesting appearance that Ashfield House presented when the three
young gentlemen arrived there.   Such descriptions are
generally skipped ; consequently, I leave it to my reader's
imagination to picture how romantic the edifice looked,
with the last faint yellow daylight glowing on its front,
and the first few stars peeping out on the green park.

Our young gentlemen, be assured, noticed nothing but
the very dismal impression that they were once more at
school.   Inquiring if the doctor were to be seen, they were
informed that he was expected in a few minutes, as it was
nearly prayer-time ; and accordingly Reginald marshalled
the way without a word to the school-room.   There was
no one in the hall or school-room, but a murmur from the
half-open door of the adjoining class-room drew them in
that direction.   The room was nearly full, for besides the
first and second classes there were many belonging to the
third class, and one or two others who had either arrived
late, or taken advantage of the little additional license
given the first few days to stay beyond their usual bed-
time.   It was too dark to distinguish faces, but the figure
of Frank Digby, who had managed with great pains to
climb the mantelpiece, and was delivering an oration, would
have been unmistakable if even he had been silent ;—who
but Frank Digby could have had spirit to do it the third
night after the opening of the school ?

The finale to Digby's speech.   Page 175.

"Gentlemen and ladies," began the merry-andrew; "I beg your pardon, the Lady Louisa not having arrived, and Miss Maria Matheson being in bed, I ought to have omitted that term—but, gentlemen, I take this opportunity, gentlemen, the opportunity of the eleventh demi-anniversary of our delightful reunion. Gentlemen, I am aware that some of you have not been fortunate enough to see eleven, but some among us have seen more. I, gentlemen, have seen eleven at this auspicious moment. I may say it is the proudest moment of my life to be able to stand on this mantelpiece and look down on you all, to feel myself enrolled a member of such an august corps. I may say I feel myself elevated at this present moment, but as, gentlemen, there is no saying, in the precarious situation I am now placed, how long I may be in a position to contemplate the elegance of his majesty and court, I hasten to propose that his majesty's health be eaten in plum-cake, and that if I fall somebody will catch me.

"With kind regards to all,

"Believe me your attached school-fellow,

"FRANK DIGBY."

A little on one side of the fireplace, which was not far from the open window, Trevannion was leaning back in a chair that he had tipped on the hind legs till the back touched the wall behind him, his own legs being stretched out on another poised in like manner on the two side legs; this elegant and easy attitude being chosen partly for the convenience of speaking to Salisbury, who was nicely balanced on the window-sill, eating plum-cake. As the young gentleman concluded his delectable harangue, he made an involuntary leap from his narrow pedestal, plunging on the top of Trevannion's legs, and, tumbling over him, struck with some violence against Salisbury, who was thrown out of the window by the same concussion that brought his more fastidious compeer to the ground, chairs and all. There was a burst of merriment at this unexpected catastrophe, but nothing could exceed the mirth of the author of the mischief, who sat in unextinguishable laughter on the floor, to the imminent danger of his person when the enraged sufferers recovered their legs.

"Really! Digby," exclaimed Trevannion, angrily, "this foolery is unbearable. You deserve that we should give you a thrashing; if it were not beneath me, I most certainly would."

"You—ha! ha!" returned Frank: "ha! ha!—you must stoop to—ha! ha!—you must stoop to conquer—for, oh! oh! I can't get up. Pardon me, my dear fellow, but—oh! ha! ha!—you did look so ridiculous."

"Get up, you grinning donkey!" said Salisbury, who, in spite of his wrath, could not help laughing.

"Trevannion's legs!" exclaimed Frank, in a choking fit of laughter.

"Get up, Digby," exclaimed Trevannion, kicking him; "or I'll shake some of this nonsense out of you."

"Do be rational, Frank," said Hamilton's voice from a corner; "you are like a great baby."

How long Frank might have sat on the floor, and what direful events might have transpired, I cannot pretend to say, for just at this juncture the further door opened, and Dr. Wilkinson entered, bearing a candle in his hand. Frank very speedily found his legs, and retired into a corner to giggle unseen. The light thus suddenly introduced brought Reginald and his brother into notice, and one or two near the door recognizing them, pressed forward to speak to them, and before the doctor had fairly attained his place, Reginald had run the gauntlet of welcomes through all his school-fellows—and Louis, half-way on the same errand, was forcibly arrested by something scarcely short of an embrace from Hamilton, who expressed himself as surprised as pleased at his appearance, and in whose glistening eyes, as well as the friendly looks of those around, Louis experienced some relief from the almost insupportable sense of dulness that had oppressed him ever since his entrance into the house. But now, the doctor having opened his book, the young gentlemen were obliged to separate and form into their places. Hamilton kept Louis by him, and Louis beckoned the sorrowful little boy who had accompanied him towards them.

"Who is that?" asked the doctor, as the child moved shyly towards Louis.

"A new boy, sir," said one.

"What is your name?" said the doctor. "Come here. Oh! I see, it is Clifton, is it not?—how do you do?"

Charles had reached Dr. Wilkinson by this time, and, encouraged by his kind tone, and the sympathizing though slightly quizzical gaze on his very tearful face, replied to his queries in a low, quick tone.

"When did you come?" asked the doctor.

"He came with us, sir," said Reginald, stepping forward.

"Mortimer here!" said the doctor. "How do you do? and Louis, too, I presume—where is he? I am very glad to see you again," he added, as Louis came forward with a blushing but not miserable countenance.   He then spoke to the other new-comers, and then, commanding silence, read prayers.

The young gentlemen were just retiring, when Dr. Wilkinson desired them to stay a moment—" I have one request to make, young gentlemen," he said, gravely ; " that is, I particularly wish when Mr. Ferrers returns that no allusion be made to any thing gone by, and that you treat him as one worthy to be among you."

The doctor paused as he spoke, and glanced along the row of faces, many of which looked sullen and cloudy : most of them avoided their master's eye, and looked intently on the ground.   Dr. Wilkinson sought Hamilton's eye, but Hamilton, though perfectly conscious of the fact, was very busily engaged in a deep meditation on the texture of Louis' jacket.

" Hamilton."

" Sir," replied Hamilton, reluctantly raising his eyes.

" I look to you, as the head of the school, to set the example.   I am grieved to see so little Christian spirit among you.   Why should you feel more aggrieved than the injured party, who has, I am sure, heartily forgiven all, and will wish no further notice to be taken of what has passed ?"

Louis looked up acquiescently, and slipped his hand into Hamilton's.   A slight pressure was returned, and Hamilton, bowing to the doctor, led the way out of the room.

On the way up stairs many rebellious comments were made on the doctor's speech, and some invoked tremendous penalties on themselves if they had any thing to do with him or any like him. Hamilton was quite silent, neither checking nor exciting the malcontents. He put his hand into Louis' arm, and, walking up stairs with him, wished him a warm good-night, and marched off to his own apartment.

This evening, as there were one or two new-comers, an usher was present in the dormitory to insure the orderly appropriation of the several couches ; and, to Louis' great satisfaction, he was able to get quietly into bed—where, feeling very dull and sad, he covered his head over and unconsciously performed a crying duet with his new friend.

Hardly had the usher departed than Frank Digby popped his head out of bed :

" I don't know," said he, " whether any one expects a feast to-night, from a few unlucky remarks which fell from me this morning ; if so, gentlemen, I wish immediately to dispel the pleasing delusion, assuring you of the melancholy fact, that my golden pippins have fallen victims to Gruffy's rapacity."

" Oh, what a shame !" exclaimed one.

" What's that, Frank ?" said Reginald.

" How did Gruffy get hold of them ?" asked Meredith : " I thought you were more than her match."

" Why, the fact is, her olfactory nerves becoming strongly excited, she insisted upon having a search, and after snuffing about, she came near my hiding-place, and found the little black portmanteau :

" ' Upon my word, Mr. Digby,' said she, ' I am surprised at your dirtiness—putting apples under your pillow !' and insisted on having the key or the apples. I disclaimed all ideas of apples, but quite failed in persuading her that I had Russian leather-covered books inside, that were placed there to enable me to pursue my studies at the first dawn of day. You should have heard her: 'Did I suppose she was an idiot, and couldn't smell apples!' and oh—nobody knows how much more. But I should have carried my point if ill-luck hadn't brought Fudge in the way, and the harpy carried off my treasures."

Frank paused, and then added, in a tone that set every one laughing, "It's a pity she can't be transported into heathen mythology; she'd have made an excellent dragon. Hercules would never have been so successful if she'd been that of Hesperia. I'll be even with her yet; but there's something very forlorn in one's troubles beginning directly."

The next morning brought with it the stern reality of school. Louis was dreaming that he was in Dashwood with Charles Clifton, when the bell-man came into the breakfast-room, crying out that the golden pippins belonging to his attached school-fellow, Frank Digby, were lost, stolen, or strayed; and that he would be even with any who should find them, and bring them to the Hesperides; and he was in the act of proving, more to his own satisfaction than to that of the bell-man, that the books in the library were what he wanted, when Reginald discovered them,—i. e., the golden apples,—peeping from under his pillow, and shook him violently for his deceit.

" Louis, Louis!—the bell, the bell."

He started up in great alarm, and discovered that he was sitting on his bed at school, listening to the sonorous clanging of the bell below.

Groans, shouts, and sleepy exclamations reverberated

round him. Reginald, rather more accustomed to good
early habits at home than some of his room-fellows, was
busy rousing those who either did not, or pretended not to
hear the summons. Among the latter was our friend Frank
Digby, who stoutly resisted being awakened, and when
obliged to yield to the determined efforts of his cousin,
nearly overwhelmed him with a species of abuse.

"That bell's a complete bugbear," he groaned. "It
ought to be indicted for a nuisance, waking people up o'
mornings when they ought to be in the arms of Morpheus—
I've a great mind to lie still. Half an hour's sleep is worth
sixpence."

"It's much better laid out with 'Maister,' Frank," suggested Meredith.

"And then Fudge will be so black about it," said Reginald. "Come, up with you, Frank."

"As for Fudge," said Frank, "I wouldn't give you twopence for him, nor his black looks neither. But you may
be sure he'll be amiable enough this morning. He has
been remarkably affectionate these few mornings—hasn't
he, Meredith?"

"*To be sure*," replied the young gentleman addressed:
"when did you know a master otherwise the first week?
They all know there's danger of our cutting their acquaintance in a summary manner, and take good care to be bland
enough till we're tamed down."

"For my part," said Frank, "I have been longing for
an opportunity of putting Fudge in a passion. If only he
or Danby would box my ears for something, that I might
fling a book at his head, and have a legitimate excuse for
taking myself off—but, alas! they are all so dreadfully

amiable, except old Garthorpe, and he's beneath all consideration."

Frank continued in this strain for some minutes, working himself into a more rebellious humor, stimulated by those among his companions who admired this demonstration of spirit. Confidentially I may remark, that though running away seems to be the desideratum of a discontented school-boy, it is far more interesting in theory than practice, and I doubt much whether any malcontent who availed himself of this as his only refuge from the miserable fate awaiting him in the dungeon to which he was consigned, ever considered in the end that his condition had been materially improved. Spangled canopies and soft turf couches do well to read of, but stiff limbs and anxious hearts are sterner realities, to say nothing of sundry woes inflicted on the culprit when discovered. But I am enlarging and must return from my digression.

Dr. Wilkinson was engaged the greater part of the morning in arranging the different classes and examining his new pupils. Great surprise was felt among those interested, in the news that Charles Clifton was to take his place in the second class. Even the doctor paused once or twice in his examination, and looked earnestly on the great forehead and small pale face of the child.

"Why, how old are you?" said he, at length.

"Twelve, sir," replied Charles, gravely.

"Very little of your age. Have you ever been at school before?"

Charles replied in the negative, and after another momentary scrutiny, Dr. Wilkinson asked a few concluding questions, and then unhesitatingly declared him a member of the second class.

Louis had, this half-year, a far better chance of distinguishing himself than before, as his brother and Meredith, with one or two others, had mounted into the first class, and John Salisbury had not returned. He was, however, not a little surprised when Hamilton informed him that he would have enough to do to keep pace with his new friend, whom he had looked upon as quite one of the lower school.

CHAPTER XIV.

THE first long dreary week had passed : quicker, however, in its peaceable monotony than many a gayer time
has been known to do, and the young gentlemen of Ashfield House were beginning to settle down soberly and
rationally to their inevitable fate. Louis' position was so
altered this half-year, that he hardly understood himself
the universal affection and consideration with which he was
treated.   He was indubitably a favorite with the doctor, but
no one was jealous, for he bore his honors very meekly,
and was always willing to share his favors with others,
neither encroaching on nor abusing the kindness displayed
towards him by his master, who seemed, in common with
his pupils, to be exceedingly desirous of obliterating all
remembrance of the misunderstanding of the last half-year.
But the doctor's affection was much more sparingly exhibited than Hamilton's, who seemed at times to forget
every thing for Louis.   He was now made the companion
of the seniors——he had free admission into all their parties.
Hamilton seemed unable to walk into Bristol unless Louis
were allowed to accompany him.   Louis' place in the evening was now by Hamilton, who did his utmost to make him
steady, and to prevent him from yielding the first place to
Clifton, who very soon proved himself to be a boy of con-

siderable genius, united with much steadiness of purpose, and who had, evidently, been very carefully educated. One evening about this time, when most of the class-room party were very busy, under the orderly supervision of Messrs. Hamilton and Trevannion, the door was quietly opened and Ferrers entered with that doubtful air that expected an unfavorable reception. When I speak of business and quietude at Ashfield House it must, of course, be understood as comparative, for the quietest evening in that renowned academy would have furnished noise enough to have distracted half the quiet parlors in the kingdom—and on this particular evening there was quite enough to cover the bashful entrance of · the former bully. Hamilton was writing, and doubly engaged in keeping Louis from listening to an interesting history, delivered by Salisbury, of a new boy who had arrived that half-year from a neighboring school. The boy in question was a cunning dunce, who had already discovered Louis' failing, and having partaken of the assistance Louis supplied as liberally as allowed, had come more especially under the ken of the seniors, and Hamilton had been administering a reproof to Louis for helping Casson before getting his own lessons ready.

Ferrers had nearly reached the upper end of the table before any one was aware of his vicinity, when Trevannion, looking up from his writing to dip his pen anew in the ink, caught sight of him, recognizing him so suddenly that even his equanimity was almost surprised into a start. He colored slightly, and coldly acknowledging his presence by a stiff bow and a muttered "How do you do," returned to his work, not, however, before his movement had attracted the attention of one or two others. The intimation of his presence was conveyed almost talismanically round the room, and a silence ensued while the young gentlemen looked at one another for an example. These unfriendly symptoms added considerably to Ferrers' embarrassment. Pale with anxiety, he affected to notice nothing, and looked for a place at one of the tables where he might lay the books he had brought in with him. The silence, however, had made Hamilton now very conscious of what, till this moment, he had been in blissful ignorance—that his voice was raised to nearly a shouting pitch to make his admonitions sufficiently impressive to his protegé—and the sonorous tones of his voice, delivering an emphatic oration on weakness and perseverance contrasted, were so remarkable that the attention was a little drawn from Ferrers by this unusual phenomenon.

"What a burst of eloquence!" exclaimed Frank, who, on the first sound of the kingly voice, had begun to attitudinize ; while Trevannion gazed on his friend with a quiet, gentlemanly air of inquiry, that was not to be put out of countenance by any circumstance how ludicrous soever. "His majesty's in an oratorical vein to-night. Such a flow of graceful language, earnest, mellifluous persuasives dropping like sugar-plums from his lips!"

"Three cheers for his majesty's speech," cried Salisbury.

These comments were hailed by a hearty laugh, mingled with clapping of hands, and an effort on the part of a few to raise a cheer. Hamilton joined in the laugh, though he had been so intent upon his lecture that at first he hardly comprehended the joke.

"Your majesty's been studying rhetoric since we had the pleasure of a speech," remarked Reginald, when a little lull had succeeded to the uproarious mirth. "Mercury himself couldn't have done better."

"Considering that the speeches of Edward the Great usually savor of Spartan brevity," said Smith, "we couldn't have hoped for such a masterpiece."

"You don't understand his most gracious majesty," said Frank; "depend upon it he's a veritable cameleon."

At this juncture, Louis, whose eyes had a sad habit of wandering when they should be otherwise employed, caught sight of Ferrers, and, starting up, he welcomed him with the utmost heartiness.

Hamilton looked round and colored furiously, but before Ferrers had time to make any answers to Louis' rapid questions, he rose, and, stepping forward, held out his hand—

"How are you, Ferrers?" he said, in a cheerful tone, "I neither saw nor heard you come in just now. You have not been here long, have you?"

Ferrers grasped Hamilton's hand and looked in his face, astonished and overcome with gratitude for this unexpected welcome. The silence of the few minutes before was resumed, and every eye was riveted on Hamilton, who, perceiving from the tight grasp on his hand and the crimsoned countenance of Ferrers, his utter inability to speak, and being anxious to remove the insupportable feeling of awkwardness under which he felt sure he labored, continued, without waiting for an answer—

"You are very late this half. We have expected you every day."

He then sat down and went on telling Ferrers about the new-comers, and the present condition of the first class, asking him some questions about his journey, and all so

quickly and cleverly as neither to appear forced, nor to
oblige Ferrers to speak more than he chose. While Hamilton spoke he only now and then glanced at him from his
work, which he had apparently resumed as soon as he sat
down.

"His majesty's taken Fudge's hint," said Frank, in a low,
discontented tone.

"Hamilton can, of course, do as he likes, but I won't,"
said another, with a nod of determination.   "We're not
obliged to follow his lead."

"Trevannion won't, you'll see," muttered Peters.

"Be kind enough to lend me your lexicon, Salisbury,"
said Trevannion, who had, since Hamilton's notice of Ferrers, assumed an air of more than ordinary dignity, and
now reached across Ferrers for the book, as if there were
no one there. Ferrers made an effort to assist in the tran-
sition of the thick volume, but all his politeness obtained
was a haughty, cold stare, and a determined rejection of
assistance. Louis was sure that Hamilton observed this
action, from the expression of his face, but he made no remark, and continued to talk to Ferrers a little longer, when
he laughingly pleaded his avocations as an excuse for being
silent ; but Louis was now disengaged, and Reginald had
happily followed Hamilton's example, for though at first
inclined to be on Trevannion's side, he could not help pity-
ing his evident distress, and, touched by the emotion he
exhibited, he exerted himself to smooth all down. Had all
been as cold and repulsive as Trevannion and his advocates,
Ferrers would have been dogged and proud, but now the
sense of gratitude and humility was predominant, and at last
so overpowered him, that he was glad to get away in the

play-ground by himself. As he closed the door, the buz was resumed, and an attack was made on Hamilton by those who had determinedly held back.

"Your royal clemency is most praiseworthy, most magnanimous Edward," said Frank Digby.

"Worthy of you, Hamilton," said Trevannion, sneeringly. "Ferrers is a fit companion and associate for gentlemen."

"My manners not bearing any comparison with yours,' replied Hamilton, coolly, "I am not so chary of contamination."

"That's a hit at your slip just now, Trevannion," said Smith. "How could you commit such a what-do-you-call it? gooch—gaucherie."

"You had better take lessons of the old woman over the way," said Salisbury; "she only charges twopence *extra for them as learns manners.*"

"A good suggestion," said Trevannion, laughing; "will you pay for me, Hamilton?"

"Willingly," replied Hamilton, in a low, deep tone, "if, on inquiry, I find her good manners are the result of good feeling."

"I am excessively indebted to you," replied Trevannion, coloring; "and feel exceedingly honored by the solicitude of Ferrers' friend."

"Just as you choose to feel it, Trevannion," said Hamilton; "but I had better speak my mind, gentlemen,—I do not think we have, as a body, remembered the doctor's injunction."

"How could we?" "Is it likely?" "No, indeed." "I dare say!" "Very fine!" sounded on all sides.

"Hear me to the end," said Hamilton; "I have not much to say."

"Two speeches in one night!" said Jones. "Never was such condescension."

Hamilton took no notice of the jeering remarks round him, but having obtained a little silence, continued——

"We have made enough of this business. It is cruel now to carry it on further. I confess myself to have felt as much repugnance as any one could feel, to renewing any thing beyond the barest possible intercourse with Ferrers; but let us consider, first, that it becomes us, while we are Dr. Wilkinson's pupils, to pay some respect to his wishes, whether they coincide with our feelings or not; and next, whether it is charitable to shut a school-fellow out of a chance of reformation. Let us put ourselves in his place."

".A very desirable position; rather too much for imagination," remarked Trevannion.

"It is a miserable position," said Hamilton; "therefore we should do well to endeavor to help him out of it. I have no doubt if we had been once in so painful a situation, we should not have considered ourselves as hopeless or irremediable characters—nor is he; he is quite overcome to-night because all have not been quite such savages as he expected."

"As he would have been. He wouldn't have been merciful!" exclaimed Meredith.

"That's nothing to the purpose," said Hamilton. "We have only to act rightly ourselves. Give him a chance. If he forfeit it by a similar offence, I will not say another word for him."

There was a dead silence when Hamilton had finished.

His appeal had the more effect, that he was usually too indolent to trouble himself much about what did not immediately concern him or his, but took all as he found it.

"In giving what you call a chance, Hamilton," said Trevannion, who alone, in the indecision evident, remained entirely unmoved; "in giving what you call a chance, you forget that we implicate ourselves. As honorable individuals, as gentlemen, we cannot admit to fellowship one who has so degraded himself. To be 'hail-fellow-well-met' with him, were to lower ourselves. We do not prevent his improving himself. When he has done so, let us talk of receiving him among us again. In my opinion, Dr. Wilkinson's allowing him to return is as much, and a great deal more than he could expect."

"I shall say nothing more," said Hamilton. "I do not often make a request."

"I know what Louis would say," said Salisbury, who had been watching Louis' earnest, gratified gaze on Hamilton for the last few minutes; "I think we ought to be guided by him in this matter."

"I! oh, I wish just what Hamilton has said—you know I wished it long ago."

"What Louis says shall be the law," said Jones. "We won't refuse him any thing."

"Especially in this matter," said Salisbury. "He's a brick, and so is his majesty, after all. My best endeavors for your side, Louis."

"And mine," said Jones.

"I'll outwardly forgive the culprit, at any rate," said Frank. Several others expressed their desire to abide by the same resolution; Hamilton looked his satisfaction, Trevannion sulkily recommenced his work, and Louis stole out of the room to find Casson, that he might finish telling him his lesson, according to promise. When Dr. Wilkinson arrived, he narrowly watched the manners of his pupils towards Ferrers, and was satisfied with his scrutiny, though he was, of course, unconscious of the means by which the civility shown had been procured. It is to be hoped that we have not gone so far in the delineation of Dr. Wilkinson's school, without discovering that the spirit of honor and confidence was generally high among the young gentlemen, and, consequently, having promised to be friendly to Ferrers, each individual, in duty bound, did his utmost to fulfil that promise, and in a little while the stiffness attendant on the effort wore off, and Ferrers was, in appearance, in precisely the same position as before, to the great satisfaction of the doctor, who was much pleased with his pupils' conduct on the occasion.

CHAPTER XV.

" WHERE is Louis Mortimer?" asked Hamilton, the next Saturday afternoon, about a quarter of an hour after dinner. " Does any one know where Louis Mortimer is?"

" Here I am, Hamilton, *prêt à vous servir*, as Monsieur Gregoire would say!" cried Louis, starting from behind the school-room door.

" Are you engaged this afternoon?"

" Never, when you want me!" exclaimed Louis.

Hamilton looked gratified, but checked the expression as soon as he was aware of it.

" That is not right, Louis; I never wish, and never ought, to be an excuse for breaking an engagement."

" But suppose I make your possible requirements a condition of my engagements," said Louis, archly; " you have no objection to that, have you?"

" Only I cannot imagine such a case."

" Such is the case, however, this afternoon. I had the vanity to hope you would let me walk with you, and so only engaged myself conditionally."

" To whom were you engaged in default of my sufferance?"

" I was going to stay with Casson," replied Louis, hesitatingly. " He has a cold and headache, and he asked me

. 17

if I would stay with him in the class-room, where he is obliged to stay while we are out."

"Casson !" said Hamilton, contemptuously ; "you were not talking to him just now?"

"No ; I was only listening to Ferrers. He was telling me about a wager Frank had just laid with Salisbury."

"How is it you prefer Casson to your friend Clifton?"

"Oh, Hamilton, I don't much like Casson ; but he asked me, poor fellow. Charlie's engaged to West—our days are Sunday, Monday, and Thursday."

"Which of you is first now?"

"Charles is, to-day," said Louis ; "he is so very clever, Hamilton."

"I know he is ; but you are older, and not a dunce, if you were not idle, Louis. Louis, I shall repudiate you, if you don't get past him."

"That would be a terrible fate," said Louis, slipping his hand into Hamilton's. "I cannot tell you how I should miss your kind face and help. You have been such a very kind friend to me : but I have not been so very idle, Hamilton."

"Yes, you have," returned Hamilton ; "I am vexed with you, Louis. If I did not watch over you as I do, you would be as bad as you were last half. Don't tell me you can't keep before Clifton if you choose."

Louis looked gravely in Hamilton's face, and put his other hand on that he held. Hamilton drew his own quickly away.

"Lady Louisa," he said, "these affectionate demonstrations may do well enough for us alone, but keep them for private service, and don't let us play *Damon* and *Pythia* in this touching manner, to so large an audience. It partakes slightly of the absurd."

Louis colored, and seemed a little hurt; but he replied, "I am afraid I am very girlish sometimes."

"Incontrovertibly," said Hamilton, kindly laying his hand heavily on Louis' shoulder. "But we have no desire that any one should laugh at you but our royal self."

"Are we going to the downs?" asked Louis.

Before Hamilton could answer, Frank Digby, one of the large audience alluded to, came up. "Of course," he replied; "Hamilton is one of our party."

"One of your party?" asked Hamilton.

"Your majesty's oblivious of the fact," said Frank, "that among the many offices, honorary and distinctive, held by your most gracious self, the presidency of the 'Ashfield Cricket Club' is not altogether one of the most insignificant."

"We will thank our faithful amanuensis to become our deputy this afternoon," said Hamilton; "having a great desire to refresh ourself with a quiet discourse on the beauties of Nature."

"No cricket this afternoon, Hamilton!" cried Louis; "I shall be so much disappointed if you go!"

"No cricket!" exclaimed Frank: "we will enter into a conspiracy, and dethrone Edward, if he refuses to come instanter."

"Dethrone me by all means, this afternoon," said Hamilton; "my deposition will save me a great deal of trouble. I am only afraid that my freedom from state affairs would be of short duration; my subjects appear to be able to do so little without me."

" Hear him !" exclaimed Jones, laughing ; " hear king Log !"

" No favoritism !" cried Smith ; " I bar all partiality. We'll treat you in the Gaveston fashion, Louis, if you don't persuade your master to accede to our reasonable demands."

" That would be treason against my own comforts," said Louis, laughing, and struggling unsuccessfully to rise from the ground, where he had been playfully thrown by Salisbury. " To the rescue ! your majesty ; I cry help !"

" To the rescue !" shouted Reginald, pouncing suddenly upon Salisbury, and diverting his attention from Louis who would have recovered his feet, but for the intervention of one or two of the party.

" Your majesty perceives," said Frank, " that a rebellion is already broken out. A word from you may compose all."

" I have engaged to walk with Louis Mortimer, and I declare I will not stir anywhere without him," said Hamilton.

" We cannot do without you, Hamilton," said Trevannion, who had just joined the council. " You are engaged for all the meetings."

" Which meetings have no right to be convened without the concurrence of the president ;—eh, Mr. Secretary ?" rejoined Hamilton.

" Of course you can please yourself," said Trevannion, proudly.

" Let Louis get up, Jones," said Hamilton.

" Does your majesty concede, or not ?" said Jones, who was sitting upon Louis.

" I will answer when you let him get up."

Jones suffered Louis to rise, breathless and hot with his laughing exertions to free himself from durance vile.

"I will come, on condition that Louis comes too."

"Certainly," said Salisbury.

"And join our game, mind," said Hamilton.

"Oh!" exclaimed Smith; "that's decidedly another affair. You can't play, Sir Piers, can you?"

"He can learn," said Hamilton, who was perfectly aware of his ignorance.

"I've not the smallest objection," said Jones, "as I'm on the opposition side."

"Nor I," cried Salisbury; "though I should be a loser, as is probable."

"Really, Hamilton," exclaimed Trevannion, sulkily, "it's impossible! He'll only be in the way. I never saw such a fuss about a boy; it's quite absurd. If you want him, let him look on."

"I don't like cricket," said Louis.

"Humbug!" exclaimed Salisbury.

"I shall be in the way, as Trevannion says," continued Louis; "I am sure I shall never learn."

"'*Patientia et perseverantia omnia vincunt,*'" remarked Frank; "which may be freely translated in three ways:

'If a weary task you find it,
Persevere, and never mind it;'

or,

'Never say die;'

or, thirdly,

'If at first you don't succeed,—try, try again,'"

"Louisa, I am ashamed for you," said Hamilton; "and insist on the exhibition of a more becoming spirit."

" That's right, Hamilton," cried Reginald ; " make him learn."

Louis pleaded as much as he dared, in dread of a few thumps, friendly in intent, but vigorous in execution, from Salisbury, and a second shaking from Hamilton, but all in vain, and they sallied forth. Trevannion fastened on Hamilton, and grumbled ineffectual remonstrances till they reached a convenient spot for their game. Here, under the active supervision of Hamilton, Salisbury, and Reginald, Louis was duly initiated ; and after a couple of hours' play they returned home, Louis being in some doubt as to whether his fingers were not all broken by the concussion of a cricket-ball, but otherwise more favorably disposed towards the game than heretofore. He was, likewise, not a little gratified by the evident interest most of the players took in his progress. Hamilton had entirely devoted himself to his instruction, encouraged him when he made an effort, and laughed at his cowardliness, and Salisbury had been scarcely less kind.

As they entered the playground, Salisbury held up a silver pencil-case to Frank :

" Remember, Frank," said he, warningly.

" Do you think I've forgotten ?" said Frank ; " my memory's not quite so treacherous, Mr. Salisbury."

" What's that, Salisbury ?" said Jones.

" Only my wager."

" Wager !" repeated Hamilton. " What absurdity is Frank about to perpetrate now ?"

" He is going to make Casson swallow some medicine of his own concoction. My pencil-case against his purse, contents and all, he isn't able to do it. Casson's too sharp."

" I am surprised," said Hamilton, " that Frank is not above playing tricks on that low boy. I thought you had had enough of it, Frank."

Frank laughed :—" No, he has foiled me regularly twice lately, and I am determined to pay him off for shamming this afternoon."

" I think it is real," said Louis.

" Then he has all the more need of medicine," said Frank ; " and if he supposes it, my physic will do him as much good as any one else's."

" You'll certainly get yourself into some serious scrape some day with these practical jokes, Frank," said Hamilton. " It is a most ungentlemanly propensity."

" Hear, hear," said Reginald.

" What's that ? Who goes there ?" said Frank, directing the attention of the company to the figure of a tall woman neatly dressed in black silk, with an old-fashioned bonnet of the coal-scuttle species, who was crossing from the house to the playground at the moment ; the lady in question being no other than the housekeeper, clothes-mender, &c., to Dr. Wilkinson, introduced by Mr. Frank Digby as Gruffy, more properly rejoicing in the name of Mrs. Guppy.

" It's Gruffy, isn't it ? Where is she going, I wonder."

Without waiting for an answer, Frank flew round the house, and disappeared in the forbidden regions of the kitchen.

" What is he after ?" said Meredith. " I suspect we shall have some fun to-night."

" I do wish Frank wouldn't be so fond of such nonsense," said Hamilton, angrily. " Come, Louis, and take a turn till the tea-bell rings."

They had taken two or three turns up and down in front of the school-room, when the bell rang, and Frank Digby came back full of glee.

"I've done it, Salisbury," he cried, as he threw his hat in the air. "I've done it. I shall kill two birds with one stone. I'm sure to win; it's all settled; only I must be allowed to put the school-room clock forward half an hour."

"That wasn't in the bargain," said Salisbury.

"It wasn't out of it, at any rate," said Frank.

"It's all fair," said several voices; "he may do it which way he pleases."

"Remember, *tace*," said Frank. "*Tace* is the candle that lights Casson to bed to-night."

"I promise nothing, Frank," said Hamilton.

"Nevertheless you'll keep it," said Frank, laughing.

When tea was over, Frank disappeared rather mysteriously.

Salisbury had just begun to make use of one of the pile of books he had brought to the table in the class-room, when a notification was brought to him from the school-room, that Mrs. Guppy wanted to speak to him.

"Bother take her!" he exclaimed. "Why can't she come and speak to me? Interrupting a fellow at his work! Don't take my place; I shall be back presently."

Some time, however, elapsed, and no Salisbury. Now and then a few wonderments were expressed as to how Frank's wager would be won, and as to what Mrs. Guppy could want with Salisbury.

"Where is Frank, I wonder?" said one. "Just see, Peters, if Casson's gone yet."

Peters departed, and returned with the news that Casson had gone to bed a little while before.

"The farce has begun, I suspect," said Meredith. "It's more than half an hour since Salisbury went,—and depend upon it, wherever he is, there is Frank."

At this moment Salisbury rushed into the room, and throwing himself in a sitting posture on the floor, with his back against the wall as if completely exhausted, laughed on without uttering a word, till his mirth became so infectious, that nearly all the room joined him.

"Well, Salisbury!" "Well, Salisbury!" "What is it?" "Tell us." "Have done laughing, do, you wretch, you merry-andrew." "Do be sensible."

"Sensible!" groaned Salisbury, laying his head against a form; "oh, hold me, somebody—I'm quite knocked up with laughing. It's enough to make a fellow insensible for the rest of his life."

"Well, what is it, madcap?" said Reginald, jumping up from his seat, and approaching him in a threatening attitude.

"Frank Digby!" said Salisbury, going off into another paroxysm of laughter.

"Shake him into a little sense, Mortimer," said Jones.

"Come, Salisbury, what is it?" said several more, coming up to him.

Salisbury sat upright and wiped his eyes.

"It was the clearest case of stabbing a man with his own sword I ever saw. I don't know whether I shall ever get it out for laughing, but I'll try."

Louis looked up at Hamilton, rather anxious to get nearer to Salisbury, but Hamilton wrote on as if determined neither

to let Louis move, nor to pay any attention himself, and
Louis dared not ask.

"Well, you know, Mrs. Guppy sent for me.   I went off
in a beautiful humor, as you may imagine, and found her
ladyship in a great dressing-gown, false front, and spectacles, surrounded by little boys in various stages of Saturday night's going to bed, tucking up Casson very comfortably.

"'Oh, Mr. Salisbury,' said she, 'I'll speak with you
presently,—will you be so good as to wait there a minute?'

"Well, I thought she looked very odd, but she spoke
just the same as ever ; and being very cross, I said, 'I am
in a hurry; perhaps when you've done you'll call on me
in the study.'   Whereupon her ladyship comes straight out
of the room, and says on the landing, in Frank Digby's
voice, 'Know me by this token, *I am mixing a black
draught by the light of a Latin candle.*'"

Salisbury burst out into a fresh fit of laughter, in which
he was joined by all present except Hamilton, who steadily
pursued his work with an unmoved countenance.

"Well, you may imagine," said Salisbury, when he had
recovered himself, "I wasn't in a hurry then.   I came back
and waited behind the door very patiently.   You never saw
any thing so exact—every motion and tone.   He had pulled
the curls over his eyes, and tied up his face with a great
handkerchief over the cap, as Gruffy has been doing lately
when she had the face-ache, and he went about among the
little chaps in such a motherly, bustling way, it was quite
affecting.   Sally, who helped him, hadn't the least idea it
wasn't Gruffy.   However, the best of it is to come," said
Salisbury, pausing a moment to recover the mirth which

the recollection produced :—" He was stirring up a concoction of cold tea, ink and water, slate-pencil dust, sugar,
mustard, and salt, when I thought" (Salisbury's voice trembled violently) " that I heard a step I ought to know, and
I had hardly time to get completely behind the door when
it was widely opened, and in walked the doctor !"

A burst of uproarious mirth drowned the voice of the
speaker. There was a broad smile on Hamilton's face,
though he did not raise his head. As soon as Salisbury
could speak, he continued :

" ' Oh !' said I to myself, ' it's all up with you, Mr.
Frank,' and I felt a little desirous of concealing my small
proportions as much as might be. What Frank might feel
I can't say, but he seemed to be very busy, and, as he
turned round to the doctor, put up his handkerchief to
his face.

" ' Does your face ache, Mrs. Guppy ?' says the doctor ;
and—imagine the impudence of the boy—he answered, it
was a little troublesome. ' How is Clarke this evening ?—
I hear he has been asleep this afternoon.' I imagine
Frank has as much idea of the identity of Clarke as I
have—I don't even know who he is, much less that he
was ill—but he answered just as Gruffy would do, with
her handkerchief up to her mouth, ' Rather better, sir,
I think—he was asleep when I saw him last, and I
didn't disturb him.' ' Hem,' said the doctor, ' and who's
this ?' "

The audience was here so convulsed with laughter that
Salisbury could not proceed ; Louis could not help joining
the laugh, though rather checked by the immovable gravity
of Hamilton's countenance.

"Really, Hamilton," he said, "I wonder how Frank could tell such stories."

"He doesn't think them so," said Hamilton, abruptly.

"Well, Salisbury!" "Well, Salisbury!" exclaimed several impatient voices. "The impudence of the fellow." "How will he ever get out of it?" "Get on, Salisbury." "The idea of joking with the doctor." "Go on, Salisbury." "What a capital fellow he'd make for one of those escaping heroes in romances—he'd never stay to have his head cut off."

"Well, and the doctor says, ' Who's this, Mrs. Guppy ? Casson ? How—what's the matter with you ? How long have you been here ?' ' Just come to bed, sir,' says Casson ; and then the doctor makes a few inquiries about his terrible headache, et cetera ; and Mrs. Guppy had a twinge of the toothache, and could only let the doctor know by little and little how she had thought it better to put him to bed.

" ' And that is medicine for him ?'

"The doctor looked very suspiciously at the cup, I fancy, for his tone was rather short and sulky. Frank seemed a little daunted, but he soon got up his spirits again, and, stirring up the mess, was just going to give it to Casson, when, lo! another strange footfall was heard ; doctor turned round (I was in a state of fright, I assure you, lest he should discover me) and in marched the real Simon Pure! It was a picture—oh! if I had been an artist :—there stood Gruffy, in her best black silk, looking more puzzled than angry ; Frank—I couldn't see what he looked like, but I'll suppose it, as he says—and doctor turning from one to the other with a face as red as a turkey-cock, and looking so magnificent !"

The counterfeit Mrs. Guppy.   Page 204.

" Poor Frank!" exclaimed several laughing voices.

" Well, at last Fudge found words, and in such a tone, exclaimed, 'Mrs. Guppy! who is THIS, then?' Then she stormed out: 'Ay, sir, who is it, indeed? perhaps you will inquire.' I didn't see what followed, for my range of vision was rather circumscribed—but I imagine that doctor pulled off part of Frank's disguise, for the next words I heard were, '*Digby*, this is *intolerable!*' uttered in the doctor's most magnificent anger—'What is the meaning of this?' Frank said something about *a wager* and *a little fun, meaning no harm*, et cetera; and Fudge gave him such a lecture, finishing off by declaring, that 'if he persisted in perpetrating such senseless follies he should find some other place to do so in than his house.' All the little boys were laughing, but doctor stopped them all with a thundering 'SILENCE!' and then he asked what Frank had in that cup. 'Cold tea, sir,' said Digby, quite meekly. 'And what's this at the bottom?' 'Sugar, sir.' I saw the doctor's face—it was not one to be trifled with, but there seemed a sort of grim smile there, too, when he gave the cup to Frank and insisted upon his drinking it all up; and Digby did it, too—he dared not refuse."

Another peal of laughter rang through the room, in which Hamilton joined heartily.

" Then," continued Salisbury, " doctor said he hoped he would feel a little better for his dose—and, becoming as grave as before, he desired he would return Mrs. Guppy's things, and beg her pardon for his impertinence."

" He didn't do so, surely?" said Jones.

" He did, though," replied Salisbury; " and I wouldn't

have been him if he'd been obstinate ; but he added—I wondered how even *he* dared—*I've saved you a little trouble, ma'am, there are six of them in bed.*"

" Oh ! oh ! disgraceful !" exclaimed Hamilton.

" What did Fudge say ?" asked Smith.

" ' THIS TO MY FACE, SIR !' and then, what he was going to do I don't know, but Frank was quite frightened, and begged pardon so very humbly that at last Fudge let him off with five hundred lines of Virgil to be done before Wednesday evening, and then sent him to bed—and there he is, for he was too much alarmed to play any more tricks."

" I'd have given something to have seen it," cried one, when the laugh was a little over.

" I think," said Jones, " all things considered, that the doctor was tolerably lenient."

" Oh ! Digby's a little bit of a favorite, I fancy," said Meredith.

" Not a bit," said Reginald. " What do you say, Hamilton ?"

" Nothing," said Hamilton, shortly.

' " One would think you never liked a joke, Hamilton," said Peters.

" Nor do I, when it is so low as to be practical," said Hamilton. " I feel no sympathy whatever with him."

The event furnished idle conversation enough for that evening, and it was long before it was forgotten ; and, in spite of Frank's reiterated boast that he did not care, and his apparent participation in the mirth occasioned by his failure, it required the utmost exercise of his habitual good-humor to bear equally the untiring teasing of his school-fellows, and the still more trying coldness and sarcasm of his master, whose manner very perceptibly altered towards him for some time after. Casson took care that no one in the lower school should be ignorant of Frank's defeat, and stimulated the little boys to tease him—but this impertinence, being an insult to the dignity of the seniors, was revenged by them as a body, and the juvenile tormentors were too much awe-struck and alarmed to venture on a repetition of their offence.

CHAPTER XVI.

DURING Louis' frequent walks with Hamilton, it must not be supposed that his home and home-doings were left out of the conversation; before very long, Hamilton had made an intimate mental acquaintance with all his little friend's family, their habits of life, and every other interesting particular Louis could remember. Hamilton was an excellent listener, and never laughed at Louis' fondness for home, and many were the extracts from home-letters with which he was favored; nay, sometimes whole letters were inflicted on him.

Among the many delightful topics of home history, Louis dwelt on few with more pleasure and enthusiasm than the social musical evenings, and said so much on them, that Hamilton's curiosity was at length aroused, after hearing Louis sing two or three times, to wonder what a madrigal could be like. Louis tried to satisfy this craving by singing the treble part, and descanting eloquently on the manner in which the other parts ought to come in; but all in vain he repeated, "There now, Hamilton, you see this is the *contralto* part; and when this bit of the *soprano* is sung, it comes in so beautifully, and the bass is crossing it, and playing hide and seek with the tenor."

Hamilton was obtuse, but at length, by fagging very

hard with one or two boys in the school-room, and getting one of the ushers, who generally performed a second in all the musical efforts in the school, to make some kind of bass, Louis presented his choir one evening in the playground, and made them sing, to the great rapture of the audience.

After this exhibition, the whole school seemed to have a fever for madrigals; nothing was heard about the playground but scraps of that which Louis had taken pains to drill into his party; and one or two came to Louis and Reginald to learn to take a second part. In play-hours, nothing seemed thought of but part-singing, and suddenly the propriety of giving a grand public concert was started; and after a serious debate, a singing-class was established, Louis being declared president, or master of the choir.

We will not say how fussy Louis was on the occasion; but he went about very busily trying the voices of his school-fellows for a day or two after his appointment, and picking out the best tones for his pupils. Casson owned a very fine singing voice, though it was one of the most rude in speaking, and having been partially initiated in the mystery before, by Louis was declared a treasure. Frank Digby was another valuable acquisition; for, joined to an extremely soft, full *contralto* voice, he possessed, in common with his many accomplishments, a refined ear and almost intuitive power of chiming in melodiously with any thing. Salisbury was a very respectable bass, as things went; and Reginald, who was certainly incapacitated for singing treble, declared his intention of assisting him, being quite confident that his voice would be a desirable adjunct. The members of the class having at last been decided on, a subscription was raised, and Hamilton was commissioned

to purchase what was necessary, the first convenient opportunity ; and accordingly, the next half-holiday, he obtained
leave for Louis to accompany him, and set off on his commission.   He had scarcely left the school-room when Trevannion met him, and volunteered to accompany him.

" I shall be very glad of your company," said Hamilton ;
" I am going to choose the music.   You may stare when I
talk of choosing music—it is well I have so powerful an
auxiliary, or I am afraid I should not give much satisfaction
to our committee of taste."

" What powerful auxiliary are you depending on ?" said
Trevannion ; " I shall be a poor one."

" You—oh, yes !" exclaimed Hamilton ; " a very poor one,
I suspect.   I was speaking of Louis Mortimer ; he is going
with me."

" Indeed," said Trevannion, coldly ; " you will not want
me, then !"

" Why not ?" asked Hamilton.   " We shall, I assure
you, be very glad of your company."

" So will Hutton and Salisbury," said Trevannion ; " and
I can endure my own company when I am not wanted ;"
as he spoke, he walked away.

Hamilton turned, and looked after his retreating figure,
as, drawn up to its full height, it quickly disappeared in the
crowd of boys, who were chaffering with the old cake-man.
His puzzled countenance soon resumed its accustomed
gravity, and with a slight curl of the lip, he laid his hand
on Louis' arm, and drew him on.

" Trevannion is offended," said Louis.

" He's welcome," was the rejoinder.

" But it is on my account, Hamilton," said Louis,

anxiously; " I cannot bear that you should quarrel with him for me."

" I have not quarrelled," said Hamilton, coldly.   " If he chooses to be offended, I can't help it."

" But he is an older friend than I am in two senses—let me go after him and tell him I am not going.   I can go with you another afternoon."

Louis drew his arm away as he spoke, and was starting off, when Hamilton seized him quite roughly, and exclaimed in an angry tone, " You shall do no such thing, Louis ! Does he suppose I am to have no one else but himself for my friend—*friend*, indeed !" he repeated.   " It's all indolence, Louis."

Louis looked up half alarmed, startled at his vehemence.

" Perhaps," said Hamilton, relaxing his hold, and laughing as he spoke, " perhaps if I had not been so lazy, I should have found a more suitable friend before ; as it is, I do not yet find Trevannion indispensable—by no means," he added, scornfully.

" Dear Hamilton," said Louis, " I shall be quite unhappy if I think I am the cause of your thinking ill of Trevannion. You used to be such great friends."

" None the worse, perhaps, because we are aware of a common absence of perfection in each other," replied Hamilton, whose countenance had gradually regained its calmness.   " It is foolish to be angry, Louis, but I was ; and now let there be an end of it—I don't mean to forsake you for all the Trevannions in Christendom."

They had by this time reached the playground gates, and were here overtaken by Frank Digby, who had before engaged to be one of the party.

"Better late than never," said Louis, in reply to his breathless excuses. "I had my doubts whether your pressing engagements with Maister Dunn would allow you to accompany us."

"Why, I got rid of him pretty soon," said Frank; "only just as I had wedged myself out of the phalanx, who should appear but Thally."

"*Who?*" said Louis.

"Tharah," repeated Frank.

"Sally Simmons, the boot-cleaner, Louis," said Hamilton; "you are up to nothing yet."

"She's a queer stick," said Frank.

"What a strange description of a woman!" remarked Louis. "It is as clear as a person being a brick."

"And so it is," replied Frank; "only it's just the reverse."

"Up comes Thally with my Sunday boots as bright as her fair hands could make them, and wanted me to look at a hole she had scraped in them, nor, though I promised to give her my opinion of her handiwork when I came back, was I allowed to depart till she had permission to take them to her 'fayther.'"

Nothing worthy of record passed during the walk to Bristol till the trio reached College Green. Here Louis began to look out for music-shops, while Frank entertained his companions with a running commentary on the shops, carriages, and people. It was a clear, bright day, and Clifton seemed to have poured itself out in the Green.

"Look there, Hamilton, there's a whiskered don! What a pair of moustaches! Hamilton, where is your eye-glass? Here's Trevannion's shadow—was there ever such a Paris!

Good gracious! as the ladies say, what a frightful bonnet! Isn't that a love of a silk, Louis? Now, Hamilton, did you ever see such a guy?"

Hamilton was annoyed at these remarks, made by no means in a low tone, and, in his eagerness to change the conversation and get further from Frank, he unfortunately ran against a lady who was getting out of a carriage just drawn up in front of a large linen-draper's shop, much to the indignation of a young gentleman who attended her.

Hamilton begged pardon, with a crimson face; and, as the lady kindly assured him she was not hurt, Louis recognized in her his quondam friend, Mrs. Paget, and darted forward to claim her acquaintance.

"What, Louis! my little Master Louis!" exclaimed the lady; "I did not expect to see you. Where have you come from?"

"I am at school, ma'am, at Dr. Wilkinson's, and I had leave to come out with Hamilton this afternoon. This is Hamilton, ma'am—Hamilton, this is Mrs. Paget."

"Our rencontre, Mr. Hamilton," said the lady, "has been most fortunate; for without this contretemps I should have been quite ignorant of Master Louis' being so near— you must come and see me, dear. Mr. Hamilton, I must take him home with me this afternoon."

"It is impossible, ma'am," said Hamilton, bluntly; "I am answerable for him, and he must go back with me."

"Can you be so inexorable?" said Mrs. Paget. "Will you come, too, and Mr. Francis Digby—I beg your pardon, Mr. Frank, I did not see you."

"I beg yours, ma'am," replied the affable Frank, with a most engaging bow; "for I was so taken up with the tempting display on the green this afternoon, that I only became aware this moment of my approximation to yourself."

"The shops are very gay, certainly; but I should have thought that you young gentlemen would not have cared much for the display. Now, a tailor's shop would have been much more in your taste."

"Indeed, ma'am, we came out with the express purpose of buying a silk for the Lady Louisa."

"I wonder any lady should commission you to buy any thing for her."

"Oh!" replied Frank, "I am renowned for my taste; and Hamilton is equally well qualified. Can you recommend us a good milliner, ma'am?"

"I am going to look at some bonnets," said the lady. "But, Mr. Frank, I half suspect you are quizzing. What Lady Louisa are you speaking of?"

Frank had drawn up his face into a very grave and confidential twist, when Mrs. Paget's equerry, the young gentleman before mentioned, offered his arm, and, giving Frank a withering look, warned the lady of the time.

"You are right. It is getting late," she said. "Goodbye, dear boy. Where are you now? Dr. Williams?"

"Dr. Wilkinson's, Ashfield House," said Louis.

"Henry, will you remember the address?" said the lady.

The young gentleman grunted some kind of acquiescence; and, after due adieus, Mrs. Paget walked into the shop.

"Frank, I'm ashamed of you," said Hamilton.

"I am sure," replied Frank, "I've been doing all the work; I'm a walking exhibition of entertainment for man and beast."

Hamilton would not laugh, and, finding all remon-strances unavailing, he quickened his pace and walked on in silence till they reached the music-seller's, where, after some deliberation, they obtained the requisite music, and, after a few more errands, began to retrace their steps.

The walk home was very merry. Louis, having un-fastened the bundle, tried over some of the songs, and taught Frank readily the contralto of two. Then he wanted to try Hamilton, but this in the open air Hamilton stoutly resisted, though he promised to make an effort at some future time. After Frank and Louis had sung their duets several times over to their own satisfaction while sit-ting under a hedge, all the party grew silent: there was something so beautiful in the stillness and brightness, that none felt inclined to disturb it. At last, Louis suddenly began Eve's hymn:

"How cheerful along the gay mead
  The daisy and cowslip appear!
The flocks, as they carelessly feed,
  Rejoice in the spring of the year:
The myrtles that shade the gay bowers,
  The herbage that springs from the sod,
Trees, plants, cooling fruits, and sweet flowers,
  All rise to the praise of my God.

"Shall man, the great master of all,
  The only insensible prove!
Forbid it, fair gratitude's call!
  Forbid it, devotion and love!

THEE, Lord, who such wonders canst raise,
    And still canst destroy with a nod,
My lips shall incessantly praise,
    My soul shall be wrapped in my God."
                                        DR. ARNE.

Frank joined in the latter part of the first verse, but was silent in the second.

"Why did you not go on, Frank?" asked Hamilton.

"It was too sweet," said Frank. "Louis, I envy you your thoughts."

"Do you?" said Louis, looking up quickly in his cousin's face, with a bright expression of pleasure.

"When you began that song," continued Frank, "I was thinking of those lines,

' These are Thy glorious works, Parent of good,
    Almighty, Thine this universal frame,
Thus wondrous fair; Thyself how wondrous then!'"

"'Thyself how wondrous then!'" repeated Hamilton, reverentially.

"I don't know how it is, Louis," said Frank; "in cathedrals, and in beautiful scenery, when a grave fit comes over me, I sometimes think I should like to be religious."

Louis squeezed his hand, but did not speak.

"Take care, Frank," said Hamilton with some emotion. "Be very, very careful not to mistake sentiment for religion. I am sure it is so easy to imagine the emotion excited by beauty of sight or sound, religious, that we cannot be too careful in examining the *reason* of such feelings."

"But how, Hamilton?" said Frank. "You would not check such impressions?"

"No; it is better that our thoughts should be carried

by beauty to the source of all beauty ; but to a poetical, susceptible imagination this is often the case where there is not the least vital religion, Frank. The deist will gaze on the splendid landscape, and bow in reverence to the God of nature, but a Christian's thoughts should fly to his God at all times ; the light and beauty of the scenes of nature should be within himself. When a person's whole religion consists in these transient emotions, he ought to mistrust it, Digby."

"But, dear Hamilton," said Louis, after a few minutes' silence, " we ought to be thankful when God gives us the power of enjoying the beautiful things He has made. Would it not be ungrateful to check every happy feeling of gratitude and joy for the power to see, and hear, and enjoy, with gladness and thankfulness, the loveliness and blessings around ?"

" The height of ingratitude, dear Louis," said Hamilton, emphatically. " But I am sure you understand me."

" To be sure," said Louis. " Many good gifts our Almighty Father has given us, and one perfect gift, and the good gifts should lead us to think more of the perfect ONE. I often have thought, Hamilton, of that little girl's nice remark that I read to you last Sunday, about the good and perfect gifts."

Hamilton did not reply, and for a minute or two longer they sat in silence, when the report of a gun at a little distance roused them, and almost at the same instant, a little bird Louis had been watching as it flew into a large tree in front of them, fell wounded from branch to branch, until it rested on the lowest, where a flutter among the leaves told of its helpless sufferings.

19

"I must get it, Hamilton!" cried Louis, starting up "It is wounded."

"The branch is too high," said Hamilton. "I dare say the poor thing is dying; we cannot do it any good."

"Indeed I must try!" exclaimed Louis, scrambling partly up the immense trunk of the tree, and slipping down much more quickly. "I wish there were something to catch hold of, or to rest one's foot against."

"You'll never get up," said Hamilton, laughing; "if you must get it, mount my shoulders."

As he spoke he came under the tree, and Louis, availing himself of the proffered assistance, succeeded in reaching and bringing down the wounded bird, which he did with many expressions of gratitude to Hamilton.

"I am sure you ought to be obliged," said Frank. "Royalty lending itself out as a ladder is an unheard-of anomaly. Pray, what are you going to do with cock-sparrow now you have got him?"

Louis only replied by laying some grass and leaves in the bottom of his cap, and putting the bird on this extempore bed. He then seized Hamilton's arm and urged him forward. Hamilton responded to Louis' anxiety with some queries on the expediency of assisting wounded birds if pleasant walks were to be thereby curtailed, and Frank, after suggesting, to Louis' horror, the propriety of making a pie of his favorite, walked on, singing

     " A little cock-sparrow sat upon a tree,"

which, with variations, lasted till they reached the playground gates, where Louis ran off to find Clifton, that he might enter into proper arrangements for due attendance on his sparrow's wants.

CHAPTER XVII.

" In the multitude of words there wanteth not sin ; but he that refraineth his lips is wise."—*Prov.* x. 19.
" Let another man praise thee, and not thine own mouth ; a stranger, and not thine own lips."—*Prov.* xxvii. 2.

WE are now considering Louis Mortimer under prosperity ; a state in which it is much more difficult to be watchful, than in that of adversity. When he first came to school, his struggle was to be consistent in maintaining his principles against ridicule and fear of his fellow-creatures' judgment. In that he nearly failed ; and then came the hard trial we have related, the furnace from whose fires he came so bright : and another trial awaited him, but different still.

By the beauty of conduct Divine grace *alone* had enabled him to observe, he now won the regard of the majority of his school-fellows ; and no one meddled with him or his opinions. He was loved by many ; liked by most, and unmolested by the rest. We are told, " When a man's ways please the Lord, even his enemies are at peace with him ;" and this was Louis' case. If a few remarks were now and then made on the singularity and stiffness of his notions, the countenance of the seniors, and the general estimation in which he was held, prevented any annoyance or interference. His feet were now on smooth ground, and the sky

was bright above his head; and he began to forget that a
storm had ever been.

One day between school-hours, when Louis and his brother were diligently drilling the chorus, they were summoned to the drawing-room, where they found the doctor
standing talking with a lady, in the large bay-window.
Her face was turned towards the prospect beyond, and she
did not see them enter; and near her, leaning on the top
of a high-backed chair, stood a tall gentlemanly youth,
whom Louis immediately recognized as Mrs. Paget's es-
quire.   The lady was speaking as they entered, and her
gentle lady-like tones fell very pleasantly on Louis' ears,
and made him sure he should like her, if even the words
she had chosen had been otherwise.

"I have been quite curious to see him; my sister has
said so much, poor little fellow!"

Dr. Wilkinson at this moment became aware of the presence of his pupils, and, turning round, introduced them to
the lady, and the lady in turn to them, as Mrs. Norman.

"I am personally a stranger to you, Master Mortimer,"
said Mrs. Norman; "but I have often heard of you.   You
know Mrs. Paget?"

"Oh, yes!" replied Louis.

"She is my sister, and, not being able to come herself
to-day, she commissioned me to bring an invitation for you
and your brother to spend the rest of this day with her, if
Dr. Wilkinson will kindly allow it."

Louis looked at Dr. Wilkinson; and Reginald answered
for himself—

"I am much obliged, ma'am; and, if you please, thank
Mrs. Paget for me, but as it is not a half-holiday, I shall

The Invitation.   Page 220.

not be able to come this afternoon. I shall be very glad to come when school is over, if Dr. Wilkinson will allow me."

Dr. Wilkinson smiled. "Mrs. Norman will, I am sure, excuse a school-boy's anxiety to retain a hard-earned place in his class," he said. "I have given my permission, you may do as you please."

"Mrs. Paget will be so much disappointed," said Mrs. Norman; "are you anxious about your class, too, Master Louis?"

Louis blushed, hesitated, and then looked from Reginald to the doctor, but Dr. Wilkinson gave no assistance. Louis demurred a little; for he had a place to lose that he had gained only the day before, and that, probably, he might not be able to gain from Clifton for the rest of the half-year. But at length, on another persuasive remark from Mrs. Norman, he accepted the invitation in rather a confused manner; and, it being decided that Reginald was to join them at dinner, he went away to make some alteration in his dress. When he returned, Mrs. Norman carried him off in her carriage, which was waiting at the door, having first introduced him to her companion, as her son, Henry Norman.

During the ride to Clifton, Louis became very communicative. He liked Mrs. Norman very much, she was so very sweet, and now and then made little remarks that reminded Louis of home; and then he was sure she liked him; even if he had not guessed that the few words he first heard from her lips referred to him, her very kind full eyes and affectionate manner spoke of unusual interest, and Louis felt very anxious to rise in her estimation. Things that are not sinful in themselves, become sins from the accompanying motives ; the desire of favor in the eyes of so excellent a person was not wrong, had it been mixed with a wish to adorn the doctrine of Christ, and thankfulness for the love and favor given ; but now Louis talked of things which, though he really believed them, and of feelings which, though he had once really experienced them, were not now the breathings of a heart that overflowed with all its fulness of gratitude. He had quickness enough to see what was most precious in his new friend's sight, and tried to ingratiate himself with her, by dwelling on these subjects, and showing how much he had felt on them. *Had felt*, for he had " left his first love."

Let it not be supposed that Louis meant to deceive—he deceived himself as much as any one ; but he was in that sad state when a Christian has backslidden so far as to live on the remembrance of old joys, instead of the actual possession of new.

The carriage stopped, at length, at a house in York Crescent, where the trio alighted. Mrs. Norman led Louis up stairs into the drawing-room, while her son, who had scarcely spoken a word during the drive, stayed a minute or two at the house-door, and then ran down the nearest flight of steps leading to the carriage-road, jumped into the carriage, which was just driving off, and paid a visit to the stables.

The room into which Louis entered was very large, and littered so with all descriptions of chairs, stools, and nondescript elegancies, that it required some little ingenuity to reach the further end without upsetting the one, or being overthrown by the others. Near one of the three windows, reclining on a sofa, was Mrs. Paget, who welcomed Louis with her usual warmth.

"You see," said she, "I am a prisoner. I sprained my ankle the very day I saw you; and I am positively forbidden to walk. But where is Master Reginald?"

Louis informed Mrs. Paget of his brother's intentions, and, after expressing her regrets at his non-appearance, the lady continued:

"Now, sit near me, and let us have a little talk: I want to hear how you are going on, and how many prizes you are likely to get. But, perhaps, my dear, you would like to go on the downs, or into the town, or to———Where's Henry, I wonder: where is Mr. Norman?" she asked of a servant who came to remove a little tray that stood beside her.

"Just gone round to the stables, ma'am."

"Dear, how unfortunate! You can't think what a beautiful little horse he has; I tell him it is quite a lady's horse. He will show it to you. I can't think how he could go away this afternoon. You'll be very dull, my dear—but my sister will take you out."

Louis assured her he should enjoy sitting with her.

"That is very kind of you; very few of your age would care about staying with a lame, fidgety, old woman."

Louis protested against the two last epithets, and as Mrs. Norman had left the room he began talking of the pleasant ride he had had with her, and how much he loved her.

Mrs. Paget warmly admitted every thing, only adding that in some things she was a little too particular.

"But, dear me! you must be very hungry," she exclaimed, interrupting herself. "How could I forget? Just ring the bell, dear boy—there's lunch down stairs. Oh, never mind, here is Charlotte."

As she spoke, Mrs. Norman re-entered, and took Louis down to lunch.

When he returned to the drawing-room, Mrs. Paget had her sofa moved so as to face the window, and a little table was placed in front of her. A low armchair was near her for Louis, and another quite in the window Mrs. Norman took possession of, when she had provided herself with some work.

"Oh, what a beautiful view!" exclaimed Louis, as he looked for the first time out of the window. "How very, very beautiful! I think this is the pleasantest situation in Clifton."

"It is very beautiful," said Mrs. Norman. "But you have a magnificent prospect at Dr. Wilkinson's."

"Dr. Wilkinson's is a very nice place, I believe, is it not?" said Mrs. Paget. "It is a pity such a pretty place should be a school."

"Nay," said Mrs. Norman, smiling; "why should you grudge the poor boys their pleasure?"

"I don't think they appreciate it," said Mrs. Paget; "and, poor fellows, they are always so miserable that they might as well be miserable somewhere else."

"We are not at all miserable after the first week," said Louis.

"I thought you were not to go to school again, my dear," said Mrs. Paget.

"So I thought, myself, but papa wished me to go, and he is the best judge."

"Well, dear, it's a very nice thing that you are wise enough to see it,—and you are happy?"

" I should be very ungrateful not to be so, ma'am ; Dr. Wilkinson and all the boys are so kind to me this half. It is so different from the first quarter I spent at school."

" They are kind, are they ? Well, I dare say ; they couldn't help it, I'm sure," replied Mrs. Paget. " I suppose you will have the medal again this half year. I am sure you ought to have it to make up."

" Oh, but I shouldn't have it to make up for last half, ma'am," said Louis, smiling.

" But you will get it, I dare say," said the lady.

" I don't know," said Louis ; " perhaps—I think I have a very good chance yet, but we never can tell exactly what Dr. Wilkinson thinks about us. There are only one or two I am afraid of."

" I should think you needn't be afraid of any," said Mrs. Paget. " I told you, Charlotte, about that story we heard at Heronhurst last summer—dear boy—you know he bore—"

" Yes," interrupted Mrs. Norman. " You have a large number of school-fellows, Master Louis," she added.

" Yes, ma'am, there are seventy-six of us this half, so many that we hardly know the names of the lower school."

" Is that Mr. *Ferrar* or *Ferrers* there still ?" asked Mrs. Paget.

" Yes, ma'am, and he is so much improved, you cannot think."

Louis looked very earnestly at her as she spoke, and she put her hand on his forehead, stroking his hair off, while she replied,

" He is very happy in having so kind a friend, I am sure ; he ought to have been expelled."

"Oh no, ma'am—I think kindness was much the best way," said Louis; and remembering how incautiously he had spoken of him before, he said all that he could in his praise.

The conversation then turned upon the school in general, and it was astonishing to watch how much Louis said indirectly in his own praise, and how nearly every thing seemed to turn in the direction of *dear self*, in the history of his lessons, progress, and rivals—and even when it branched off to his friends, among whom in the first rank stood Hamilton.

"You would so like Hamilton, he is so kind to me. I told you about him before," said Louis, eagerly.

"Is that the young gentleman who had charge of you the other day?" asked Mrs. Paget.

Louis answered in the affirmative.

"I did not much like him, only one doesn't judge people fairly at first, often."

"Oh, Hamilton's such a good creature!" exclaimed Louis, in his energy letting fall one end of a skein of silk he was holding. He gathered it up, apologized, and resumed his defence of his friend.

"He is, perhaps, a little blunt, but he is so sincere, and so steady and kind, Dr. Wilkinson is very, *very* fond of him, I know; he makes me sit by him every night, and I learn my lessons with him. I am sure if it were not for him I should be terribly behind Clifton."

"I saw them coming out of Redland Chapel yesterday morning," said Mrs. Paget. "At least I saw Mr. Hamilton, but I did not see you."

Louis informed her of the division of the school on Sunday, and she continued,

"I noticed a very aristocratic young gentleman with Mr. Hamilton—quite a contrast, so very handsome and elegant; who was he?"

"Was he tall?" asked Louis; "and dressed in black, with a light waistcoat?"

"I don't know what waistcoat he had," said Mrs. Paget, laughing. "His dress was in perfect gentlemanly taste. He was, I should think, tall for his age, and had dark hair and eyes."

"I have no doubt it was Trevannion; he is the handsomest fellow in the school, except Salisbury."

"That he is not," said Mrs. Paget, significantly.

Louis blushed, and felt rather foolish, certainly not wholly insensible to the injudicious hint.

"Only Fred Salisbury is so different: he is not elegant, and yet he is not awkward; he is rough and ready, and says all kinds of vulgar things. He is very much liked among us, but I don't think Trevannion is, though he gets his own way a great deal: he thinks nobody is equal to himself, I know, but I am sure he is not a favorite."

"Why not?" said Mrs. Paget.

"He is so very selfish, and so contemptuous, and so dreadfully offended if Hamilton does not treat him with the deference he wants. I think we know more of each other than any one else does, and no one would think, in company, when Trevannion is smiling and talking so cleverly, that he is so unamiable."

"He does not look like an ill-tempered person," said the lady.

"I don't think he is what is generally called an ill-tempered person; for he never puts himself into passions, nor does he seem to mind many things that make others very angry. But he is sometimes dreadfully disdainful and haughty when any one offends him, and especially when Hamilton seems to like anybody as well as himself. Only last Saturday he was so much affronted because Hamilton had asked leave for me to go into Bristol with him. When he found I was coming, he wouldn't go with us. I think he is very jealous of me, though I begged Hamilton to let me stay at home, and I was just going after him to call him back, only Hamilton wouldn't let me. I did not like to see such old friends quarrel. I am sure I would very gladly have stayed at home to keep peace."

"I am quite sure of that," said Mrs. Paget. "But how came your perfect Mr. Hamilton to choose such a friend?"

"I have often wondered," said Louis; "and last Saturday, when that happened that I told you of just now, and Hamilton (he is so kind) said he wouldn't give me up for anybody, he said he thought he made Trevannion his friend because he was too lazy to find another for himself."

"*Too lazy to find another?*" repeated Mrs. Paget.

"Hamilton does not like taking trouble, generally," said Louis: "it is his greatest fault, I think. He takes things as they come. I have often wished he would concern himself a little more about the wrong things that go on among us. You know it would be of no use my speaking about them, though I try sometimes; it is so much easier to do right when the great boys support you."

"So it is, dear," said Mrs. Paget, kindly.

Mrs. Norman had scarcely spoken during the whole

conversation, though she had once or twice laid down her
work and looked very gravely at Louis ; but he had not
noticed it ; for he was so elated with himself, and the relations of his own importance at school, and the idea of his
superiority above his school-fellows, that there was no
room for any thing else in his head, and he went on with
the firm conviction that both the ladies were, like every
one else, extremely delighted and interested in him and his
sentiments.   There had been another auditor in the room
almost ever since the beginning of the long chat, and that
was Henry Norman, who, when he had seen his horse and
lunched, entered the room unperceived by Louis or Mrs.
Paget, and passed noiselessly along to the furthest window, where he sat, with a book, hid by the curtains from
a careless glance.   A few words caught his ear as he was
finding out his place ; and, whether the matter of the first
page required deep consideration and digestion or not, we
cannot pretend to determine, not knowing the nature of the
chosen volume, but it is certain that that leaf was not
turned over that afternoon, and the eyes that professed to
convey its meaning to the mind of the reader not unfrequently wandered on the hills in the distant prospect, or,
on being recalled, on the nearer objects of Mrs. Paget's
sofa—the skein of silk and the pair of hands, which were
the only portions visible to him of the loquacious little vis-
itor.   That he was listening with interest of an equivocal
nature might be gathered from the frequent, impatient
knitting of the brow, biting of the lips, and sudden laying
down of the book altogether ; but there he sat till Louis,
having flown off from Hamilton to the general school failings, had finished relating the history of Frank Digby's

memorable Saturday night's exploit, and concluded by an emphatic delivery of his upright sentiments on the heinousness of practical jokes. He paused a minute to take breath, after a Philippic that elicited a small dose of flattery from Mrs. Paget, and, with a face flushed with satisfaction and excitement, stooped to pick up a fallen pair of scissors, when Mrs. Norman, laying down her work, looked again at him and uttered a sound indicative of an intention of speaking. This time Louis was fully aware of an expression in her countenance far from satisfactory, but she had not time to express her sentiments, for at this moment Reginald was announced, and a general move took place. Henry Norman came forward and welcomed him, and then took him and Louis out on the Crescent till dinner-time. Here they were joined by some of Norman's acquaintances, whom he introduced to his visitors. Louis thought uncomfortably, for a few minutes, of Mrs. Norman's look of disapprobation ; but he persuaded himself that there was nothing meant by it, and soon became very lively. There was something he did not like about Norman, who, though perfectly well-bred and attentive, showed a degree of indifference and disregard to any thing he said or did, that did not altogether suit Louis' present state of mind. If Louis addressed him, he listened very politely, but with a slight, sarcastic smile, and either returned a very short and cool reply, or, if the remark did not require one, an inclination of the head, and turned immediately to one of his other companions. Reginald did not much fancy him ; but, upon the whole, they managed to pass the time very pleasantly till they were summoned to dinner.

Several persons came in in the evening, and Louis was

called upon by Mrs. Paget to sing, " *Where the bee sucks.*"
This led to other songs, and Louis attracted the notice of a
musical gentleman, who was much pleased with him, and
who gave him a general invitation to his house. Louis
was in the midst of his thanks when Reginald summoned
him to go home, and, in spite of Mrs. Paget's remon-
strances and offers of her carriage, carried his point.

" Well, Louis, how did you get on ?" said Reginald, as
they were walking home ; " I think you must have been
dreadfully bored with holding skeins and talking fine for
Mrs. Paget's edification for two hours at least, to say
nothing of all the stuffing you have had this evening."

" Oh ! I have been very happy," said Louis. " Do you
know Mr. Fraser has invited me to his musical parties ?"

" I wish you joy, I am sure. What a nice woman Mrs.
Norman seems !"

" Yes," said Louis, doubtfully.

" *Yes*—that sounds very much like *no*," said Reginald.

" I did not mean it." Louis recalled her manner lately
towards him, and mentally went over the conversation of
the day.

" Well, what's the matter ?" asked Reginald.

" I am afraid I have been very foolish ; I talk so foolishly
sometimes, Reginald—I said so many foolish things this
afternoon. I don't think Mrs. Norman likes me."

" Rubbish ! stuff and nonsense ! Just like you, Louis,
always imagining somebody's displeased with you—I won't
hear a word more ; I have no patience with you."

" Then you don't think she seemed vexed with me ?"

" Not I ; and if she were, what's the odds ? What difference need she make in your happiness ? What a wretched

creature you'll make of yourself, Louis, if you think so much of the opinion of every one—a person, too, you may never see again."

Louis was relieved, and talked on other matters with his brother till they reached home. He was a little annoyed to hear that Hamilton had expressed considerable vexation at his going with Mrs. Norman before afternoon school, and this, combined with the excitement and vanity under which he labored, disturbed considerably the tranquillity of his slumbers, and prevented his earnestly seeking that aid he so much needed.

CHAPTER XVIII.

" A talebearer revealeth secrets; but he that is of a faithful spirit concealeth the matter."—*Prov.* xi. 13.

" He that covereth a transgression seeketh love, but he that repeateth a matter separateth very friends."—*Prov.* xvii. 9.

" When pride cometh, then cometh shame."—*Prov.* xi. 2.

" A haughty spirit goeth before a fall."—*Prov.* xvi. 18.

PERHAPS those who have read the first part of the story of Louis Mortimer will remember that I there endeavored to explain the nature of the Christian's warfare, and that I stated that there were sad periods when the Christian, too confident in his own strength, perhaps too much inclined to exult in his victories as evincing some latent power in *himself*, becomes less watchful, and gradually falls back in his glorious course. It is certain, that if we do not advance we go back, and oh, how sad it is that redeemed sinners, called by so holy a name as that of Christian, should, in any degree, forget to whom they owe all their might to do well, as well as their final salvation, that they should relax, in the least, their prayers, their efforts in the strength of the Holy Spirit to press forward towards the mark of the prize of their high calling. It is not that all those who thus sadly backslide are allowed to fall into open sin. Many, by the great mercy of their Lord, are preserved

from thus dishonoring His holy name and cause; but alas!
too often is there a falling off in devotion, in singleness
of heart, in perseverance, in watchfulness against besetting sins, when the prayers are fewer and colder, the
praises fainter, and the Christian, after languishing for a
time in this divided state, hardly making an effort to return,
becomes conscious, to his alarm, how far he has wandered,
and feels with our sweet poet, in the bitterness of his spirit,

" Where is the blessedness I knew,
    When first I saw the Lord?
Where is the soul-refreshing view
    Of Jesus and His word?

" The peaceful hours I once enjoyed
    How sweet their memory still!
But they have left an *aching void*
    The world can never fill."

For the next fortnight the singing class was indefatigable,
and owing to the cultivated taste of Louis and Reginald,
and the superior musical education of one or two others,
among whom Mr. Witworth and Frank were not the least
in importance, the members at length considered themselves
competent to exhibit before an audience.

Accordingly, after Dr. Wilkinson had been favored with
a specimen of their skill, his permission was obtained to in-
vite such of their friends as they chose.

Tickets of admission, which had been prepared before-
hand, were then sent out in various directions, accompanied
by notes of invitation. As soon as Mrs. Paget's arrived at
its destination, a most kind answer was dispatched to Louis
as president, adding a request to be allowed to provide

refreshment for the performers ; and, as her proposal was hailed with three cheers, and gracefully accepted by Louis, on the morning of the eventful day came grapes, peaches, biscuits, and wine, which were very elegantly set out in the class-room by the committee.

The concert passed off as propitiously as could be wished. Hamilton, who, from utter want of ear, was totally incapacitated for singing, acted the part of steward with Trevannion, Meredith, and one or two others, with great decorum, and actually stood near Mrs. Paget during part of the performance, listening quietly to Louis' praises with such evident interest, that a few words of commendation he uttered quite won the lady's heart, though she had certainly been prejudiced against him before. It was remarked by some, that the doctor did not seem much pleased with Louis' manners on this occasion ; for, when Mrs. Paget, between the parts, began to praise Louis' extraordinary musical talents (as she was pleased to call them), and to relate how much he pleased the company at her house, Dr. Wilkinson coolly replied, that he considered he had been well taught, but doubted his having more than an average good taste and general ability ; and as his eye turned upon Louis, who was moving rather affectedly and conceitedly from rank to rank on his way to the refreshment-room, his forehead wrinkled ominously, and his lips became more tightly compressed. He was observed to watch Louis for a minute, and then turn suddenly away as if disgusted.

The madrigal concert took place about the end of the quarter, and on the following Saturday afternoon, the monotony of Ashfield House was varied by the arrival of a new scholar, in the person of Mr. Henry Norman, who was placed as a parlor boarder with the doctor.

When Hamilton and Louis returned from the playground together, they discovered this young gentleman sitting on the table, carefully balancing the doctor's chair with one of his feet, deeply immersed in the contents of a new book with only partially cut leaves, left by accident on the table. His back was turned towards them, and he was so engrossed in the twofold occupation of reading and keeping the heavy chair from falling, that he did not notice their entrance, and Louis, not recognizing his figure at first, nor knowing that he was expected, left the business of welcoming the stranger to his senior.

"Our new school-fellow, Louis, I suppose," said Hamilton, in a low tone, as he scrutinized the lengthy figure before him. "I know that fellow, Louis—he is a friend of yours."

Before Louis had time to answer, the low murmur had disturbed Norman; and, looking up without altering his position in the least, he acknowledged his acquaintance with Louis by a nod, and a careless "How do you do?"

Louis advanced directly with a warm welcome and outstretched hand that was met by two fingers of Norman's left hand, tendered in a manner so offensive to Hamilton that he debated whether he should turn the intruder out of window, or walk himself out of the door; and concluded by drawing back in disdainful anger.

Louis was not so ready to take offence, though he was sensitive enough to feel a little hurt; and, turning round to his friend, introduced Norman to him.

Norman took a steady quick glance at Hamilton, and, though his lips were full of propriety, there was something like a sarcastic smile in his eyes.

"You are not altogether a stranger to me, Mr. Hamilton, though, I imagine, I am to you," he said, as he allowed the chair to regain its legs, and got off the table, throwing the book on another, several yards distant.

"I must confess you have the advantage of me," said Hamilton, coldly. "I was not aware that I had the honor of being known to you."

"I assure you, then, that you had that honor.—Dear me!" he added, as he threw himself into the doctor's chair, stretching out his legs to their utmost length : "absurd of me to sit on that table, when I might have initiated myself so admirably into the art of reading made easy. Comfortable chair this of Fudge's—I beg his pardon, Dr. Wilkinson's. I am so accustomed to that elegant *nom du guerre* that I occasionally forget myself. The old gentleman knows how to make himself comfortable ; I suppose that book belongs to him. I took the liberty of cutting a few leaves."

"Which will be a peculiar satisfaction to him, doubtless," said Hamilton ; "and perhaps you may have the pleasure of hearing so from his own lips."

"*Verbum sat*," replied Norman. "It is a peculiar gratification, Mr. Hamilton, to discover that your natural good sense is overcoming your usual disinclination to notice those things which are not *comme il faut* in your school-fellows, thereby depriving them of the aid of your countenance and example in their little endeavors ; and I feel peculiar satisfaction in thus early becoming the recipient of the good

services bestowed by the blunt sincerity and kindliness of
your nature."

Hamilton crimsoned and stared ; but there was nothing
insolent in the tone : it was inexplicable. That something
was meant he could not doubt ; and presently, perceiving that
Louis was uncomfortable and embarrassed, he said haughtily,

" I really am at a loss to understand you, sir ; but your
manner towards your friend and mine is particularly unpleasant. What you may have been used to I cannot
pretend to know ; but, whatever it be, you will be kind
enough to remember that here we are accustomed to the
society of gentlemen, and to treat each other as such."

" My dear Mr. Hamilton," said Norman, blandly,
slightly moving as if to arrest Hamilton's progress towards
the door, " you entirely misunderstand me. Master Mortimer and I now understand each other better. Indeed, I
am laid under a weighty obligation to Master Louis for my
acquaintance with your royal self and various members of
your court ; and could not possibly have any intention of
quarrelling with so kind a benefactor. As for you, I have
made up my mind to know and like you. Shake hands,
will you ?"

Hamilton hesitatingly touched the proffered hand, and
looking at his watch at the same moment, wondered to
Louis why tea was not ready.

" There's the bell !" exclaimed Louis ; and seizing Hamilton's arm, he hurried off, leaving Norman to follow at his
leisure, as neither Hamilton nor himself felt at all inclined
to be ceremonious.

Louis felt a little afraid of Norman, though he did not
exactly know why.

Norman did not follow them immediately; and Hamilton had nearly emptied his first cup of tea when he came in, in company with Trevannion and Frank Digby, the latter of whom had a marvellous facility for making acquaintances on the shortest notice. They sat down at the end of one of the three long tables, and continued laughing and talking the whole of the tea-time, after which Norman went to his own tea with the doctor.

"So, Louis, Norman's come!" exclaimed Reginald, pouncing upon his brother just as he reached the school-room door.

"Is he a friend of yours?" asked Trevannion.

"He is, and he is not. Make that riddle out at your leisure," replied Reginald, gayly.

"Oh, that settles the matter!" said Trevannion.

"What matter?" asked Louis.

A look of the most withering description was the only answer Louis received; it was enough, however, to deter him from repeating his question.

Happily, Reginald did not see it.

"How do you like our new-comer, Trevannion?" asked Hamilton, linking his arm in his friend's, preparatory to a short, after-tea turn in the playground. "There is something very peculiar about him—insolent, I think."

"He's a nice fellow, in my opinion," said Trevannion.

"A very knowing chap," said Salisbury. "Has he been here before?"

"No," said Frank Digby; "but somebody's been kind enough to give the full particulars, history, and lives, peccadilloes, *et cetera, et cetera, et cetera*, of the gentlemen, generally, and individually, at Ashfield Academy. Why,

Hamilton, he called Trevannion and Salisbury by their names, without any introduction, and is as much up to every thing here as yourself, I believe."

" I don't much fancy him," said Hamilton ; " and strongly suspect he won't add much to our comfort."

" He doesn't like your pet, I suppose, then," said Trevannion, marking the slight color that rose in Hamilton's face. " He told me of your strange rencontre in the class-room ; he has taken a fancy, I am sure, to you."

Hamilton did not look particularly delighted, and changed the subject to one on which he and Trevannion conversed most amicably till past their usual time for re-entering the study.

Norman did not come among them that evening till prayer-time ; and, to his great satisfaction, Louis saw very little of him for the next day or two.

One day, during the first week of Norman's initiation, at the close of the morning school, a party similar in size and kind to that which had the honor of greeting Louis on his arrival the preceding half-year, was assembled on the raised end of the school-room. Frank and Salisbury were both of them seated on the top of a desk ; the former, generally silent, relieved himself by sundry twists and contortions, smacking of the lips, sighs, and turnings of the eyes, varied by a few occasional thumps administered to Salisbury, who sat by him, apparently unconscious of the bellicose attitude of his neighbor, listening attentively, with a mixed expression of concern and anger on his honest countenance, to Norman, who, on this occasion, was the principal speaker. Louis was in the room, at his desk, hunting for a top ; but too intent upon his search, and too far off to hear more of the topics that engrossed so much attention, than a few words that conveyed no impression to him, being simply, "Ferrers—my aunt—clever—hypocritical."

Just as he had given up all hope of finding his top, Hamilton came up to him. "Louis," said he, "if Trevannion goes out with me, I shall have time to hear your Herodotus before afternoon school, directly after dinner, mind."

"I shan't forget;—oh, Hamilton, you haven't such a thing as another top, have you? Reginald's broken two of mine, and I can't find my other."

"I do happen to have taken care of yours for you, you careless boy. Here is my desk-key, you will find it there; you can give me the key after dinner."

With many thanks, Louis proceeded to Hamilton's desk, and Hamilton went up to Trevannion, who was one of the party at the upper end of the room. Louis was now so near the speakers, as to be unavoidably within hearing of all that passed; and, astonished by the first few words, he proceeded no further in his errand than putting the key into the lock.

"Are you inclined for a walk, Trevannion?" asked Hamilton, as he reached him.

Trevannion was leaning against the doctor's desk, in a more perturbed state than his calm self usually exhibited. As Hamilton spoke, he turned round, stared, and drew himself proudly up, replying, in a tone of great bitterness, "Thank you, Mr. Hamilton, but perhaps if you *will* take the trouble, you may find some one better suited to you than myself."

"What is the matter?" said Hamilton.

21

"Some of your friends appear to have better memories than yourself," replied Trevannion, folding his arms, and assuming an indifferent air; "you will, perhaps, not find mine quite so capricious; I am much obliged for all favors bestowed, Mr. Hamilton. Perhaps you considered me too lazy to look out for another friend; I am active enough, I assure you, to provide myself with one, and to release you from the irksome ties your indolence has imposed upon you."

Hamilton looked, as he was, seriously annoyed. He did not remember the expression that had given so much offence, and was quite at a loss to understand the mystery:— he looked from one to the other for explanation; at one time inclined to walk away as proudly as Trevannion could have done; at another, his more moderate feelings triumphing, urged him into an inquiry.

"I really cannot understand you," he said, at length; "do explain yourself. If I have done any thing to offend you, let me know what it is, and, if reasonable, I am willing to apologize."

Trevannion sneered. "Apologies can do little good—eh, Norman?"

"If you know what this is, Norman," said Hamilton, "I must beg you to enlighten me."

"I have no business to interfere," said Norman, carelessly.

"What a tragedy scene! What's the matter?" cried Reginald Mortimer, who came up at the moment. "You lazy-bones of a Louis! where are you?"

"The matter is simply this," said Frank Digby: "Norman has heard from a veracious source that Mr. Hamilton once said, in confidence (between you and me, you know), that the reason he retained Mr. Philip Trevannion in the rank of first bosom-friend, was because he was too lazy to look out for one better suited to his tastes : consequently, as Mr. Trevannion can aver that Mr. Hamilton never confided this matter to him, it is certain that some one has betrayed confidence reposed in him—oh, yes ! oh, yes !"

"What a fuss about a nonsensical report !" exclaimed Reginald. "Do you believe it ?"

"Does he deny it ?" said Trevannion, turning to Hamilton.

Hamilton's color rose ; and, after a little pause, in which he carefully considered what he had said, he replied, " No, I do not deny having said something like this one day when Trevannion and I had fallen out ; but how much it was more than a momentary fit of anger our long friendship ought to decide. Trevannion, we have been friends too long for such a silly thing as this to separate us. I am very sorry it should ever have escaped my lips ; but if every thing we say in a moment of impatience and vexation were repeated and minded, there would be very little friendship in the world. Come, Trevannion, shake hands, and forget it for auld lang syne, as I will do when any one brings such a tale to me."

As Hamilton spoke, his eye rested on Norman, fired with indignation, and lighted a second on the principal offender, but no longer, for he did not wish to draw Louis into notice.

"It may seem a little nonsensical matter to you, Hamilton," said Trevannion, putting his hand behind him ; "but these little things exhibit more than the greatest professions. I am not too lazy to cure myself of old habits, if you are."

" I never make professions," said Hamilton, proudly; " and I have done."

He was turning away, when a sudden motion from Jones arrested him. Jones had been standing silently by Trevannion, and now, leaping over a desk, seized Louis, and dragged him in the centre of the group, to the great astonishment of both himself and his brother, exclaiming :

" Here's the offender, the tell-tale, the hypocrite, the meek good boy, so anxious of Ferrers' reputation !"

" What do you want with me ?" exclaimed Louis, angrily, struggling to free himself from his captor.

" Hands off! Leave him alone, Jones," shouted Reginald. " What's all this about ?"

" Do let him go," said Hamilton. " Can't you let him alone ?"

" He's the traitor, Hamilton."

Hamilton could not deny it, for it could have been no one else.

" Well, it is past, and the punishment he has in his own feelings will be enough," he said. " Let him alone."

" Louis, *you* haven't been telling tales and making mischief ?" cried Reginald.

" I don't know," said Louis. " I said something to Mrs. Paget, I believe — I didn't know there was any harm. Hamilton didn't say he didn't want any thing said about it."

" *Didn't say !*" echoed Jones, scornfully.

Hamilton's look was more in reproach than anger. Louis felt struck to the heart with shame and anger ; but so much had he lately been nursed in conceit and self-sufficiency, that he drove away the better impulse; and, instead of at once acknowledging himself in the wrong and begging pardon, he stood still, endeavoring to look unconcerned, repeating, "I didn't mean any harm."

"Oh, Louis!" exclaimed Reginald, reproachfully, "I didn't think you could."

"Let the boy go, Jones," said Hamilton, trying to remove the grasp from Louis' shoulders.

"Not so fast, an't please your majesty," said Jones: "I like to see hypocrites unmasked. Here, gentlemen, forsooth, here in this soonified youth, the anxious warden of Ferrers' reputation, you see the young gentleman who not only tells the story, but gives the name of the party concerned to a dear, good, gossiping soul—"

"Gently, gently there, Jones," remarked Norman.

"A gossiping old soul," repeated Jones, "who'd have the greatest delight in retailing the news, with decorations and additions, all over the kingdom with the greatest possible speed."

"I don't believe a word of that, Jones," said Reginald. "It is impossible!"

"What! is it impossible?" asked Jones, giving Louis a shake.

"What business have you to question me?"

"Did you?" repeated Jones, with another shake.

"Fair questioning, Jones," cried Reginald. "No coercion, if you please."

"Hold him back, Mason, if you please. Norman, will you hold him back? Now, Louis, if you don't answer I'll give you a thrashing."

"You and I are friends, Mortimer," said Salisbury, jumping off the desk and coming close up to Reginald; "but I mean to have fair play in this matter. He shan't be hurt —but, if you interfere till they've done questioning him, I shall help them to hold you back."

"Don't meddle with it, Salisbury," said Hamilton; "it's nobody's affair."

"Nobody's affair, indeed!" exclaimed Frank. "Here we've been making a *cher ami*, a *rara avis*, or something or other of this boy, because he professed to be something superior to us all—and now, when we find he has been telling tales of all of us, we are told it's *nobody's affair*. He's been obtaining credit upon false pretences. We're the strongest party, and we'll do what we please."

Reginald restrained himself with a violent effort, and Jones proceeded.

"Now, sir, answer directly—is this impossible?"

Louis felt very much inclined to cry, but he replied without tears very reluctantly, "Mrs. Paget would make me tell her some things—she had heard almost all from others. I don't know how the name slipped out; I didn't mean to tell, I am sure."

"WHAT?" said Hamilton; "you tell *that* story, Louis!"

Louis felt that Hamilton despised him; and perhaps, had they known all the circumstances relative to the Heronhurst disclosure, the clamor would not have been so great; so much evil is done by repeating a small matter, exaggerated, as these repetitions usually are, according to the feelings of the speaker. But in every case now bearing so unexpectedly down upon him, had Louis, thoughtless of himself, been less anxious for admiration, he would not have committed himself; had he not attracted Norman's attention by his folly and conceit, the circumstance of his having disclosed the name of the offender, at Heronhurst, would, most probably, not only have been unknown to his school-fellows, but to Norman also.

" Oh, Hamilton, I didn't tell all the story!" he exclaimed.

" No, only just enough to appear magnanimous," said Frank.

" Seeing that such is the case," continued Jones, " it cannot be a matter of great astonishment, that the same meek crocodile should also deliver to the same tender mercy various particulars of minor import respecting sundry others of his school-fellows; among which, we discover the private conversation of an intimate and too indulgent friend. Upon my word, young gentleman, I've a great mind to make you kiss Ferrers' shoes. Where's Ferrers ?"

Jones turned round with his victim towards the door, perceiving that Ferrers was not in the room, but neither Hamilton nor Reginald would permit matters to procced further.

" Let him go," said Norman; " it is not worth while taking so much trouble about it. You know whom you have to deal with, and will be careful."

" Thanks to you," said Hamilton, in a tone of the most cutting irony.

He released Louis, and stood still till he saw him safely in the playground, whither he was followed by the hisses and exclamations of his inquisitors, and then turned in the opposite direction to the class-room.

" Mr. Hamilton!" exclaimed Norman, " may I ask what your words meant just now ?"

"You may," said Hamilton, turning round and eyeing the speaker from head to foot, with the most contemptuous indifference. "You are at liberty to put whatever construction you please upon them; and perhaps it will save trouble if I inform you at once that I never fight."

"Then, sir," said Norman, whose anger was rising beyond control, "you should weigh your words a little more cautiously, if you are so cowardly."

Hamilton deigned no reply, and proceeded to the classroom, where he shut himself up, leaving the field clear for Reginald, who, before long, was engaged in a pitched battle with Norman.

Louis retreated to his play-fellows who were yet unconscious of his disgrace with the higher powers; and, after playing for a little while, wandered about by himself, too uneasy and sick at heart to amuse himself. He found now, alas! that he was alone; that he had lost all pleasure in holy things; and, conscious of his falling away, he was now afraid to pray,—foolish boy. And thus it is—Satan tempts us to do wrong, and then tempts us to doubt God's willingness to forgive us, in order that, being without grace and strength, we may fall yet deeper.

As Louis wandered along, he heard sounds familiar enough to him, which portended a deadly fray, and when he came upon the combatants, he discovered that one of them was his own brother. He knew it was useless to attempt to stop the fight, and he wandered away again, and cried a little, for he thought that something would happen, and he and Reginald would be placed together in some unpleasant situation; and he dreaded Dr. Wilkinson's hearing of either affair.

I must be excused for stopping my story to remark here, that in this world, it is certain that we have great influence on one another, and that for this influence we are responsible. Had Louis' school-fellows acted more kindly, endeavoring to set before him the fault of tattling, the effect would have been to raise a feeling of gratitude in his mind, which would have been far more effectual in preventing the recurrence of the fault, than the plan of repudiation they had adopted. Had they, even after a day or two's penance, given him an opening into their good graces, he would not have felt, as he did, that he had lost his character, and it was "no use caring about it," and so gone from bad to worse, till his name was associated with those of the worst boys in the school. It may be said, How can school-boys be expected to have so much consideration? but this a school-boy may do. He may mentally put himself in the position of the delinquent, and considering how he would wish to be treated, act accordingly.

Every thing seemed to go wrong with Louis that day. The Herodotus that Hamilton was to have heard, was scarcely looked at; and Louis lost two or three places in his class. Hamilton never noticed him, and even Reginald was offended with him. Louis tried to brave it out, and sung in a low tone, whistled, and finally, when he was roughly desired to be quiet, walked into the school-room, and finished his evening with Casson and Churchill.

CHAPTER XIX.

" Be not deceived; evil communications corrupt good manners."-
1 *Cor.* xv. 32.

For the next few days Louis was regularly sent to
Coventry, and though Hamilton took no part in any thing
that was said against him, his manner had so entirely
changed, and his tone was so cold when he addressed or
answered him, that Louis needed no further demonstration
to feel assured of the great difference in the feeling with
which he was regarded. Clifton alone remained unchanged,
but he was so much absorbed in his dear classics that he
had hardly time to notice that any thing was the matter :
and as Reginald, thoroughly disappointed, was also highly
displeased with his brother, Louis was either thrown entirely
upon his own resources, or driven to seek the society of the
lower school ; and, as he was in a very unhappy state, and
could not bear to be left alone, he naturally chose the latter.
For the first two days he struggled to assume an independent air, and, changing his place of his own accord from
Hamilton to Clifton, talked incessantly, though nearly un-
heeded by the latter, to show how perfectly well able he
was to do his own business without assistance. Hamilton
missed him, and glanced down the table with a gaze of

mingled disappointment and displeasure. A few words from him might have recalled Louis, but they were not spoken, and the only impression conveyed to the poor truant was, that the friend he most cared about, in common with the rest, considered him beneath his notice.

The third evening some affair was to be taken into consideration, of which the proceedings were intended to be kept very secret. Louis was sitting by Clifton, when Trevannion, who was to open the business, entered with a folded paper and a pencil in one hand, and took his place at the head of the long table. He looked down the table, and his eyes meeting Louis', he laid down his pencil, and taking up a book, began, or pretended to begin, to read.

" Hey ! What's that, Trevannion ?" asked Salisbury. " Are we to be prepared with a choice quotation from Thucydides, or is it a hint that we are to remember duty first and pleasure afterwards ?"

" Rather," said Frank, " that some people have long ears and tongues."

" Perhaps," said Trevannion, looking over the top of his book, " Louis Mortimer will have the civility to hasten his studies this evening, as we have pressing business to perform."

" And why need I prevent it ?" said Louis, crimsoning.

" Simply for this reason," said Trevannion, " that we do not choose to have every thing that passes our lips this night carried over the country ; therefore, Master Louis, we can dispense with your company."

" Without so much circumlocution, either," said Jones. " We like your room better than your company just now, Louis Mortimer ; so please to decamp."

" Evaporate !" said Meredith.

" I have my lessons to learn," said Louis.

" Is there any moral or physical impossibility in your lessons being learned in the school-room ?" asked Smith.

" I don't choose."

" Don't choose!" repeated Jones.   " We'll see about that. Do you choose to go quietly, or to be turned out, eh ?"

" You have no right to do it," exclaimed Louis.   " I have as much right to be here as you."

" Ho, ho !" exclaimed Jones.   " You'll find might is right here, my pretty young gentleman.   Salisbury, will you have the kindness to put the door between us and his impertinence ?"

" The procacity of the juvenile is progressing," remarked Frank.

Hamilton was not in the room, and there was no one to assist Reginald in his resistance to the numbers by whom he was soon overpowered, and in a few minutes, in spite of his exertions, he found himself turned out with Louis, whom he had vainly endeavored to defend.

Boiling with fury, Reginald at first attempted to kick open the door, and then, being called to his senses by the interference of the usher in the room, walked into the playground, and getting in at one of the class-room windows, opened the door to Louis before his antagonists had recovered from their surprise.

There was another scuffle, which was at length settled by the usher's taking Louis' side, and desiring him to go in ; but Louis found the study so thoroughly uncomfortable, that in a few minutes he returned to the school-room, and seated himself, in a restless, idle mood, by Casson.

The idle conversation of an idle, uprincipled boy is sure to be of a hurtful description, and after Casson had heard Louis' grievances, and condoled with him in the fashion of encouraging him in all that was bad, the discourse fell upon Casson's last school, and many things Louis heard and learned of which he had remained, till then, in blissful ignorance. One or two ushers usually sat with the boys in the evening. One of these was an elderly man, uncouth and ungainly in person, and possessed of a very unfortunate temper, that was irritated in every possible manner by those whose duty it was to have soothed the infirmities and considered the trials of one whose life was spent in their service. Louis had felt a great pity for the poor solitary man who never seemed to have a friend, and now and then had spared a few minutes of his play-time to talk to him, and would ask to be allowed to cut the pencil that was employed so constantly in ruling the ciphering books ; and when his flowers were in bloom, a half-open rosebud was usually presented to Mr. Garthorpe to put in his button-hole on Sunday morning. The poor usher loved Louis as warmly as any one else in that house, nor would he have believed that " that good lad," as he called him, could have spent a great part of an evening in laughing at practical jokes played off on him, though Louis could not yet be prevailed upon to take part in them.

The next few days were spent as might be expected. Louis had now put himself under the guidance of some of the worst boys in the school, and the consequence was (for the downward path is easy) the neglect of all that was good, and the connivance at, if not actual participation in, all that was wrong. His place was lost, his lessons so ill prepared, that, as formerly, he was kept in day after day and Casson, his chief adviser, persuaded him that Mr. Danby was unjust and tyrannical, and instigated him to impertinence as a retaliation. Louis was miserable, for miserable must he be who sins against light.

It was not long before Dr. Wilkinson became aware of a change in Louis' conduct, and he took an early opportunity of speaking very seriously to him on the subject. Louis was very humble, and longed to throw open all his troubles to his master, the only person who had spoken kindly and sensibly to him since his disgrace, yet foolishly afraid to declare the whole truth to him, especially as, by the doctor's recommendation to him to follow the example of his friends Hamilton and Clifton, he found that his master was not aware that Hamilton was so much displeased with him. Unhappily, Dr. Wilkinson did not know of Louis' intimacy with Casson, nor had Casson been long enough with him to enable him to know more of him than as an idle, troublesome dunce. The doctor's admonitions were so far beneficial to Louis, that besides producing decidedly better behavior for a few days, they were instrumental in restraining him afterwards from the commission of many things which might have been both hurtful to his well-doing and future peace of mind ; but unassisted by prayerful efforts on Louis' part, they could go no further than this ; and as he had not strength of mind to shake off his evil companions, he soon fell back into much of his idle, giddy habits, and was classed with some of the worst boys by those of the upper school who had formerly so unwisely flattered and spoiled him. Oh, had they known how often his sad, restless, though at times reckless mind, yearned for a little kindness from them, that he might feel that every chance of retrieving their esteem had not gone! Once, after standing some time by Hamilton, he ventured to ask if he were still offended with him. Hamilton coldly disclaimed any idea of offence, and declining all discussion on the matter, hinted that Louis' conduct was too disreputable to be noticed. Louis turned from him with a proud resolve never to speak to Hamilton again. Hamilton's conscience smote him when he saw him a short time after in company with Casson and Harris, whispering and laughing in a corner, at no good, assuredly; but though he inwardly felt that he had forced Louis, in some measure, to take refuge with these boys, he was too proud to stoop from his throne of dignity to save him.

That day, when the boys returned from their walk, they entered at the back of the playground from a lane, on the opposite side of which lay some fields belonging to Dr. Wilkinson, and close on the edge of the field nearest to the ditch bounding the lane, were some out-houses, consisting of a cow-house, stables, and barn. As the lane was public property, the boys were forbidden to wander beyond the boundary of their playground, which on this side was a high wall, a wooden door shutting out all communication with any thing beyond. Notwithstanding the prohibition regarding this lane, there were now and then excursions over the wall in the direction of the cottage of an old woman, who kept a small day-school, and sold bull's-eyes and gingerbread, with other dainties of a doubtful description, and who was, more than all, willing, for "a consideration," to perform any hazardous errand for the young gentlemen. Other sallies of a still more doubtful character occasionally took place, and Dr. Wilkinson felt sure that his orchard had been robbed more than once, though by what hands he did not always discover.   On this day the boys had just entered from the lane, and, as the ushers had not been careful in seeing the door closed, it stood open for some time, while several of the boys availed themselves of the crowd of their school-fellows near it to slip out on their various errands to old Mary Simmons.   Louis had been collecting mineralogical specimens during his walk, all of which he had consigned to the depths of a large green baize bag which he carried with him.   He stopped a few minutes near the gate to talk about his treasures to Clifton, who had been walking with him, but the concourse becoming rather greater than Clifton found convenient, he presently moved away, and Louis was following him, his bag in one hand and two unpromising-looking stones in the other, when Casson arrested him with,

"I say, Louis, what a famous bag—lend it us a minute. I'm going to old mother Simmons's; it would hold half her shop."

"There are stones in it," said Louis, drawing back.

Casson verbally execrated the stones, and, declaring it was of no consequence, snatched the bag out of Louis' hand and ran away.

Rather startled by this abrupt manner of proceeding, Louis followed Casson to the verge of the lane, and waited there till he came back.

"I haven't eaten your bag, you see, but I can't spare it till we get in."

"But are the stones there?" said Louis.

"To be sure; what do you suppose I've done with them?

What a famous receptacle! I say, Louis, did you ever see the inside of the stable over the way?"

"No—I am not very fond of stables."

"But I suspect there's something worth seeing there," said Casson; and he proceeded to tell Louis, under a promise of the strictest secrecy, in a manner so exceedingly vulgar and improper that I do not choose to write it, that he believed that the doctor kept his winter apples in the loft of that stable, and concluded by hinting that some of them meant to find them out and help themselves. "We used to do it regularly at old Stennett's, where I went before, Louis," he continued. "It's such fun: you must lend us your green bag, and come with us."

"Oh! Casson, how can you think such a thing of me!" exclaimed Louis, shrinking back.

The exclamation was so loud that Casson laid his hand upon his mouth with a muttered angry ejaculation.

"One would think I had spoken of breaking open a house," said Casson.

"It's stealing," said Louis, in a tone of anger.

"Nonsense."

"I tell you, Casson, it is—don't talk to me any more about it—I wish I had never known you!"

Casson burst out laughing. "What a ninny you are!" he exclaimed. "You are as easily frightened as a bird with a pop-gun. And now, I suppose, you will go with this nice little story to some good friend and make something interesting and romantic out of nothing."

"Is it *really* nonsense?" said Louis, after a pause. "Tell me, Casson, truly, did you mean nothing just now?"

" Nothing, upon honor," said the unprincipled boy.   " 1
wanted to see you horrified."

Louis looked doubtfully at him.   " Well, please give me
my bag."

" What a hurry you are in !—you must wait till I've un-
loaded."

Louis followed him to the school-room, but, Casson's
crowded desk not holding all the contents of the bag, he
was obliged, notwithstanding his anxiety, to wait for his
property for a day or two, at the expiration of which time
it was returned to him, and borrowed the next day for
another expedition to Mary Simmons.

CHAPTER XX.

"Open rebuke is better than secret love."

It now wanted little more than three weeks to the holidays. Sticks for notching were in great request, and "days" cut in paper were fastened to the testers of the several beds, to mark more securely the weary time that must elapse before the joyful breaking-up. Reginald and Louis had jointly decorated theirs with an elegant drawing of Dashwood Priory, with a coach and four in the distance, which drawing would remain uninjured till even the last of the twenty-eight strips of paper had been detached, when the owners tore the remainder for excess of joy. The subjects for examination had already been given out, and those who had any interest at stake had already commissioned Maister Dunn for candles, and begun to rise early and sit late, or as late as was allowed, at their various studies. It was with some little dismay that Louis looked down the long list of subjects for the examination of his class, for he felt that, though (thanks to Hamilton at first, and latterly some degree of perseverance on his own part) he had made some progress during the half-year: his friend Clifton's indefatigable industry had placed him so far first, that it would be almost impossible to hope for any advantage.

Hamilton was now busily engaged in the composition of a prize poem in Latin, besides the many other things with which (to use his own expression) he found it necessary "to cram himself;" for, however easy, comparatively, he had found his post the preceding half-year, he had now competitors sufficiently emulous and talented in Norman and Frank Digby——the latter of whom had shown a moderate degree of diligence during the half-year, and now, exerting to the utmost the great powers with which he was gifted, bid fair, if not to distance all his rivals, at least to claim the lion's share of the honors held out.

As Hamilton scarcely allowed himself time to run once round the playground in the day, it cannot be supposed that even had he condescended to notice Louis he would have found much time to attend to him. More than once, however, he looked rather anxiously down the long table where Louis now sat (Reginald having insisted on his leaving the school-room and his companions to their fate), and, apparently satisfied that he was doing something, resumed his own work. Louis' mind was more than ever occupied now——every moment was taken up with lessons of one kind or another. The first waking thoughts, which were formerly, at least, a consciousness of the presence of his Maker, were now so mixed up with Latin verses, English translations, French plays, ancient and modern history, that a very short time sufficed for his cold prayer——and then poured in the whole flood of daily business, only checked by as cold a semblance of a petition at night. The former half-year the case, though similar in many respects, differed in the greatest essential. Louis was not less diligent than now, but he was more prayerful; he had not more time, but he used it better; he did not leave his religion for a few minutes at night and morning, and forget it for the rest of the day; he did not shut up his Bible, and scarcely look at it from Sunday to Sunday. He who waits closely upon his God is sure to be enabled to serve him in the beauty of holiness: and those who thought at all about Louis could not but be struck with the wide difference between the gentle, humble, happy-looking boy, who bore so meekly what was unkindly done and spoken, and the equally industrious, but fevered, restless, anxious, and now rather irritable being, who toiled on day after day almost beyond his strength.

The first day of the examination, Charles Clifton and Louis were walking together, between school-hours, settling the order in which their labors were to be undertaken. As they turned the corner of the playground, near the kitchen, they encountered Harris, Casson, and Churchill, who, with Sally Simmons and her basket of apples, blocked up a narrow passage between the side of the house and the kitchen-garden wall.

"Aint they beauties, Louis?" said Churchill, at the sight. The mention of apples sufficiently disturbed Louis in the present company, and he made a violent effort to get past Harris, who was, however, so much engaged in choosing an apple from the basket, that he did not move an inch. Finding it useless at present to attempt the pass, Louis was turning back, when Sally offered the basket to him, with "Mathter Louis, you mutht hide it; I donnoh what mathter would thay."

"There are plenty more where they came from, Sally," said Casson.

"Here'th a nithe one, thir," said Sally, looking in Louis' alarmed face, and pointing to one of the apples.

"They are not yours to give, Sally," said Louis, stepping back against the wall. "Harris, Casson, Churchill, don't take them—it's dishonest."

Sally protested in great dismay, that it was only one or two, and Dr. Wilkinson wouldn't mind.

"You know he would, Sally, or why did you say I was to hide it?" said Louis.

"Do you mean to tell him you have given away any?" asked Clifton.

"Not she; she knows better—don't you, Sally?" said Casson.

"You are not to be trusted," said Clifton.

"Mathter Louis, you won't be going and making mith-chief?" said the girl.

"If he does," ejaculated Harris, " I'll—"

What he would do Louis never heard, for he had by this time freed himself from the basket and run away, followed more leisurely by Clifton.

"I am sure," he said, when Clifton rejoined him, " that Sally Simmons ought not to be employed here; she is always doing forbidden things for the boys."

"If you know of any thing wrong in her, why don't you tell Dr. Wilkinson?" said Charles.

"The next thing I know of, I shall. But I should get the boys into such a scrape," said Louis.

"If they are bad boys they deserve it," replied Clifton; " my father says, if we conceal evil, when we may remove it by mentioning it, we make ourselves partners in it."

"The boys would call me a sneak if I did," said Louis.

Charles looked at Louis in simple wonderment. "That wouldn't hinder you from doing what is right, would it? What does it matter what such fellows as those think or say?"

"Yes, but I shouldn't like to get them into a scrape," repeated Louis, uneasily.

"Why don't you tell your friend Hamilton of it, and ask his advice?"

"Oh, Clifton! surely you know that Hamilton won't speak to me."

"No, I didn't," said Clifton, in a tone of surprise. "Why not? he used to be so fond of you."

"He's offended now," replied Louis, looking down.

"He doesn't like me, I know," said Charles; "but he used to be so very fond of you." -

"*Used*—that's long ago," said Louis, with a suppressed sigh.

"Well, but," remarked Clifton, without showing the least curiosity to discover the cause of Louis' quarrel with Hamilton, "if you can't consult him, ask your brother."

"I know very well what Reginald would do; he wouldn't think it right to tell of them, or of her either."

"Then, Louis, make up your own mind."

"It's not so easily done," replied Louis; "oh, Charlie, I wish I were like you!"

"Oh, why?" said Charles, gravely; "you have a great many more friends, and are much better liked than I am. I have no friend but you—not that I care at all about it, but I should think you would."

"Yes; but I wish I *could* make up my mind. I am not half so happy as you are, for I cannot make up my mind to do a thing because it is right. You only think about that and do it at once ; and because I have so many friends, and even care about pleasing those I do not like, I am always getting into scrapes, and always doing wrong. I think there never was anybody so bad as I am. I wish papa hadn't sent me to school."

"I like you very much," said Clifton ; "and I am sure you have done me good—on Sunday, at least."

"Ah, it is much easier to know and talk of what is right than to do it," replied Louis, sighing very deeply. "Oh, *domum, dulce domum !* But there is Reginald, and I must go and ask him a question."

For several days after this occurrence, Louis was too busy, and too much with his brother, to see much of his evil advisers ; and very pleased in having, as he imagined, thus got rid of them. The examination was going on in earnest ; Louis had now nearly regained his old place, and was, on the whole, favorably reported of : but Clifton was not to be overcome. Thoroughly prepared, and thoroughly understanding all he had learned, he kept the first place undaunted by any difficulty, and apparently unexcited by the crisis ; at least, Louis remarked to Reginald, that Clifton was so cool, he didn't seem to care whether he won or not. He had a little more color than usual, and the only beauty his face possessed—his intelligent eyes—wore perhaps a keener and more anxious expression, but this was not noticed by a casual observer ; nor was the violent palpitation of the heart, when the chances ran so closely between him and the next, at the close of a two days' struggle for the mathematical prize. There were few that congratulated him on his almost unparalleled success; but few that did not respect his ability and steadiness. Never once, from the first day he came to school, had he on any occasion incurred the displeasure of his masters; and yet no one cared for him, for he had lived only for himself.

But to return to Louis. The mathematical contest was finished, and there was a little lull before the second class would be again called on, and Louis determined to spend this little interval of leisure in giving a finishing scrutiny of the history likely to be in demand. Full of his purposes, he burst into the class-room, where only Hamilton and Reginald were, the former writing very fast, and the latter looking carefully over an English essay he had just finished. Louis flew to the shelves and ransacked them in vain: almost every book he wanted was gone. At length, in despair, he asked Reginald if he knew who had Rollin's History. Reginald absently replied in the negative, as he noted down something in the page he was reading.

"The books are always gone," said Louis, pettishly. "I suppose Charlie has it. He had it yesterday—he might as well let me have it to-day."

"Trevannion has it, I think," said Reginald.

"You may have mine," said Hamilton.

Louis stood still; he wanted the book very much, but was too proud to accept the offer.

"It is in my room," continued Hamilton, without looking up.

"Thank you, I don't want *yours*," replied Louis, proudly, walking out of the room.

As he entered the school-room he confronted Dr. Wilkinson, who, having given orders for a brisk walk, was

23

inquiring for Hamilton. Louis had scarcely taken his hand from the lock when Hamilton abruptly opened it and came quickly out of the room.

"You are the person I want," said the doctor, laying his hand on his arm. "Hamilton, I want you to come out with me this bright day."

"To-day, sir?" said Hamilton, whose countenance expressed any thing but delight at the proposition.

"And why put off till to-morrow what may be done to-day so well?" said the doctor, smiling. "I suppose you have hopes of the weather making a walk impracticable to-morrow: but I must have you all out, or some of you will be laid up before you go home."

His eye fell upon Clifton, who was sitting with his elbows on a desk close by, his fingers pushed through his hair, wholly absorbed in " *Gibbon's Decline and Fall.*" Dr. Wilkinson addressed him twice, but, producing no impression, he removed one of the props of his head, and turned his face towards himself.

"What are you doing there?"

"History, sir," said the boy, getting up mechanically, and looking very much as if he were not pleased at the interruption.

"I hear your name is very high in the list to-day."

"Yes, sir," replied Charles, gravely; and, as the doctor released him, he settled down precisely in the same attitude, without showing the least satisfaction at the notice he had received.

Hamilton turned away with an impatient gesture.

"Are you going immediately, sir?" he said. "Can you spare me a few minutes?"

"I shall be at the garden-gate in a quarter of an hour from this time," replied the doctor.

"I will not fail, sir," said Hamilton ; and, crossing the room in immense strides, he flew up stairs, and returned almost immediately with a large volume under his arm. He made some inquiries of Trevannion's whereabouts, and, learning that he was in the playground, went in search of him. He very soon found him, walking briskly up and down with Norman, making extracts from an old book in his hand, and questioning his friend alternately. Hamilton and he had scarcely exchanged a word since their quarrel, and it was with some surprise that he saw Hamilton present himself, and still more, when a request was made that he would exchange books.

"I particularly want this just now," he replied.

"This is Rollin," said Hamilton. "I should feel obliged if you would exchange copies."

Trevannion opened his eyes wider, but after a second's pause, he took Hamilton's and gave him his book in exchange, without any comment.

"What a strange whim!" remarked Norman, when Hamilton had left them, after shortly expressing his thanks.

"What can he mean, Norman?" said Trevannion. "This is his own, too."

"Perhaps some new way of trying to make up an old quarrel," said Norman, sneeringly.

"I don't think so," replied Trevannion ; "he would not have tried so odd a plan—no, there's something deeper than that."

"Are the histories alike?" asked Norman.

"I believe so," answered Trevannion; "if there's **any** advantage, I am sure to have it, at any rate."

"You have a very high opinion of him."

"VERY," said Trevannion. "If Hamilton did mean this to make up our quarrel, I am sure I shall be willing."

"Upon my word," said Norman, "this is dignity."

Trevannion made no answer, for something had attracted his attention on the opposite side of the playground.

"Holloa! Norman, look there!" he exclaimed.

"Where? what! oh, horror!" cried Norman.

"There they are—they're hid: now, there they are again!—now look, who is it? Stand behind this tree a minute—now let us look out."

Obedient to his instructions, Norman looked, and saw three boys drop down one after another from the branch of a tree, that had evidently assisted their descent from the playground wall, and then run across the playground.

"Who are they?" said Trevannion, putting up his eye-glass (which, gentle reader, be it known he carried for use). "One is Churchill, I'm sure! Who's that long fellow? Why, it's Harris, isn't it? It can't be, surely!"

"It is," said Norman; "and the other's Casson."

"I'm sure they are at no good," said Trevannion; "I shall make a note of this remarkable occurrence."

So saying, he made a memorandum of the circumstance in his pocket-book, and had just finished when the boys poured out cloaked and great-coated, and informed him of the doctor's desires.

The reader will be at no loss to discover Hamilton's reason for exchanging the books. As Louis was out, he took Dr. Wilkinson's with him into the class-room, and sat down to finish the six last words of his poem; and then, folding it neatly up, enveloped it in half a sheet of writing-paper. He was just pressing the seal upon the wax, when his watch, which he had laid open before him, warned him that the last minutes of the quarter of an hour had arrived. He just pushed his things together, and left them on the table; and snatching up his hat as he ran through the hall, scarcely arrived at the garden-gate in time to save his character for punctuality.

It so happened that Casson was Louis' companion during the walk, and entertained him with a flowing account of all the vulgar tricks he had been in the habit of playing at his former school. Louis could not help laughing at them; nor would his vanity allow him to refrain from boasting of—what he had before been properly ashamed—his own share in some of Casson's late exploits. So afraid was he of seeming inferior, even to a person he despised, and in those things which his better feelings taught him equally to despise. Casson inwardly laughed at Louis' boasted feats, as he had always done to others when Louis was out of hearing; but he now quizzed him, stimulating him, by applauding his spirit and ingenuity; and by the time they had reached the house, Louis was in a thoroughly giddy humor, ready to try, at the risk of disgrace, the new scheme to which he had just been listening.

The boys stayed in the playground till the dinner-bell rang, which was a few minutes after they had entered the playground; but these few minutes sufficed for Louis, in his present humor, to get himself in a scrape, the consequences of which, at the time, he certainly did not contemplate. He had been complaining to Casson, in the beginning of their walk, that he could not get "Rollin's History," and, as Casson persisted that it was in the study, Louis took him there to show him his error, when they returned home.

"Ha, ha! Mr. Louis Mortimer, who's right?" cried Casson, holding up the book.

"That can't be; I wonder how it got there," said Louis, approaching the table in a mystified manner. "These must be Trevannion's things, I suppose; only Hamilton was writing here; and here is his dictionary,—I wonder what he wanted with it—he never said he had it—he let me suppose Trevannion had it—kind of him—I suppose he wanted to prevent my getting it; but I'll have it now—he's got one of his own."

"I'd be even with him," said Casson; "what a heap of things! See, here's an exercise of his; or a letter, I suppose—it's too neat for an exercise. A good thick letter—sealed, too. I'll tell you what, Louis—"

Accordingly, what Casson did tell Louis was, what a "capital dodge" it would be to abstract Hamilton's sealed packet, and to leave another folded like it in its place.

"We often used to trick the boys at old Stennett's with their exercises," continued he; "they never wrote in books there—we used to tear the leaves out of the exercise-books, and write on them. It was such jolly fun to see them open the paper and find nothing in it, or only some rubbish."

"How did you do it?" asked Louis.

"Oh, we doubled up a bit of an old exercise-book, and exchanged, that's all!" replied Casson; "see, why here's half a sheet of paper, that'll do for the cover; and now then, Louis, more paper—he'll never miss it—that's it—fold it up just the size; how beautifully you have done it!"

"But there's no seal," said Louis.

"He'll forget he sealed it," replied Casson; "oh, how jolly!—here's a piece of sealing-wax—it is sealed with the top of a pencil-case."

"I have one just like that," said Louis; "oh, no; here's E. H. on this—that won't do, Casson."

Casson presently relieved this difficulty by discovering Hamilton's pencil-case; and the paper was quickly sealed, when Louis began to doubt:

"But we don't know what it is, Casson."

"If it turns out to be any thing, send it by post, directed to him, at his father's," said Casson; "he'll get it safely enough."

The dinner-bell rang loudly at this moment, and with a little laugh at the idea of the oddity of sending it to Hamilton's home, and a strong feeling of doubt as to the wisdom of his proceeding, Louis hastily exchanged the packets, and ran out of the room. On his way to the dining-room he paused—

"If it should be of any consequence, Casson," he said.

"Well, if it is, so much the better fun; he won't treat you so shabbily another time."

"Ah, but—I don't want to revenge myself, and I don't like playing tricks on Hamilton exactly, either: I think I must give it back."

"I thought you were such a dab at these kinds of things," said Casson, sneeringly.

"What have I done with it now?" Louis exclaimed suddenly, as they reached the dining-room door, after stopping a few seconds in the hall to hang up his coat. "What can I have done with it? I must have slipped it into my desk just now, when I put my Livy in."

He was not able to turn back then; and, in the mean time, Hamilton had paid a hasty visit to the class-room, to collect his things, and had locked up carefully the false packet; and Louis had not courage to make any inquiries, though he hoped that he might have found the right one, which, with all his care, he could not discover himself. Louis had, in his hurry, left Rollin on the study-table, and after school he ran into the room, and finding it in nearly the same place where Hamilton had been guarding it for him, he carried it off, and Hamilton, seeing the action, made no remark on the matter.

The next evening, the Latin poems were sent in to the doctor's study for comparison, and Hamilton's blank counterfeit was titled on the cover, and dispatched with a degree of nervous anxiety that certainly would not have been called forth by a subject so empty. Louis was in an agony of remorse, when the truth burst on him. His only hope was, that Hamilton might have found the right packet. He heard the speculations around him as to the probability of success, and saw the last paper put into Norman's hand to be carried away, but he dared not say any thing. He had never dreamt of the importance of the paper he had so carelessly dropped or mislaid, and would have given all he possessed to have remembered what he had done with it.

Nothing more was done that evening. Study had helped to drive away the smaller qualms of conscience the day before; but he was now so sick at heart, that he remained with his head on his hand doing nothing, puzzling himself in vain to remember what he had done with the poem.

CHAPTER XXI.

It was Saturday night when the manuscripts were delivered to the doctor, and it was not till Monday that the absence of Hamilton's poem was discovered. As much of Sunday as he was able, Louis spent with Casson, trying to discover what could have become of the poem, and in devising all manner of schemes for its recovery and restoration. Little comfort he received from his tempter—Casson alternately laughed at his fears, and blamed his cowardice—and, in order to escape this, Louis affected to be indifferent to the consequences, concealing his heaviness of heart under assumed mirth and unconcern. He had lately spent many cold, careless Sabbaths, but one so utterly wretched as this he could not remember.

The boys had just left the dining-room on Monday, after dinner, when a summons to the doctor's study came for Hamilton. As this was not an uncommon occurrence, Hamilton betrayed neither curiosity nor uneasiness, but quietly gave a few directions to his little brother, and then leisurely left the room. He was soon in the presence of Dr. Wilkinson, Mr. James Wilkinson, and an old gentleman who had a day or two before been examining his class, and who usually assisted in the half-yearly examinations. The countenances of these gentlemen were not very promising, and he instantly saw that something unpleasant might be expected. Before the doctor lay a number of folded papers, which Hamilton recognized as the poems under consideration, and in his hand was a blank sheet of paper, the envelope of which had fallen on the floor.

" Mr. Hamilton," said the doctor, " I have sent for you to explain this strange affair. Pray can you tell me what was in this envelope?" He stooped, and, picking up the paper as he spoke, handed it to Hamilton.

" My poem, sir," replied Hamilton, quietly.

" You are sure that is your writing?"

" Quite," said Hamilton, confidently.

" I have been able to discover nothing more than this," said the doctor, with something like annoyance in his tone. " I do not know whether you have been writing with invisible ink. This is a mistake, Hamilton," he added, turning the blank sheet in all directions. " Where is your poem?"

" That in *my* envelope, sir!" exclaimed Hamilton, reddening to the roots of his hair. " In *my* envelope!" he reiterated, taking up the envelope and re-examining it in a state of tremulous excitement. " I *cannot* have made such a mistake—it is utterly impossible."

" I should say so—impossible, unconsciously, to make so great a mistake," said the old gentleman.

" And equally so, sir, to make it *consciously*," replied Hamilton.

" But where is the poem?" asked Dr. Wilkinson.

" I expected it was here," said Hamilton—" and, as it is not, I cannot answer that question, sir." He again turned over the paper, but could find no clue to the mystery.

" Is the paper the same as you used ?" asked Mr. James.

" It is," replied Hamilton ; " and the seal is my own, as well as the writing."

" What is the seal ?" asked Dr. Berry, the old gentleman.

" E. H. It belongs to this pencil-case," answered Hamilton, producing his pencil-case. " I always carry it about with me."

" That's awkward again," said Dr. Berry, exchanging a ..ok with Mr. James.

" Have you never left your pencil-case about lately, nor lent it to any one ?" asked Dr. Wilkinson.

Hamilton considered.

" I believe I left it with all my things on the class-room table last Friday, when I went out with you, sir."

" Ah !" said Dr. Berry, " what did you leave there ?"

" Some writing-paper, pens, a few books, and my poem, which I had just finished."

" That was careless of you, Hamilton," said Dr. Wilkinson.

" I had only just sealed it in time to run after you, sir," replied Hamilton ; " and, as every one was out, I thought there could be no harm in leaving them there till I returned."

" How much paper did you leave there ?" asked Mr. James.

" About half a quire."

" *About* half a quire ; then, I suppose, you do not know whether any of that paper was taken while you were away ?"

"No, I do not," replied Hamilton. "If any one changed it, it must have been then ; as, after I came home it was locked up in my own writing-desk till Saturday evening."

"It might have been changed on the way," suggested Mr. James.

Hamilton was silent for a few seconds, when he answered :

"I do not think so ; for I am sure this is my writing : I must unwittingly have directed an empty packet."

"Unless," said Dr. Wilkinson, quietly, "some one has imitated your writing ?"

"I only know one who could," replied Hamilton, coloring ; "and, I am confident, he was not the party : besides, sir, I do not think there was time, between Norman's departure and his return, to have done it, and that was the only time any one would have had after I had directed it. I did not direct it till Saturday evening."

"But you said the boys were all out at the same time with yourself ; and, in fact, I know they were : I saw them going in as we turned into the playground," said Dr. Wilkinson. "Did no one stay at home ? Stay— Friday—Digby was at home ; I remember he pleaded his cold."

Dr. Wilkinson looked down on the paper he held : there was a strong expression of suspicion in his countenance. The other gentlemen exchanged looks, and Mr. James remarked, that he considered Frank the probable culprit.

"I am glad he does not hear you say so, sir," exclaimed Hamilton. "I am sure Digby would sooner put his own on the fire! I'd trust Frank's honor as much as my own; and, I am sure, sir," he added, turning to Dr. Wilkinson, "*you* know Frank too well."

To Hamilton's annoyance, Dr. Wilkinson did not reply immediately.

"Frank is too fond of practical jokes," he said, at last; "I wish I could give him a lesson he would remember. He will never be cured till it touches him severely."

"But Frank would not joke on this, sir," expostulated Hamilton. "If he were not so high it might be so, but I'm sure it is not now."

"Well, there is no time now to consider of this any more," said Dr. Wilkinson, getting up. "I could bring forward many instances of Digby's disregard of feelings and appearances when his fancy for joking interferes. Dr. Berry, will you be kind enough to attend to these for me, this afternoon? I shall be glad to call upon you on Wednesday for my second class, if you can spare me the day."

Dr. Berry signified his ready acquiescence; and Dr. Wilkinson turned to Hamilton:

"It is just school-time," he said; "but I wish you, after school, to make a search in every desk for your poem. I do not imagine it is destroyed. Mr. James will assist you. In the mean time, in the event of your poem not being discovered, you had better rewrite it as well as you can; I will give you till nine o'clock on the last morning."

Hamilton bowed, thanked his master, and retired, exceedingly uncomfortable. His own loss was slight compared with the vexation he felt at any suspicion of Frank's honor being raised. A very different surmise would now and then try to rise in his own mind, but was vigorously opposed as ungenerous in the extreme. An idea of the real culprit never once occurred to him, nor to any other person. The first class being disengaged that afternoon, Hamilton employed himself with the new edition of his poem, but his thoughts wandered ; and, had it not been for a good memory and the force of habitual concentration, he would have found it almost impossible to resume a task he had considered as finished, in circumstances so very disagreeable to him.

As soon as the business of the day was concluded Dr. Wilkinson commanded every one to remain in his place, and then desired Hamilton to begin the search, carefully refraining from mentioning the object in quest. There was considerable excitement in the school when the doctor's command was made known, and it was strictly enforced, that no one should touch the desks till after the search had been made.

" Frank Digby, come here !" shouted the doctor from his post. " Did I not desire that none of those desks should be touched at present ?"

" I was only putting my slate away, sir," said Frank, in much amazement.

" I will not have your desk touched ; stay here."

" What's in the wind ?" muttered Jones, sulkily. " The magister's in a splendid humor. What do you want in my desk, Hamilton ?"

" A trick has been played on me," said Hamilton, hastily ; " my poem has been exchanged ; but——" he added, hesitating, " I cannot bear this."

" Nonsense, Hamilton !" said Mr. James, who was turning over the contents of Jones's desk. "There is nothing there."

"Stand back, and let Hamilton look, pray!" exclaimed Reginald Mortimer. "What a shame it is!—you don't suspect *us*, Hamilton?"

"*To be sure not!*" said Hamilton, warmly; "but I am desired to do this."

"So much the better," said Salisbury; "you'll find mine locked, but here are my keys: we'll go up to the doctor. I say, Hamilton, don't upset my bottle of lemon kali, or my blue ink; you mightn't see them, perhaps, among the other things."

Hamilton took the keys with some embarrassment, and the first class moved in a body to the upper end of the room, where they remained till every desk had been subjected to a fruitless ransacking.

Louis' state of mind may be easily imagined. He had guessed the reason of the doctor's command the instant it was given; and had also heard the few words that passed between Hamilton and his friends. Oh! what would he have given that he had considered before he committed such folly! He could not bear to face Hamilton, and yet he must be near him when his own desk was examined, for he dared not move from his place. He had looked carefully there himself, but still he was afraid it might, by chance, be there. He hardly dared look round, for fear he should betray his secret; and yet his distress sadly longed for vent. "I did not mean to do any harm," was his reiterated thought; "I am sure, I thought it was a letter—I did not mean it." And then he wished to confess his fault; but, with his usual vacillation of purpose, he deferred it, till he

should see how things went.   It did seem strange that,
with all the lessons he had had, he should have put off his
confession; yet he dared not, and tried to quiet his conscience with, "I shall tell Hamilton alone;" and, "It's no
use telling, when I can't find the poem."   But his trouble
was tenfold increased when Hamilton and Mr. James came
near him, and finding his desk locked, inquired who's it
was, and where the keys were.

Hamilton remarked in a low tone, not aware that Louis
was so near, "I suppose for form's sake we must look, but
I am sure, poor fellow, he has nothing to do with it."

Louis just then handed his key; and, as Hamilton's hand
came in contact with his, he was struck by its cold clammi-
ness, and just looking at him, noticed the troubled expression, and the almost tearful eyes that were fixed on him.
He attributed Louis' anxiety to his natural timidity, as well
as to his having probably overheard the remark on himself;
and his heart smote him, for he still loved him, and had
felt once or twice lately, that he had not done his duty
towards him.

The poem was not found.   Louis ran out into the playground, despite the cold and twilight, to cry; and hurried
in again in a few minutes, for fear of discovery.   The members of the first class gathered round Hamilton to learn the
story and to condole with him, and even Trevannion made
some remark on the shamefulness of such a trick.

"I am sure, whoever gets the prize will not feel com-
fortable unless your poem is found and compared," said
Frank; "write away, Hamilton; no one shall disturb you.
I don't wonder Fudge was in such a passion."

Louis was very glad when bed-time came, and he could

hide his tears and misery under the bed-clothes. Reginald had been too busy to notice that any thing was the matter with him ; but Hamilton, occupied as he was, had seen it, though Louis had kept out of his way as much as possible. He dared not tell Reginald his trouble ; and he felt afraid to pray—he did not remember that, though our Heavenly Father knows all our thoughts and wants, He requires that all our care and sin should be poured out before Him. The Christian does not love sin ; and when, through unwatchfulness or neglect of prayer, he has been betrayed into the commission of it, let him remember, that He alone can remove it and restore peace to his wounded conscience, who has said, "Return, ye backsliding children, and I will heal your backslidings."

Louis got on very ill the next Wednesday, and Reginald, extremely vexed, spoke very angrily to him. Louis answered as unkindly, and walked proudly away from him to the other end of the school-room, where, in spite of his abhorrence of such company, he was soon surrounded by his worst companions. Hamilton was standing near Reginald at the time ; he watched Louis in his proud descent, and saw that, though he turned away with an erect head and high words, his step soon grew more listless, and an expression of indefinable weariness usurped the place of the independence he had assumed.

"Louis is unwell, I am sure, Reginald," he said.

"He is well enough," said Reginald, abruptly ; "but he is sadly altered : I never saw a boy so changed. He is quite ill-tempered now, and so horridly idle. Why, Hamilton, you'd never believe that in to-day's examination in

Prometheus Vinctus, he got down below Harris !—he's positively at the bottom.   He hardly answered any thing, and seemed quite stupefied."

"The more reason to think he's not well," said Hamilton ; "for, to my certain knowledge, he would have stood an examination on Prometheus better than that, a week after we came back.   Why, Harris and Peters, and half the rest, are not to be compared with him."

"I know it," said Reginald ; "and that makes it the more vexatious.   It's bad enough to think that Clifton should get ahead of him, but one may comfort one's self in the idea of his genius ; but when it comes to those donkey-fied ignorami, it is past endurance.   He has not tried a bit : I have seen him lately with his book before him, dreaming about some wonderful story of some enchanted ass, or some giantess Mamouka, I suppose ; or imagining some new ode to some incomprehensible, un-come-at-able Dulcinea.   He is always shutting himself up in his air-castles, and expecting that dry Latin and Greek, and other such miserable facts, will penetrate his atmosphere."

"Don't be angry with him ; something is the matter. You only drive him to herd with those boys," said Hamilton.   "Look there !—there they are !—oh, Reginald ! it is not right to leave him with them."

"Speak to him yourself, Hamilton," said Reginald, a little sobered.   "He will mind you.   You have had a great deal to bear with him, but I know you make allowances."

Hamilton did not reply, but he had determined on making the effort to detach Louis from his evil counsel-ors, when the latter suddenly left the room with Casson, and did not return till Hamilton had gone into the class-room.

Casson was the only one to whom Louis could relieve his mind on the subject that weighed him down so heavily —and he had, at the time Hamilton was watching him so intently, been whispering some of his fears, only to be laughed at. Suddenly he paused—" Casson, just come with me ; I think I recollect—yes, surely—"

He did not wait to conclude his sentence, but, pulling Casson into the hall, sought his great-coat, dived to the bottom of the pocket, and, to his great joy, drew forth Hamilton's poem.

" It's here ! it's here ! it's here !" he cried. " How could I have put it here without knowing ? Oh, my dear Casson, I am *so* glad !"

" Well, what now ?" said Casson, rudely. " What good is it ? What do you mean to do with it ?"

" Give it back, of course—I think Hamilton will forgive me, and if not, I *must* give it back to him, and then, per-haps, I shall be happy again ; for I have not been happy for a long, long while : I have been very wrong," he added, in a low, sorrowful tone.

" If ever I saw such a sap in my life," said Casson ; " this comes of all your fine boasting ; a nice fellow you are —why you're afraid of your own shadow ! Do you know what you'll get if you give it back ?"

" Whatever happens," said Louis, " I feel I have done wrong—wrong in listening to you, too, Casson. Oh, if ever it please God to make me happy again, I hope I shall be more careful ! I have been afraid to do right—I am afraid to think of all that has happened lately."

" I always thought you were a canting hypocrite," said Casson, sneeringly. " I never see that you religious people do any better than any one else. Go and get a thrashing, as you deserve, for your cowardice, only don't tell any lies about me. Remember it was all your own doing."

Casson opened the hall-door as he spoke, and ran into the playground, where most of the boys had assembled, the weather having cleared a little for the first time for the last two days.

Louis sat down on a chair to think what he should do, and the long-restrained tears coursed slowly down his face. His first and best thought was to go at once to Hamilton, acknowledge his fault, and restore the poem. Then came the idea of renewed disgrace, and his head sunk lower on his breast, and the parcel fell from his powerless hands. So intense was his grief, that he was as unconscious that Dr. Wilkinson passed through the hall while he sat there, as that he had heard the conversation between himself and Casson ; for, unknown to them both, he had been in a recess of the hall, nearly covered by the cloaks and coats, looking there for something in a little corner closet. Louis at last took up the paper, and went to Hamilton's room ; but a servant was there, and he did not like to leave it. Next he thought of the doctor's study, but he dared not venture to approach it. At length, after wandering about from the bed-room to the class-room door several times, he ventured to peep into the latter room, and, throwing the parcel in, ran to the playground as fast as his feet could carry him.

CHAPTER XXII.

"Bear ye one another's burdens, and so fulfil the law of Christ."—
Gal. vi. 2.

As soon as Hamilton had decided that it was of no use following Louis, he called his brother to him and marched with him into the class-room, to explain, according to promise, some classical allusions that occurred in his Latin grammar. Reginald took his arm, and several of the first class, who saw them move, accompanied him, for the glass-door opening at the moment, admitted more cold air than was agreeable to those who did not feel inclined to visit the playground. They almost expected to find the doctor in the study, as they knew he had been there a short time before, but the sole occupant of the chamber was Frank Digby, who, to the astonishment of all, was standing in a very disconsolate attitude near the fireplace, leaning his head on the mantelpiece, and neither moved nor spoke when they entered.

"Holloa, Momus!" exclaimed Reginald, "what's the row? as Salisbury would say; only, more properly we might ask, in your case, what do the tranquillity and genteel pensiveness of your demeanor denote?"

"We're going to have a change in the weather," said Jones.

"What's the matter, Frank?" asked Hamilton.

"Nothing," replied Frank, raising his head quickly, and endeavoring, rather unsuccessfully, to smile, amid something that looked very much like tears; at least, if we must not be allowed to hint at such appearances, there was certainly much agitation in his countenance—so unusual a phenomenon, that a dead silence followed the ghastly effort.

"Nonsense," said Hamilton, kindly; "you won't persuade me that nothing is the matter, Frank."

"Nothing particular," said Frank, fidgeting with a penny that lay on the mantelpiece; "only the doctor has been giving me a lecture for the good of my morals, that's all."

"A lecture?" repeated Norman.

"What's been the matter, Frank?" said Reginald.

"A small moral discourse upon the sin and danger of practical jokes," said Frank, swallowing down such an evident degree of emotion as convinced his auditors that the discourse had been no ordinary one. "His hints were rather peculiar, Hamilton—too decided for so quick-sighted a youth as myself. I don't wonder he has such a horror of a joke; I should think the dear man never was guilty of such a crime in his life himself; or he has a strong imagination; or, perhaps, a bad opinion of your humble servant—all the same—the cause doesn't much signify; the effect's what one looks at."

"Something dreadfully mysterious," said Reginald.

Hamilton was silent. He watched anxiously Frank's varying countenance, the twitching of which, as well as the thick, quick tone in which he spoke, betrayed great excitement.

"The fact is, I suppose, the doctor has reasons for his

suspicions," continued Frank, still more quickly, while his face grew redder, and his eyelids twinkled painfully, and the penny was fairly spun into the fender.

"I haven't been quite so sage as I might have been, and, perhaps, jokes may not be quite gentlemanly—but,—but, Hamilton,—he thinks,—he thinks—and almost said it— that *I changed your poem.*"

"What a shame!" they cried.

Frank stooped to pick up the penny, and was some minutes finding it. When he rose, he said:

"One will grow old in time, but it's hard to pay so dearly for good spirits. However, you couldn't expect such a flow cheap, I suppose," he added, with a little laugh.

"You must have mistaken him," said Trevannion; "he couldn't have meant it."

"I am not in the habit of taking offence at nothing," replied Frank. "Nay, I can be as purposely obtuse as any one when I choose, but one couldn't be blind."

"What did he say?" said Reginald.

"I don't exactly remember—a heap about 'pain inflicted,' of 'misconstructions being placed on motives,' of 'transgressions against honor and kindliness;' and then, when I was at a loss to comprehend him, he said, 'he could not understand the gratification of seeing another disappointed and annoyed—when he discovered that his school-fellow, whom he confidently trusted, had substituted a blank sheet for a carefully, laboriously-written work;' and then I asked him if he supposed I had tricked Hamilton? and he said he couldn't think of another who was so likely to do it as myself—that 'the constant indulgence in these senseless follies was likely to blunt the sense of honor,' 'that I must excuse him'—excuse him, forsooth—'if he spoke his mind on the subject:' and then he raked up an old affair, that happened ages ago, about an exercise—Salisbury, you remember—you were the victim; but that was a paltry, every-day affair, only he didn't seem to understand the difference. I'll back the doctor up for as good a memory as any man in the three kingdoms. I had forgotten that piece of moral turpitude, and might have been excused for imagining that the caning I got then had wiped out the offence. Hamilton," he added, with a faltering voice, laying his hand on Hamilton's shoulder—" you don't believe I did it ?"

" To be sure not, Frank," said Hamilton, heartily shaking Frank's hand. " I know you too well—I am as confident of you as I should be of myself in the same case. Don't think any more of it. I am sure the doctor doesn't believe it himself: he only wants to show what might be thought if you get a character for playing tricks. I am excessively vexed at this."

" I don't feel at all certain he believes me yet," said Frank; " but this I declare, that unless your poem is found, I will withdraw all claim—I won't touch the prize for any consideration."

" Don't do that, Frank," said Hamilton; " I'll give you some trouble yet with my new one."

" If that gets it, so much the better," said Frank, "and I dare say it will; but you all hear—my mind is made up —I won't have a prize for this poem unless it is gained over Hamilton's first."

" How came the doctor to begin this rigmarole ?" asked Salisbury.

Frank blushed, and replied, with a conscious laugh: " I

did an abominably foolish thing last night, in dipping all the bed-room candles that were standing in the pantry, into a tempting basin of water; and Mrs. Guppy was malicious because the candles sputtered and wouldn't light, and, as usual, determined that I had done it; and Fudge taxed me with it this morning."

"I wish," said Hamilton, emphatically, "I could discover the author of this shameful piece of business. It was vexatious enough in the first place, but this is painful to us all. Frank, every one knows you."

"Doctor best of all," put in Frank.

"I will give myself up to discovering who has done it," said Hamilton.

"You had better give yourself up to finishing your poem," said Reginald; "for it's my humble opinion if you haven't found it now, your eyes won't discover the clue, if you were Argus himself."

The others then began a rather noisy debate on the impropriety of their master's behavior; and little Alfred, finding his brother was not speaking, ventured to remind him of his promise. Contrary to his usual habit, Hamilton turned quite crossly to him:

"What an idle fellow you are! Why don't you get *Lemprière* and find them out for yourself?—you ought not to be beginning now."

"I tried, Edward, but I couldn't understand it, and it went out of my head. I want to know about Cecropia again—I forget what country it was, Edward," said the child, timidly, noticing an ominous reddening of his brother's face.

"A great deal of use it is giving you any information,

25

is it not, sir ?   I have a great mind to make you write out every word I say.   And pray what else have you forgotten ?"

"Not *forgotten* any thing," said Alfred, meekly; "but I wanted to know, please Edward, who was Hannibal's father, and whether it was true about Hannibal's making the rocks red hot, and pouring vinegar on them ?   I don't think it could, for I don't know where he could get so much."

"A great deal he carried in his own countenance," said Frank, "and the rest was made from the wine supplied for the Carthaginian officers.   There's nothing like white-wine vinegar, Alfred ; and the Carthaginians were renowned for parting with luxuries on an emergency."

"Now I know that's your nonsense," said Alfred, looking very puzzled.   "And, please Edward, who was Philomela and—"

"That's enough—one at a time !" exclaimed Hamilton ; "get *Lemprière*, and my Roman History, and you shall look them out with me.   It's to be hoped you are not dreaming of a prize."

"Poor infant !" said Salisbury ; "it's hard work, I know, to remember the difference between those heathen chaps."

Alfred had just brought the required books, and was opening them by his brother's desire, and Hamilton was standing near him at the table, when suddenly a packet was thrown into the room, and fell at his feet.   Changing color, he picked it up with the rapidity of lightning, and, with an exclamation, rushed out of the room, before any one but Alfred had seen the transaction.   Louis had just gained the threshold of the door leading to the play-ground, when Hamilton hailed him, and his long strides gaining on Louis' terror-impeded steps, he presently reached him, and, grasping him tightly by both arms, bore him back to the class-room, sternly desiring two or three boys, who attempted to follow, to stay behind. Louis did not make any resistance, and Hamilton, after locking the door and putting the key into his pocket, brought him irresistibly to the front of the fire, and, placing him with his back against the table, opposite the assembled group, desired him, under pain of instant punishment, to remain where he was.

"What is the matter with him, Hamilton?" asked Reginald.

"You shall see presently," said Hamilton; "I mean to have some inquiries answered: and please, Mortimer, however unpleasant it may be to you, let us have fair play."

"I only stipulate it for Louis too," said Reginald.

"He shall have it," said Hamilton, calmly; "but if he attempts to move till I have done, I will carry him at once to Dr. Wilkinson."

Hamilton glanced at the windows, where five or six heads were darkening the lower panes, in their eagerness to discover the cause of Louis' forcible abduction; and, walking coolly up to them, bolted them, and drew down both blinds. He then returned to his place, and, drawing his coat-tails under his arms, arranged himself with his back to the fire, exactly opposite to Louis, who stood passively where he had been placed, very pale, but otherwise showing little emotion.

"Now, sir," began Hamilton, "explain how you got this."

As he spoke, he produced, to the astonishment of his school-fellows, the parcel—rubbed at the edges, but still the identical parcel, as he proved, by breaking the seal, and showing the writing inside.

"What! Louis Mortimer!" exclaimed Jones.

"*Et tu Brute!*" ejaculated Frank, in a tone of mingled surprise and reproach.

"Louis!" said Reginald, coloring deeply; "oh, Louis! How did you find it, Hamilton?"

"Did you not see it come in through the half-open door just now?" said Hamilton.

"I fancied I saw something fly along," said Meredith.

"I thought I heard something fall," said another.

"Too cowardly to come openly," said Trevannion.

The room seemed to turn round with Louis.

"How did you come by this?" said Hamilton.

There was no answer.

"I will have an answer, Louis," he said: "and if you don't give it to me, you shall to Dr. Wilkinson!"

Louis murmured something that no one heard.

"What?" said Hamilton, sharply; "speak so as we can all hear. If you have brought it back for some one else," he added, in a softened tone, "say so at once; only let me know who took it."

"I took it," replied Louis, with a great effort.

"You ungrateful viper!" exclaimed Jones.

Hamilton appeared a little moved, but checking the emotion, continued:

"You! for—your—own—especial—gratification? And

pray, when might you have accomplished that adroit and praiseworthy feat?"

"Last Friday," said Louis, in so low a tone, that nothing but the silence that reigned could have made it audible.

"And what was your motive?" asked Hamilton, leaning back against the mantelpiece, and putting one foot on the fender behind him.

"Only a little fun!"

"Pretty respectable *fun!*" said Hamilton, contemptuously.

"Gratitude might have restrained you, one would think," said Jones, "if nothing else would. A pretty return for all Hamilton's kindness, to set to work to lose him his prize!"

"I didn't, Jones," said Louis, warmly; "I thought it was a letter; I didn't mean any harm. And as to gratitude—when Hamilton was kind to me, I was grateful—and I do feel grateful for his kindness now; but he has been unkind enough lately to make me forget that."

"And reason enough he had," said Meredith. "Unkind, indeed! why no one else stood your friend when we found out what a tell-tale you were."

"I am sure nobody knew he was my friend then," said Louis, assuming an air of independence that ill became him. "Only last Friday, he let me believe that Trevannion had the doctor's Rollin; he offered me his, but I wasn't likely to take that, and—" Louis hesitated, for Hamilton's eye was upon him so calmly and inquiringly; and Louis felt he was not likely to have had such an idea in his head.

"And what?" said Hamilton, quietly.

" Nothing," replied Louis ; " I don't believe you knew, only it was rather strange, Hamilton."

" What was strange ?" said Hamilton, in the same unmoved tone.

" Only when I came back into this room, I saw it on the table with your things, and I thought you had it, perhaps," said Louis, reluctantly. " If it hadn't been for that, I shouldn't have come here, and shouldn't have thought of playing the trick."

" You little—" exclaimed Trevannion. Not being able to find a genteel epithet strong enough, he continued, " When Hamilton had just taken the trouble of exchanging his own history with me, for your service ! I see it all now, Hamilton—you ungrateful boy !"

" How should I know ? he never said so," replied Louis, touched to the heart at this proof of his friend's kindness ; and grieved very deeply that he should have thought or said so unkind a thing of him in his anger. " How am I to know what people think, if they don't speak, or if I don't see them ?"

" And so you did it out of revenge ?" said Hamilton.

Louis was silent for a minute, for he could not speak ; but at last he replied, in a quivering voice—

" No ; I told you I did it out of fun. I thought it was a letter, and—and I have been very sorry I ever did any thing so foolish. I should have brought it back sooner, but I could not remember what I did with it."

" Why did you not tell me, at least, that you had taken it, Louis," said Hamilton, " when I was inquiring for it ? It would have been more open."

" I should have done it, I believe, if I had known how

you would have heard me—but it's not so easy when every
one is against you. I brought it only a few minutes after
I found it."

" Who put such a thing into your head, Louis ?" asked
Reginald.

Louis checked the answer he had nearly given, and remained silent.

" Were you alone ?" said Hamilton. " Were you the
only one concerned in this business ?"

" I was not alone," replied Louis, rather proudly ; " but
I do not mean to say who was with me. He was not to
blame for what I did."

" How so ?" asked Hamilton. " Didn't he put it into
your head, and help you to do it ?"

" You have no right to ask such questions," said Louis,
uneasily. " He came in to help me find Rollin, and—that's
all I shall tell you."

" What, Casson help you to find Rollin !" said Hamilton,
quickly. " He wouldn't know the book from a Lexicon."

" He did," however," said Louis ; then, becoming suddenly conscious, from the intelligent glances exchanged
among his judges, of the admission he had made, he turned
very red, and exclaimed,

" It's very unfair !"

" I knew he was your companion," said Hamilton, rather
scornfully. " You have belonged to his set too much lately
to suppose otherwise—and this is the consequence."

" If it is, Hamilton," said Louis, scarcely able to speak
for the warmth of his feelings, " you might have prevented
it if you would. You wouldn't forgive my speaking carelessly once—and no one that I cared for would notice me.

He was almost the only one who would speak to me. If you had said one word, I shouldn't have been so bad. I thought you didn't care about me, and I didn't mean to stay where I wasn't wanted."

The expression of Hamilton's face was not easy, and he drowned the end of Louis' speech by knocking all the fire-irons down with a movement of his poised foot.

"It was a likely way to be wanted, I imagine," said Jones, "to go on as you have been doing. Besides, who is to know what's likely to be safe with such a tell-tale—a traitor—in the camp as you are?"

"If there hadn't been another as great," said Louis, "you would never have known of me; but you bear with him because you can't turn him out."

"Pray, sir!" exclaimed Norman, "whom do you mean?"

Louis felt sorry he had allowed himself to say so much; but he stood unshrinkingly before his interrogator, and replied :

"I mean you, Norman : you know if you hadn't told tales of me this wouldn't have happened."

What vengeance Louis might have drawn on himself by this ill-judged speech we cannot tell, had not Hamilton stepped forward and interposed.

There was a grim ghost of a smile on his face as he put his arm in front of Louis.

"Fair play, Norman," he said; "I won't have him touched here. You can go now."

As Louis left the room, Hamilton resumed his former attitude, and seemed lost in a revery of an unpleasant description, while a discussion on Louis' conduct was noisily carried on around him : some declaring that Louis had done the deed from malicious motives, others believing that it was merely a foolish joke of which he had not calculated the consequences, and a third party attributing it entirely to Casson's influence.

"Vexed as I am to find Louis has been so foolish," said Reginald, "I am glad, Frank, that you will now be cleared. Hamilton, I am sure you believe that Louis only intended a joke ?"

Hamilton nodded gravely.

"I suppose you'll clear up the matter instanter, Hamilton ?" said Jones.

"*Clear up the matter?* How! is it not clear enough already ?" said Hamilton, almost fiercely.

"Clear to us, but not to the doctor," said Meredith.

"It's as clear as it's likely to be, then," said Hamilton. "I intend to send up this poem the last evening, and say nothing about it."

"A likely story!" exclaimed Jones.

"If you don't, I shall, Hamilton," said Salisbury.

"Whoever breathes a word of the matter," cried Hamilton, "ceases from that moment to be a friend of mine. Whose business is it, I should like to know—if I choose to throw that unhappy thing on the fire, who is the loser but myself ? What satisfaction can it be to any one to get that boy into such a mess ?"

As Hamilton spoke he disdainfully flung the poem on the table, and drew the fender, contents and all, on the floor with his fidgety foot.

"The matter comes to this," said Reginald : "it appears that either Louis must be exposed, or Frank suffer for his delinquencies.   It is not, certainly, fair to Frank, and mustn't be, Hamilton, though Louis is my brother."

Hamilton cast a bewildered look on Frank.

"True, I had really forgotten Frank.   It must be so, then," he said, in a lower tone.

"No, Hamilton, no!" said Frank; "I won't have you tell of poor Louis.   I don't care a bit about Fudge's suspicions now, *you* all *know* I am clear.   Don't say a word about it, I beg."

"Frank, you're a fine fellow!" exclaimed Hamilton, grasping his hand; "but I don't think it is quite fair."

"Nonsense!" said Frank, gayly; "I owe him something for relieving me from my situation; and, besides," he added, more gravely, "Louis deserves a little forbearance from us : none of us would have done what he did, last half."

"You are right," said Hamilton, warmly; "none of us would, but all of us have forgotten that lately; even Ferrers, who ought, at least, to have befriended him, has turned the cold shoulder to him.   I feel quite indignant with Ferrers."

"Ferrers had a little reason to doubt him," said Trevannion.

"What, for letting his name slip out by accident?" said Hamilton, scornfully; "you heard how he let out Casson's just now—you wouldn't blame him for that, I imagine?"

"No," said Frank; "and I can tell you that Mrs. Paget (no offence to her nephew) is one of those dear retailers of all descriptions of news, that would worm a secret out of a toad in a stone, and Louis hasn't ready wit enough to manage her."

"He has no presence of mind, and a little vanity," said Hamilton.

"He is as vain as a peacock—a lump of vanity!" exclaimed Norman; "without an atom of moral courage to stand any persuasion short of being desired to put his head into the fire—a perfect coward!"

"And where did you get your moral courage, Mr. Norman?" said Hamilton, with deliberate gravity; "we may send you to the heathen for reproof:

> "'If thou hast strength, 'twas heaven that strength bestowed,
> For know, vain man, thy valor is from God.'"

Norman was on the point of speaking, but Hamilton continued in the same calm, irresistible manner:

"If Louis is vain, we are proud; and I should like to know which is the worst,—having an exalted opinion of ourselves, or craving the exalted opinion of others? We have not behaved well to Louis, poor fellow! we first spoiled him by over-indulgence and flattery, and when this recoils upon us, we visit all the evil heavily on him."

"I only want to remark," said Meredith, "that we had a right to expect more consistency in a professed saint."

"Perhaps so," said Hamilton; "yet, though I am sure Louis is a sincere Christian, he is not free from faults, and had still a hard work to do in overcoming them; and, because he has for a time forgotten that he had this work to do, shall we cast him off as a reprobate? Remember it was his former blameless conduct that made us expect more from him than another: the Power that guided him

then can restore him again.   But we have sadly forgotten
that great duty, of bearing one another's burdens, which
he taught us so sweetly a few months ago.   Let us forgive him," continued Hamilton, with tears in his eyes, "as
we would be forgiven; considering how we should act in
temptation ourselves."

There was a dead silence, for Hamilton's address had
something solemn in it.   He added, after a short pause—

" I feel that we seniors have an immense responsibility :
the power of doing much good or harm lies with us.   I
have been far too selfish and indifferent : Trevannion, will
you forgive the thoughtless words that so justly offended
you, but which, I assure you, had only the meaning of an
angry emotion ?"

" Willingly !" said Trevannion, starting up to meet the
proffered hand of his friend ; " I am sorry I should have
been so much offended."

Reginald was making some acknowledgments to Hamilton
and Frank, when a messenger came to summon Hamilton
to a short turn with the doctor, and after gladly accepting
Reginald's offer of performing his task towards Alfred, he
took up his poem, and went away full of deep thoughts
and regrets, that the late scene had called forth

CHAPTER XXIII.

"O Israel, return unto the Lord thy God; for thou hast fallen by thine iniquity. Take with you words, and turn to the Lord: say unto Him, Take away all iniquity, and receive us graciously; so will we render the calves of our lips."—*Hosea* xiv. 1, 2.

WHEN Louis left the class-room, his feelings of grief and shame were almost too bitter for restraint; but he had learned lately to conceal something of what he felt from those who were not likely to sympathize with him; and finding some boys in the school-room, and being subjected there to several disagreeable remarks and questions, he went into the playground, in the hope of finding either relief in change of scene, or a little more seclusion than he could hope for in-doors; and after escaping from some tormentors, who met him at the door, in their anxiety to know what Hamilton wanted with him, he went towards the side of the playground that looked upon the lane, hardly caring where he was going, or what became of him.

The door was open, and disregarding, or more properly, forgetting, the injunctions respecting it, he went up to it, and stood looking out into the lane, till at last, one of his school-fellows discovering the open door, came up, and asked him to keep watch for him, while he went on a forbidden errand.

Meantime, Dr. Wilkinson and Hamilton had, after a walk across the grounds in front of the house, turned into the lane, making as large a round as possible, on their way to the house. Hamilton was in a very silent humor, and as his tutor was equally grave, very few words passed between them during the first half of their walk; and if Hamilton had thought at all about what he had undertaken so mechanically, he might have wondered how the doctor could have wanted a companion, when he was in so taciturn a humor.

Suddenly the doctor remarked,—"Have you heard nothing of your poem, Hamilton?"

This was so unexpected a question, and Hamilton was so unwilling to make a direct answer, that he remained silent for a minute or two, his hesitation and color convincing his master that Louis had acted up to his determination.

"Well, have you forgotten all about it?" said the doctor, good-humoredly.

"I have found it, sir—here it is," he replied, producing the paper.

"How did you get it?" asked the doctor, who betrayed far less surprise and satisfaction than the occasion seemed to demand.

"It was thrown into the class-room this morning, sir," said Hamilton, reservedly.

"And you are ignorant of the party?" said the doctor, with raised eyebrows.

"No, sir, I know who has done it," replied Hamilton, after a slight pause; "but I must beg you to excuse my naming him. I think there is no danger of a repetition of the offence. Of course you will understand, sir, that I do not mean Digby, who is as innocent as I ever believed him."

There was a little silence, while the doctor ran his eye down a page of Hamilton's manuscript.

"As you wish to keep the matter secret, I shall ask no further questions; only, Digby may not think it quite fair."

"He wishes it to be so, sir," replied Hamilton, eagerly. "It is quite his wish now he knows I have *proof* that he is not the culprit."

Dr. Wilkinson's face lighted up with an expression of great satisfaction, as he said,

"It does Digby credit."

Hamilton was on the point of hazarding a remark on the impossibility of Frank's contemplating such a thing, when they turned a corner of the lane that brought them in sight of the playground wall and the farm-yard opposite. The doctor's attention was suddenly arrested by the figure of a boy, perched on the top of the high wall surrounding the latter, who was reaching downwards towards the top of a large hawthorn-tree that grew inside.

"Hey-day! Hamilton, who's that?" he exclaimed. "Do you recognize the figure? If my eyes deceive me not, it is Louis Mortimer. I have strongly suspected lately that I have been robbed more than once. It *is* Louis Mortimer."

The doctor's tone assumed its ready sternness, and he quickened his pace. Hamilton could not doubt the evidence of his senses, but he felt miserably disappointed.

"I do not think Louis Mortimer would do so, sir," he said, faintly.

"There he is, however, out of bounds," said the doctor.

"Something else may have taken him there," said Hamilton.

" I hope it may prove so, but he is surely receiving something from below—he sees us—he will be down—he will assuredly break his neck !" exclaimed the doctor, hurriedly.   " There—quick, Hamilton—run."

Hamilton needed no bidding, for, as soon as he saw Louis fall, he ran off in the direction of the stable-yard.   The doctor followed so quickly that Hamilton had only just raised Louis from the ground when he came up.   To their great satisfaction he was not much hurt, having fallen on a heap of straw that lay just under the wall.   He was much frightened, and at first so stunned as to be almost incapable of understanding what was said to him.   On the ground near him lay his green baize bag, and rolling about in all directions, some apples, one or two still remaining in the bag.

" Where is your companion, sir ?" was the first question Dr. Wilkinson asked, after ascertaining that no injury had been done to Louis.

" There was no one with me, sir," replied Louis, almost inarticulately.

" What were you doing here, sir ?"

" I came to fetch my bag, sir."

" It is a mercy you were not killed," said Dr. Wilkinson, gravely.   " Put the apples in that bag, Hamilton."

Dr. Wilkinson waited till Hamilton had performed this task, and then desired Louis to take the bag and follow him.

Louis did as he was desired, but he was evidently not yet in a condition to walk, and trembled so violently that Hamilton caught hold of him to prevent him from falling.

" He can't walk yet, sir," he said, compassionately.   " I will bring him in when he has recovered a little."

" It is too cold to sit out here," said the doctor. " Where are you hurt ?"

" I don't exactly know ; I am not much *hurt*—but, oh ! I feel so strange, Hamilton. Let me walk—I can take your arm."

Dr. Wilkinson looked anxiously at him, and assisted him, with Hamilton's aid, across the road, through the garden, into the kitchen, where, with a little hartshorn and water, he was soon in a condition to go up stairs. Dr. Wilkinson desired him to go to bed for the rest of the day, and sent Reginald to help him. The bag he took into his own possession till further occasion.

Louis was too much dismayed by his ill success, and too much exhausted by the shock of his fall, to make any remarks till he reached his room. Hamilton did not leave him until he had seen him comfortably in bed ; and then, after wrapping him up most tenderly, he leaned over him, and asked what was really the matter.

Louis endeavored to answer calmly, but in his present weak condition Hamilton's kind manner overcame him, and he burst into tears.

" Oh, dear !" he exclaimed, amid his violent sobs ; " oh, Reginald, Reginald—Hamilton, I am so unfortunate ! Every thing I do is always found out ; but others can do all sorts of things, and no one knows it."

" Is there any thing then to be found out, Louis ?" said Hamilton, gravely ; " if so, it is far better for you that it should be."

Louis suddenly threw his arms round Hamilton, as he sat near him.

" Hamilton, I did not go there to_steal, I am sure," he

said, throwing his head back, and examining his friend's face with the most intense anxiety. " I am sure, Hamilton, bad as I am, you could not believe it of me. I have been very sinful, but oh, I am very sorry ; and, Hamilton, I *could* not do so very wicked a thing. Do remember, please, how things were against me before when I was not guilty. Though it seems all against me now, I assure you, the only thing I have done wrong is going out of bounds—oh, do let me keep my arms round you, Hamilton—don't believe me guilty. I haven't—oh, I haven't had a friend for so long ! I have been very proud and self-willed—if I had been humble perhaps things would not have gone so wrong. I never even said I was sorry I repeated what you said to Mrs. Paget ; but I was sorry, Hamilton—very, very sorry, only I did not like to say so. Will you forgive me, and be my friend again ? I have been so ungrateful, I am afraid you will never love me any more."

Hamilton was completely overcome by the vehemence of Louis' appeal. He pressed the poor boy closer to him, and even kissed his forehead, as if he were a little child.

" Love you, Louis ! love you, dear boy !" he replied ; " you have had reason to doubt it, but I have always loved you. I forgive you from my heart, but you have something to forgive in me. I have not been as kind to you as I might have been."

" I am very sorry I spoke so unkindly of you this morning, Hamilton," sobbed Louis, laying his wet cheek on Hamilton's shoulder. " I was cross, and didn't think of what I was saying."

" Don't think any more about it," said Hamilton, affectionately; "lie down, and tell me quietly how you came to be on that wall just now."

"I was standing at the wooden door," said Louis, "when Sally Simmons told me that she had seen my bag on the great hawthorn-tree, by the wall on the other side. And when I asked her how it got there, she said, she supposed I knew, but it was too high for her to reach; and if I didn't get it, the doctor would find me out. At first, I thought I wouldn't go," said Louis, hesitating; "and then I was afraid I should be getting into a scrape—I am sometimes so unfortunate—and so I went across the lane, and got over the gate, and went into the yard to see if it were there. And there it was, Hamilton, with some apples in it, too, hanging partly, and partly lying, near the top of the tree; it was so high that I was obliged to get upon the cow-house roof, and as the cow-house was on the wrong side, I was obliged to get on the wall to reach it. And I was pulling it off when you first saw me, and then—I was afraid, and as I was rather over-reaching myself, I tried to get down in a hurry, and fell down. I think the tree broke my fall; but I don't know how it was, for I hardly understood any thing, even when you came up."

"You had better have let it alone," said Reginald.

"What were you doing at the gate?" said Hamilton; "keeping watch?"

"One of them asked me," replied Louis.

Hamilton shook his head.

"Have you any idea how your bag came there?"

"Please don't ask me any questions about that, Hamilton. Will you not believe I am innocent?"

"I fully believe your story, Louis, but I know you have

been in bad company lately, and I wish to help you to clear yourself. Tell me all you know. If you have ever had even the least hand in any thing like this, make a friend of me, and tell me at once. Have you not some idea who put your bag there ?''

" I may guess, you know," said Louis, evasively ; " but, Hamilton, I do assure you, I never had any thing to do with any robbery here at all—never once."

" If you do not know who has done it, then," said Hamilton, " I am sure your *guess* is a very accurate one—whom do you *guess ?*"

" I cannot tell you, Hamilton ; you mustn't ask me."

" This is only nonsense," said Reginald, impatiently. " Are you going to make a martyr of yourself for a set of bad fellows who are a disgrace to the school ?"

" They may tell themselves, perhaps," said Louis, " but I will not."

" Louis !" said Hamilton, seriously, " this is folly ; don't let a mistaken notion of honor induce you to skreen these bad boys from their just punishment. By doing so, you are doing an injury to others as well as yourself. You must remember, that these evil-disposed boys are still mixing with others, to whom their example and principles may do much harm, independently of the evil done to themselves by being allowed to sin with impunity. Louis, you were saying just now, that you were very unfortunate— they are the most unfortunate whose crimes are undiscovered, and therefore unchecked. If you are, as you say, innocent of any participation in this affair, why should you wish to conceal what you know, or, at least, telling me whom you lent your bag to ?"

"I did not lend it at all lately," said Louis, raising his face from the pillow, where he had hidden it. "The thing is, Hamilton," continued he, very sorrowfully, "I am called a tell-tale, and I know I deserve it; but the worst is, they call me a hypocrite, and say that religious people are no better than others. I could bear it if it were only myself, but it is more, and I have given reasons for them to say all kinds of things," he added, and burst anew into tears. "But do not make me tell any more tales. I have promised, Hamilton—I dare not—I *will* not break my promise!"

Hamilton made no immediate reply, and the loud ringing of the dinner-bell obliged him to leave Louis to himself.

"If it is a promise, Louis," he said, as he left the room with Reginald, "I won't urge you to break it; but remember well how the promise was made—remember the consequences."

"Reginald," he added, when they had closed the door, "I have a clue; depend upon it, he won't be much the worse, poor fellow. But the doctor knows him well, I am sure."

Reginald stole away after dinner to sit with Louis, and to endeavor to persuade him to disclose all his suspicions, but all he could obtain was a kind of half-promise to clear it up, after he had seen how the matter would end; and the subject caused him so much distress, that Reginald at length left it alone.

"Sit down by my side, dear Reginald," said Louis, "and tell me again that you forgive me. I cannot think how I could be so unkind to you as I have been lately, when you were so anxious about me. I have been ungrateful to everybody."

"Don't make yourself miserable," said Reginald, as gayly as he could. "I know I am hasty and cross, and don't go the right way to help you; but you had spoiled me by being so very gentle before, and I didn't understand your having any spirit."

"It was a very wrong spirit," replied Louis; "the fact is, Reginald, I have not been serving God lately, though at first I did not know it myself. I thought I did a great many things when I came back to school, because it would glorify God; when, I really believe now, the reason was—to be praised for it. Every one seemed to think so much of me, and that every thing I did was right. I have wished so many times lately, that all the trouble of last half-year might come again if I should be so happy. But, Reginald, when the boys would not speak to me, then I knew by my angry feelings that I only cared for myself; and I saw that I had not been serving God, and I became afraid to pray. Sometimes so strangely, when I knew I was in the wrong, and that I ought to pray for help to be better, yet I wanted to look grand, and to show I didn't care, and I never used the time I had, and that's very little here, Reginald. I have been thinking of myself almost ever since I came back—I have been thinking of glorifying myself!" He paused, and then added, in a lower tone, "I fancied I was not selfish, but now I *know* I am!"

When Reginald went away, Louis had long and quiet time to trace the reason of his sad falling away, and to make his peace with Him whose great name he had so dishonored. Earnestly, humbly, and sorrowfully did he confess his faults. How bowed to the earth he felt, in the consciousness of his utter impotence! He remembered how confident he had been in his good name; and now he became aware, in this silent self-examination, how mixed his motives had been, how full of vanity and vain-glory he had been, how careless in waiting for " more grace," how little he had thought of pressing forward, how wanting he had been in that single heart that thought only of doing the work committed to him regardless of the approbation of men—that only desired to know what was right in order fearlessly to follow it; and unutterable were the tearful desires of his heart that he might be strengthened for the time to come to walk more worthy of the vocation wherewith he was called.

CHAPTER XXIV.

"I will heal their backslidings, I will love them freely; for mine
    anger is turned away from him. Ephraim shall say, What have
    I to do any more with idols !"—*Hosea* xiv. 4, 8.
"I will hear what God the Lord will speak: for He will speak
    peace to His people, and to His saints, but let them not turn
    again to folly."—*Psalm* lxxxv. 8.

Louis awoke from a calm, sound sleep very early the
next morning, with a dim, indistinct recollection of having,
when half awake during the night, seen Dr. Wilkinson
standing by him, and of a consciousness of a hand being
laid on his forehead and his hands; but, as he did not feel
certain, much less suppose it likely, he settled that he
must have dreamed it. It was quite dark when he awoke,
and it was some few minutes before the events of the preceding day ranged themselves in any order in his mind;
and then his thoughts flew to that rest whence they had
been so long absent.

In about half an hour, several of his school-fellows
began to rouse themselves, and, a candle or two being
lighted, dressing was hastily accomplished; and, rolling
themselves up in counterpanes and blankets, shawl fashion,
they proceeded to pore over the books they had brought
up the night before.

"I don't mean to get up," growled Frank; 'it's a great deal more comfortable in bed. Clifton, bring me my candle here, and put it on that chair—I shall make a studium of my couch."

"Dr. Wilkinson asked if we read with candles near the beds," said Clifton. "He said he wouldn't have us read in bed unless it were daylight, Digby."

"Well, we'll suppose he didn't," said Frank, "so come along."

"No, I won't," said Clifton, sitting down near a chest of drawers, on which was a candle, the joint property of himself, Reginald, and Louis.

"You won't, won't you?" said Frank, coolly; "Reginald, my candle's near you, I'll trouble you for it."

"You must take the consequences, then," said Reginald, "for I heard the doctor say so."

"*I* didn't," said Frank, snuffing his candle, and opening a book; "Meredith, I'd advise you to follow my example."

"I followed it yesterday, and fell asleep in uncomfortable snoozes till the bell rang," yawned Meredith. "Reading one word and dreaming six may be entertaining, but it is certainly not instructive."

There was very little noise, and Louis lay for some time in deep thought. At length he moved as if with the intention of getting up, when Reginald started up and planted his beaming face over him so as to prevent his rising:

"Awake at last, Louis?"

"Yes, I have been awake a long time."

"You've been very quiet."

27

" How happy you look !" said Louis ; " I could almost fancy you had something to tell."

" What will you give me for my news ?"

" I am afraid I can offer nothing but thanks," replied Louis, smiling.

" What should you say if I were to tell you Casson was gone ?"

" Casson *gone !*" exclaimed Louis, starting up in spite of his brother's incubian overseership. " Where ?   When ?   How ?   Was he ill ?   What was the matter ?"

" He went home yesterday evening by the London coach.   He was in perfect bodily health.   The matter was, that the magister wouldn't keep him."

" What ! *expelled*, Reginald ?" said Louis, aghast.

" Expelled, Louis," Reginald replied, gravely ; " don't look so frightened ; he deserved it."

" Oh, Reginald ! it is so terrible !   But how—why was it so sudden ?"

" Ah, Beauty !" said Frank, " a few wonders have happened while your ladyship has been sleeping there.   What will you say to Harris going, too ?"

" Harris ! no, surely not, Frank ?   Tell me, do tell me what's been the matter."

" We promised to let Hamilton tell the story," said Reginald.   " He has been, in a great measure, the cause of finding all out ; so make haste and go to him, for I want you back again."

Louis did not need any further bidding—he hurried his toilette, and flew to the room that Hamilton enjoyed to himself.   Hamilton was up.   An open Bible lay near him, which he closed as Louis entered.

"How are you, foolish boy, this morning?" he said, kindly—very kindly, Louis thought, as he squeezed his hand.

"I am very well, thank you. Reginald's been telling me strange news this morning."

"News?" said Hamilton. "He promised me—"

"Oh! I only know that Casson's gone, and Harris going, but he would not tell me any more."

"Well, then, I will."

"Hamilton," said Louis, gently laying his hand on Hamilton's, "may I ask one thing?"

"What is it?"

"Will you read a little of this with me first?" he said, timidly, touching the Bible. "I have neglected it so lately. It would be so pleasant before we begin any thing else. You do not know how difficult it is in our room to be a minute quiet."

Hamilton had opened the Bible before Louis had finished, and bade him select a chapter, which he asked him to read aloud.

Louis read the 7th Psalm, and the 14th of Hosea; and when he had finished, he and his friend remained very silent.

Hamilton felt for Louis, though he did not know how soothingly the sweet words fell on the soul of the erring boy; how unspeakably precious had been the promise, that the backslider should be healed, and the dew of the Spirit refresh him, and make him grow in grace. Louis felt a wish to prolong those gracious words, "Ephraim shall say, What have I any more to do with idols? I have heard and observed him; I am like a green fir-tree, from me is thy fruit found!"

"Dear Hamilton," he said, at length, "I have a very great favor to beg of you—would you let me come in a little every morning to read with you? It would do me so much good."

"By all means," said Hamilton, perhaps a little shily; but it was promise enough to call forth Louis' heartfelt thanks.

Hamilton then made Louis don a cloak of his, and stretching his own legs, so as to rest them comfortably on the window where Louis was sitting, he entered into a minute detail of the events of yesterday afternoon, equally surprising and interesting to Louis.

It appeared that Hamilton, acting on his own strong suspicions, went immediately after dinner to Dr. Wilkinson, whom, strange to say, he found equally inclined to listen to them; for he confessed to Louis that he did not exactly know what had made Dr. Wilkinson so suddenly take such a decided view of Casson's character as he appeared to have done. They went to the stable and examined it very carefully. They found the door unfastened; but on further consideration, discovered that the staple, which was rusty, had been broken off, so that, though the key had been turned, it could be opened as easily as if it had had no lock. They went up through the trap-door, but found nothing to assist them, till, just as they were descending, Hamilton picked up part of a Greek exercise. It was very small, not more than two inches square; a more careless observer might not have noticed it, but Hamilton seized it as a treasure, and, with the doctor's advice, set to work to discover whose handwriting it was.

The few words he deciphered carried him to the second

class for the owner: " And oh, Louis ! Dr. Wilkinson looked so grave when I told him it was Kenrick. But I knew it was not your writing. With very little trouble, and without discovering any thing, I soon found Harris to have been the writer. Having settled this point about an hour after school had begun, I took the first opportunity of informing the doctor, who immediately entered the school-room, suspended all business, summoned every one, and in an able speech, as the papers would say, prefaced the proceedings by declaring how painful it had been to him to discover that any of his pupils were not trustworthy, *et cetera ;* and his determination to arrive at some conclusion on the point, to know whether his orders were or were not to be obeyed. He then mentioned having found you, and his firm belief, that even supposing you had gone there for the purpose of abstracting the apples, *which he could not believe*, you must have been tempted and persuaded to it by older hands; he called upon the offenders to come forward and clear the matter. Well, no one answered ; and then the doctor just alluded to you, and what you had suffered last half, and said that he had determined that every one should be aware of the grounds of accusation, and he desired, if any one knew of any thing that would throw a light on the matter, he would come forward.

" Then, to every one's surprise, comes up Charles Clifton, and tells him coolly, that he was sure you had not stolen the apples, and that it was very likely to be Harris, Casson, and Churchill, and that Sally Simmons had, in his presence, given them apples, and they joked about the place where they came from. Sally was called, and at last confessed that she had let Casson know where the apples were kept;

and they frightened her, or something, for she tried to bring you in as an accomplice, only Clifton was so manful, and braved her with so much spirit, that she soon quitted that ground, and departed under sentence of dismissal."

"Oh, poor Sally! I am very sorry."

"She is a bad girl," said Hamilton; "I never liked Clifton so well as I did yesterday: there is a great deal of truthful independence about him."

"Oh, Charlie's a very nice fellow!" said Louis, warmly "Well, Hamilton."

"Well, Casson and Harris bullied, talked of characters defamed, and stoutly protested innocence. The doctor looked so indignant; I think I never saw him so thoroughly convinced of the evil-mindedness of any one, as he appeared to be of Casson's. He heard all they had to say, and spoke to them seriously of the crime they were adding. Harris looked abashed, but Casson declared there was not enough to convict him in the evidence of a 'liar like Sally, and a self-sufficient fellow like Clifton;' when, to my astonishment, Trevannion came forward, and gave his pocket-book open into the doctor's hands." Hamilton then proceeded to tell Louis what Trevannion had seen on the memorable Friday, and the great effect produced upon the school by the reading of the memorandum. Churchill confessed every thing, and cried, and begged pardon.

It seemed that they had gone no further than the gate leading to the field, on the Friday morning, as they saw some one in the distance; but that the plan had been re-newed on Monday at twilight, when they were disturbed by a man with a lantern, coming into the yard as they left the stable, and, instead of going out the usual way, they scrambled over the wall, dropping the bag in their hurry, and had no opportunity the ensuing day to look for it.

"Harris," continued Hamilton, "turned as white as a sheet, and murmured something that no one could understand. The doctor spoke really beautifully. I hope something of what he said may remain with them, at least, be remembered at some future time."

"What did he say?" asked Louis.

"He spoke about the heinousness of the offences they had committed, and of his sorrow; and, Louis, he spoke as if he were sorry," said Hamilton, looking down, and speaking gravely. "I felt as if I were wrong in being so rejoiced at their detection. He spoke of the necessity he was under, not simply of making an example of such offenders, which was a duty he owed to the others under his charge, but of that of marking also to themselves the great abhorrence he entertained of their conduct. He then spoke of the consequences of unchecked sin, and, in a few words, mentioned a very sad history of a former pupil of his who turned out very ill—he is dead, Louis; the manner in which he spoke of that prayer of the Psalmist's, 'Make me not a rebuke unto the foolish,' was very solemn; I assure you there were very few dry eyes."

Louis' were filled with tears.

"Well, Hamilton," he said, slowly.

"He then desired Casson to go directly and make preparations for leaving his house in less than an hour, and told Harris that he should not allow him to return after the holidays. There was not a sound when Casson left the room, Louis, except the sobbing of one or two of the little boys. I think I never felt any thing so solemn. It is a serious, a very serious thing."

"Very, very," said Louis. "Did Casson seem sorry, Hamilton?"

"He was very pale and silent—I think frightened, not sorry. Harris stood like a statue while the doctor was speaking; but, when he told him he was not to return, I heard him sigh so deeply, it was quite painful."

"And Churchill?" said Louis, with difficulty.

"Churchill is to stay a week behind the others, and to write exercises every day till he goes home."

"Oh, Hamilton, Hamilton!" cried Louis, bursting fairly into tears, "I am not crying wholly for sorrow; for I am, and ought to be, thankful that I have not been made a 'rebuke unto the foolish.'"

Hamilton pressed his hand.

"I hope," he continued, "that this may be a blessing to me; but I am very much afraid of myself, Hamilton, for I am constantly making good resolutions and breaking them—but, Hamilton, do you think they would suppose I had told of them?"

"Dr. Wilkinson told them you would not break your promise and clear yourself by betraying them," replied Hamilton; "and he also said a great deal on the folly of rash promises, and the evil of covering sin. I wish you had heard it; but we must not talk any more, for here is Alfred, and we shall have the prayer-bell presently; so, if you have any thing to do before you go down, you had better make haste."

Louis dried his tears, and obeyed the hint, after submitting, with no very great reluctance, to a mighty hug from

Alfred, who would have given vent to his delight in a great flow of words had not his brother been present and waiting for him. There was little time for talking when Louis returned to his dormitory ; but he and his brother made the most of it, and, arm in arm, they issued forth when the summons was heard. All the way down stairs Louis received the congratulations of his school-fellows. Everybody, even Trevannion, seemed to have forgiven him, and Norman held out his hand at the hall-door with a "Shake hands, old fellow !"

Louis felt rather afraid of entering the school-room, but Dr. Wilkinson made no comment, and, as far as he could judge from the doubtful light of a few candles struggling with the coming daylight, scarcely looked at him. The names were called over. At Harris's name there was a pause—some one answered, "Not here, sir ;" and, as Dr. Wilkinson, without any comment, proceeded, Louis caught a few whispered words near him :

"He's been moaning nearly all night, poor fellow ! he's in a terrible way now ;" and then the reply, "Ah, the doctor never unsays any thing !"

When prayers were over, Dr. Wilkinson called Louis into the study, and kept him till breakfast-time with him. What passed, never transpired ; but that it was something serious was conjectured from Louis' exceedingly humble manner and red eyes, when he left the room—though every one was sure, from the subsequent manner of both master and pupil, that all was entirely forgiven, and Louis reinstated fully in Dr. Wilkinson's good graces.

But I must hasten to finish my story. The prize day arrived. It was a dismal, wet, dreary day ; but the boys

cared nothing for that, except that the audience was
smaller than usual.   Charles Clifton carried away all the
first prizes of his class, except that for French, which was,
contrary to his expectation, adjudged to Louis.   Hamilton
having privately signified to the doctor his wish to withdraw all claim to the medal, it was likewise bestowed on
Clifton.   Reginald was not successful in any branch this
half-year, having so recently entered the highest class.   As
for Frank and Hamilton, the poems were considered so
equal—Hamilton's being the more correct, and Frank's
displaying the greater talent and brilliancy—that they
each received a prize exactly alike.   The doctor passed a
high encomium on Frank's industry, and that original
young gentleman had the satisfaction of bearing away
two prizes in addition to that already mentioned, leaving another for Hamilton, one for Ferrers, and one for
Norman.

Just as the boys had dispersed, and Reginald and Louis
were arranging a snug place in their carpet-bag for Louis'
prize, a letter was put into the hand of the former.

"From home, Reginald?" cried Louis ; " I suppose it is
to say who is coming for us."

But, no ;—it was to tell them of the illness of a lady
who had been staying at Dashwood Priory, which had
assumed so much the character of typhus fever, that Mr.
Mortimer considered it unsafe for his boys to return ; and
the letter, which was from their mother, informed them,
with many expressions of affectionate regret, that their
father had written to ask Dr. Wilkinson to keep them a
few days, till it could be decided how they were to be disposed of.   Poor Louis was grievously disappointed, and

Reginald, not less so, inveighed aloud on the folly and impertinence of ladies going to friends' houses to fall ill there and prevent their sons from enjoying their holidays, so long, that Louis at length could not help laughing.

"But what shall we do, Reginald? it will be so dull here."

"I shall die of the vapors, I think," said Reginald.

"Come home with me," said Salisbury, "both of you—I am sure my father and mother will be very glad to see you."

"I should like nothing better," replied Reginald; "provided your father and mother prove of the same accommodating opinion when you sound them."

"Charlie asked me last week to go with him, Reginald," said Louis; "if you go with Salisbury, I shall go with him; but if you remain here, I shall stay with you."

The brothers received invitations on all sides when their desolate condition was known, but none could be accepted without the consent of their parents, or in the mean time of Dr. Wilkinson, as their guardian. It was finally settled, that as both Salisbury and Clifton lived in the neighborhood, their invitations might be accepted till further notice from Dashwood.

The lady proved very ill, though, as it was not any infectious disease, the brothers probably might have been sent for, had not a heavy fall of snow rendered the roads near Dashwood impassable.

Louis spent nearly the whole of his holidays very happily with Charles; becoming, during his stay with them, a great favorite with Mr. Clifton and his little girls, as well as their nurse. Salisbury had the benefit of Reginald's company for a fortnight, the rest of his time being bestowed upon Meredith.

When the holidays were over, Hamilton returned for his last half-year. The reflections induced by the preceding term were not transient. He struggled manfully with the constitutional indifference of his character; and though there were many failings, for the habits were too deeply rooted to be suddenly overcome, yet the effort was not without its use, both to himself and others. To Louis, he was a constant and useful friend, never flagging in his efforts to make him more manly and independent in his conduct, as regarded the opinion of others; and also quietly strengthening, by his example and encouragement, every good feeling and impression he noticed. There were no tears shed, but Louis felt very low when he bade good-bye to Hamilton, at the close of the next half-year.

"Oh, Hamilton! I owe you a great deal. What shall I do next half without you? Who will help me?"

"Thy God, whom thou servest," said Hamilton, reverentially. "The thanks are not to me for the help of the last few months, Louis. Good-bye, my dear fellow—our friendship does not end here; we are friends forever."

They shook hands warmly and parted.

Louis continued at school for two or three years longer, and passed through the ordeal of school-life with credit to himself and his relations. I would not be thought to mean that he never did wrong, or was always equally steady in his Christian course; for the Christian's whole life is a continued fight against the evil of his nature. He still retained his strong desire to enter the ministry of the Church, and his studies and pursuits were principally directed to that

end. It was one of his fairest day-dreams, to be his
father's curate when old enough to be ordained, and though
that might not be, he still felt, wherever he might be
placed, his language would be that of the Psalmist, when
he said—

" My soul hath a desire and a longing to enter into the
courts of the living God." " For I had rather be a door
keeper in the house of my God, than to dwell in the tents
of wickedness."

THE END

PETER PARLEY'S JUVENILES.

I.

A WINTER WREATH OF SUMMER FLOWERS. By
S. G. GOODRICH. 1 vol. 8vo. cloth, illuminated, gilt
edges. Price $2 50.

From the Boston Transcript.

A very handsome Souvenir for girls, printed, bound, and illustrated in
an exquisite manner. It consists of alternate verse and prose, entertaining, unexceptionable and often instructive. It is a beautiful gift-book,
and we believe the only one intended for the same class of readers that has
appeared this season. The novel style of engraving and typography will
attract purchasers whom the contents will not disappoint.

II.

THE WANDERERS BY SEA AND LAND. By PETER
PARLEY. Illustrated with 12 engravings. 1 vol. 12mo.
$1 12; cloth, gilt, $1 50.

From the Palladium.

If any of our young friends wish to go to Paris, let them by all means
get this volume. Peter Parley will give the most authentic and entertaining accounts of the delights of that great capital which can be found
without taking a Collins' steamer, and we trust our juvenile friends prefer
to remain at home and study their books until they are old enough to have
finished their education.

III.

FAGGOTS FOR THE FIRESIDE; OR, FACT AND FANCY.
By PETER PARLEY. 1 vol. 12mo. cloth. Illuminated
Price $1 12; cloth, gilt edges, $1 50.

Come, girls and boys—black eyes and blue—
And hear a story told for you.
Lay down your books, John, Tom and Bob;
Be seated, if you please. No laughing Bob!
Just stir the fire, Ben. Steady—steady!
Hand me my specs, Tom. So all's ready
There goes the tongs again, slam bang,
And pussy's tale has got a whang!
Poor puss—be wise—of boys beware,
And keep your tail with better care.
Sit still now, all, and hear the story
Old Peter Parley's rhyme would set before ye.

IV.

PARLEY'S PRESENT FOR ALL SEASONS. By S.
G. GOODRICH. Illustrated with 16 fine engravings.
12mo. bound in illuminated covers, $1; gilt edges,
$1 25.

This is a very rich and choice work, consisting of many pleasant stories
by that most popular of all writers for the young folks, Peter Parley, and
illustrated with a dozen or more superior engravings.—*Albany State Reg*

MORTIMER'S COLLEGE LIFE. By E. J. MAY, author of "Lewis's School Days," etc. With illustrations, 1 vol. 16mo. 75 cents; gilt edges, $1.

A very pretty story prettily told. A vein of humor runs throughout the volume, tinctured with just enough of religious sentiment to make it agreeable and instructive to the reader. The plot is evidently founded on fact, with now and then a dash of romance to make it interesting.—*Pennsylvanian.*

LOUIS'S SCHOOL DAYS. A Story for Boys. By E. J MAY. 16mo. illustrated with engravings, 75 cents.

The School-days of Louis present a great variety of incident and character. The story is naturally and effectively told, and is calculated to encourage the young to persevere in the path of Christian duty.—*Morning Post.*

Written in the right spirit, by one who can recall his own youth, describe its feelings, revive its joys and sorrows, and speak its language, there is nothing in literature more attractive.—*London Literary Journal.*

THE SUNSHINE OF GREYSTONE. A Story for Girls. By E. J. MAY, author of Louis's School Boy Days. 1 vol. 16mo. illustrated, 75 cents.

Here little girls is a sweet book, made on purpose for you, in neat gilt binding with nice engravings; a delightful story, with just the least bit of romance for those of you who are about shedding pantalettes, a little love by way of warning, and every chapter prefaced with a text from scripture, appropriate to its contents, and designed to inculcate the virtues which will serve to adorn you when you become women, and make your homes happy, and your lives useful.—*Detroit Inquirer.*

Uniform with Louis's School Days.

EDGAR CLIFTON; OR, RIGHT AND WRONG. A Story for Boys. By C. ADAMS. 16mo. elegant cloth, with numerous illustrations, 75 cents.

₊ The story of "Edgar Clifton" will be found a most appropriate companion to that of "Louis's School Days," the aim of the works being alike. The same lessons of right and truth are inculcated in each. The contents, however, of the books, and the heroes of the stories are so entirely different, as to render them not only free from sameness, but full of distinctive attractions and claims.

BOYS AT HOME. By C. ADAMS, author of "Edgar Clifton," etc., etc. Illustrated by John Gilbert. 1 vol. 16mo. 75 cents.

"A very entertaining volume, just the kind to make boys read, whether they will or not; and there is no reason why girls should not read it too."

Popular Tales.

By Mary Howitt, Mrs. Ellis, Hannah More, &c., &c.

ALICE FRANKLIN. By Mary Howitt.	$0 38
HOPE ON, HOPE EVER. By do.	38
LITTLE COIN, MUCH CARE. By do.	38
LOVE AND MONEY. By do.	38
MY OWN STORY. By do.	38
MY UNCLE, THE CLOCKMAKER. By do.	38
NO SENSE LIKE COMMON SENSE. By do.	38
SOWING AND REAPING. By do.	38
STRIVE AND THRIVE. By do.	38
THE TWO APPRENTICES. By do.	38
WHICH IS THE WISER? By do.	38
WHO SHALL BE GREATEST? By do.	38
WORK AND WAGES. By do.	38
DOMESTIC TALES. By Hannah More. 2 vols.	75
DANGERS OF DINING OUT. By Mrs. Ellis.	38
FIRST IMPRESSIONS. By do.	38
SOMERVILLE HALL. By do.	38
MINISTER'S FAMILY. By do.	38
SON OF A GENIUS. By Mrs. Hofland.	38
EARLY FRIENDSHIP. By Mrs. Copley.	36
POPLAR GROVE. By do.	38
CHANCES AND CHANGES. By Chas. Burdett.	38
NEVER TOO LATE. By do.	38
CROFTON BOYS. By Miss Martineau.	38
PEASANT AND PRINCE. By do.	38
FARMER'S DAUGHTER. By Mrs. Cameron.	38
TIRED OF HOUSEKEEPING. By T. S. Arthur.	38
TWIN SISTERS. By Mrs. Sandham.	36
LOOKING-GLASS FOR THE MIND.	38
GOLDMAKER'S VILLAGE. By H. Zschokke.	36
OCEAN WORK. Ancient and Modern. By J. H. Wright.	38

MARY HOWITT'S JUVENILE TALES.

NEW EDITIONS, BOUND TOGETHER, ENTITLED:

POPULAR MORAL TALES. 16mo.	75
JUVENILE TALES AND STORIES. 16mo.	75
MY JUVENILE DAYS, and other Tales. 16mo.	75
TALES AND STORIES FOR BOYS AND GIRLS.	75

LIBRARY FOR MY YOUNG COUNTRYMEN.

ADVENTURES OF CAPT. JOHN SMITH. By the Author of "Uncle Philip."	38
ADVENTURES OF DANIEL BOONE. By do.	38
LIFE AND ADVENTURES OF HENRY HUDSON. By do.	38
DAWNINGS OF GENIUS. By Ann Pratt.	38
LIFE AND ADVENTURES OF HERNAN CORTEZ. By do.	38
PHILIP RANDOLPH. A Tale of Virginia. By M. Gertrude.	38
ROWAN'S HIST. OF THE FRENCH REVOLUTION. 2 vols.	75
SOUTHEY'S LIFE OF OLIVER CROMWELL.	38

COUSIN ALICE'S HOME SERIES.

OUT OF DEBT OUT OF DANGER. 1 vol. 16mo. Illustrated, cloth, 75 cents.

This is a new volume of Cousin Alice's charming tales for the young folks. The same wonderful talent is here evinced which has been so successfully shown in all her writings for young children.

NOTHING VENTURE NOTHING HAVE. By Cousin Alice. 1 vol. 16mo. Price 63 cents.

One of those charming little stories for which Cousin Alice is so famous—simple, natural, graceful, interesting without effort, full of pathos, and teaching in a manner not to be forgotten, what marvels may be accomplished by self-denial, self-reliance, and trust in God.—*National Era.*

ALL'S NOT GOLD THAT GLITTERS; OR, THE YOUNG CALIFORNIAN. By ALICE B. NEAL. 1 vol. 16mo., neatly illustrated, 75 cents.

Those who have read the former works of this charming authoress will anticipate a rich treat in this, in which we venture to predict their expectations will be fully realized. The title of "Home Books" is peculiarly appropriate and happily chosen by the writer, judging from the series and they will, doubtless, exercise a most beneficial influence on the hearts of those for whom they are designed.—*Home Journal.*

PATIENT WAITING NO LOSS: OR, THE TWO CHRISTMAS DAYS. 1 vol. 16mo. neatly illustrated. 63 cents.

We have not met with a volume for a long while so intensely interesting as the one bearing the above title. The book is evidently intended to impress upon young persons, particularly children, the necessity of energy, and the result of a firm reliance on the goodness of God. It will also prove a source of assistance to mothers, in teaching them the necessity of early instilling into the minds of their children, the principles of truth and honesty. The style is simple and elegant.—*Observer.*

CONTENTMENT BETTER THAN WEALTH. 1 vol. 16mo. neatly illustrated. 63 cents.

The tale is a delightful narrative: it is presented in an effective manner; and the lesson it inculcates, is one of truth and duty. It is that a high and manly resolution, persisted in with a fixed determination, will meet with its reward in the final attainment of all reasonable purposes. The volume is beautifully published.—*Com. Adv.*

NO SUCH WORD AS FAIL; OR, THE CHILDREN'S JOURNEY. 1 vol. 16mo. neatly illustrated. 63 cents.

Mrs. Neal has seldom written a story so pathetic, and with such healthful meaning as that contained in this elegant little volume. The minds of children who read it cannot fail to be strengthened and inspirited for the encounter with the troubles and trials of life.—*Tribune.*

Juvenile Books.

PUSS IN BOOTS. Finely illustrated by Otto Speckter. Square 18mo, boards, 25 cents. Cloth, 38 cents. Extra gilt, 50 cents.

ROBINSON CRUSOE. Pictorial edition. 300 plates, 8vo, $1 50. Gilt edges, $2.

ROSE and LILLIE STANHOPE: or, THE POWER of CONSCIENCE. By MARIA J. McINTOSH. 1 vol., 38 cents.

SEDGEMOOR; or, HOME LESSONS. By Mrs. MANNERS. 16mo. Cloth, 75 cents.

STORIES of an OLD MAID. By Madame DE GIRARDIN. 16mo, Illustrated, cloth, 75 cents.

SUNSHINE of GREYSTONE. By the author of " Louis' School Days." 16mo, illustrated, 75 cents.

UNCLE JOHN'S FIRST BOOK. Illustrated with numerous pretty engravings. Square 16mo, neat cloth, 31 cents.

UNCLE JOHN'S SECOND BOOK. Illustrated with numerous pretty engravings. Square 18mo, in neat cloth, 38 cents.

VICAR OF WAKEFIELD. A Tale. By OLIVER GOLDSMITH. 1 vol, 12mo, with numerous illustrations, 75 cents. Gilt edges.

WANDERERS (The): by SEA and LAND, with Other Tales. By Peter Parley. Illustrated with exquisite designs. 1 vol. 12mo. $1 12.

THE WEEK'S DELIGHT; or, GAMES and STORIES for the PARLOR and FIRESIDE. 1 neat volume. 16mo, engravings. 75 cents.

WILLIAM TELL, The PATRIOT OF SWITZERLAND: to which is added, Andreas Hofer, the " Tell " of the Tyrol. Cloth, 50 cents. Half cloth, 38 cents.

A WINTER WREATH of SUMMER FLOWERS. By S. G. GOODRICH. Illustrated with splendid colored plates by French artists. 1 superb vol. 8vo, extra cloth, gilt edges, $3.

YOUNG STUDENT (The); or, RALPH and VICTOR. By Madame GUIZOT. From the French, by Samuel Jackson. 1 vol. of 500 pages, with illustrations, 75 cents.

YOUTH'S CORONAL. By H. F. GOULD, 16mo, 63 cents.

———— **STORY BOOK.** 16mo, 75 cents.

Juvenile Books.

MIDSUMMER FAYS: or, THE HOLIDAYS at WOODLEIGH. By SUSAN PINDAR. 1 vol. 16mo, 63 cents.

MORTIMER'S COLLEGE LIFE. With neat illustrations, 16mo, cloth, 75 cents. Extra cloth, gilt edges, $1.

MYSTERIOUS STORY BOOK: or, the GOOD STEPMOTHER. Illustrated, 16mo, cloth, 75 cents. Gilt edges, $1.

NEAL (ALICE B.) CONTENTMENT Better than WEALTH. 16mo, illustrated, 63 cents. Gilt edges, 90 cents.

———————— **PATIENT WAITING NO LOSS.** 16mo, illustrated, 63 cents. Gilt edges, 90 cents.

———————— **NO SUCH WORD AS FAIL.** 16mo, illustrated, 63 cents. Gilt edges, 90 cents.

———————— **"ALL'S NOT GOLD that GLITTERS,"** or, the YOUNG CALIFORNIAN. 1 vol. 16mo, neatly illustrated, 75 cents. Gilt edges, $1.

———————— **NOTHING VENTURE, NOTHING HAVE.** 1 vol. 16mo, beautifully illustrated, 63 cents. Gilt edges, 90 cents.

———————— **OUT OF DEBT, OUT OF DANGER.** 16mo, illustrated, cloth, 75 cents. Gilt edges, $1.

———————— **A PLACE for EVERYTHING.** 16mo, cloth, 75 cents

———————— **THE COOPERS, or, GETTING UNDER WAY.** 12mo, cloth, 75 cents.

NIGHT CAPS. By the author of "Aunt Fanny's Christmas Stories." 1 vol. 18mo, cloth, 50 cents.

NIGHT CAPS (The New). Told to Charley. By the author of "Aunt Fanny's Christmas Stories."

OUTLINES OF CREATION. By ELISHA NOYCE, author of "The Boy's Book of Industrial Information." 12mo, profusely illustrated, extra cloth, $1 50.

PARLEY'S PRESENT for ALL SEASONS. By S. G. GOODRICH, (Peter Parley.) Illustrated with 16 fine engravings. 12mo, elegantly bound in a new style, $1. Gilt edges, $1 25.

PELL'S GUIDE for THE YOUNG to Success and Happiness. 12mo, cloth, 38 cents. Extra cloth, gilt edges, 50 cents.

PHILIP RANDOLPH. A Tale of Virginia. By MARY GERTRUDE. 18mo, 38 cents.

PICTURE PLEASURE BOOK (The). Illustrated by upwards of five hundred engravings from drawings by eminent artists. 4to. size, beautifully printed, on fine paper, and bound in fancy covers. First and Second Series, each $1 25.

Juvenile Books.

HISTORY OF PETER THE GREAT, CZAR OF RUSSIA. **By** SARAH H. BRADFORD. 16mo, illustrated, cloth, 75 cents.

HOUSEHOLD STORIES. Collected by the Brothers GRIMM Newly translated, embellished with 240 illustrations by Wehnert. 1 vol., cloth, $2 00. Gilt edges, $2 50.

HOWITT'S (MARY), SERIES of POPULAR JUVENILE WORKS. 14 vols. uniform, in a case, in extra cloth, neat style.

HOWITT'S (MARY), PICTURE AND VERSE BOOK, commonly called Otto Speckter's Fable Book. Illustrated with 100 plates. Cheap edition, 50 cents. Cloth, 63 cents. Gilt leaves, 75 cents.

JESSIE GRAHAM; or, FRIENDS DEAR, BUT TRUTH DEARER. By MARIA J. McINTOSH. 1 vol., square 16mo, 88 cents.

LITTLE DORA; or, THE FOUR SEASONS. By a Lady of Charleston. Beautifully illustrated, 25 cents. Cloth, 88 cents.

LITTLE FRANK, and other TALES. Square 16mo. Cloth, 25 cents.

LOSS AND GAIN; or, MARGARET'S HOME. By COUSIN ALICE.

LOUIS' SCHOOL DAYS. By E. J. MAY. Illustrated 16mo. 75 cents.

LOUISE; or, THE BEAUTY OF INTEGRITY, and other TALES. 16mo, boards, 25 cents. Cloth, 88 cents.

McINTOSH'S NEW JUVENILE LIBRARY. 7 beautiful vols. With illustrations. In a case, $2 50.

——————— META GRAY; or, What Makes HOME HAPPY? 16mo, cloth.

MARY LEE. A Story for the Young. By KATE LIVERMORE. 1 neat vol. 16mo, illustrated. Extra Cloth, 63 cents.

MARTHA'S HOOKS and EYES. 1 vol. 18mo, 37 cents.

MARRYATT'S SETTLERS IN CANADA. 2 vols. in one, colored, 62 cents.

——————— SCENES IN AFRICA. 2 vols. in one, colored 62 cents.

——————— MASTERMAN READY. 8 vols in one, colored. 62 cents.

Juvenile Works.

A PLACE FOR EVERYTHING, and EVERYTHING IN ITS PLACE. By COUSIN ALICE. 16mo, illustrated, cloth, 75 c.

AMERICAN HISTORICAL TALES. 16mo, 75 cents.

APPLETON'S BOYS' AND GIRLS' AMERICAN ANNUAL for 1860. 1 vol. 12mo, illustrated. Cloth, gilt, $1 50.

AUNT KITTY'S TALES. By MARIA J. MCINTOSH. 12mo, 75 cents.

AUNT FANNY'S STORY BOOK FOR LITTLE BOYS AND GIRLS. 18mo, illustrated, boards, 31 cents. Cloth, 38 cents.

BARON MUNCHAUSEN'S SURPRISING TRAVELS AND ADVENTURES. A new and beautiful edition. Illustrated with characteristic designs, by Crowquill. (Several colored.) 1 vol. 12mo. Extra cloth, gilt edges, $2 50.

BERTRAM NOEL. A Story for Youth. By E. J. MAY, author of "Louis' School Days," &c. 16mo, 75 cents.

BLIND ALICE. A Tale for Good Children. By MARIA J. MCINTOSH. 1 vol. square 16mo, 38 cents.

BOYS (The) AT HOME. By the author of "Edgar Clifton." 16mo, illustrated, 75 cents.

BOY'S BOOK OF MODERN TRAVEL AND ADVENTURE. By Meredith Johnes. 1 neat vol. 16mo, illustrated, cloth, 75c.

BOYS' AND GIRLS' AMERICAN ANNUAL. Edited by T. Martin. With finely colored illustrations. 1 vol. 12mo, in extra cloth, gilt edges, $1 50.

BOY'S (The) BIRTH-DAY BOOK: a Collection of Tales, Essays, and Narratives of Adventures. By Mrs. S. C. HALL, WILLIAM HOWITT, AUGUSTUS MAYHEW, THOMAS MILLER, G. A. SALA, &c., &c. 1 vol. crown 8vo, illustrated with 100 engravings. Cloth, gilt edges, $2.

BOY'S BOOK OF INDUSTRIAL INFORMATION. By ELISHA NOYCE, author of Outlines of Creation. Illustrated with 370 engravings. 12mo, extra cloth, $1 25.

BOY'S (The) OWN TOY MAKER. Square 16mo. 50 cents.

BIBLE STORIES: or, Tales from Scripture. 1 vol. square 12mo.

BOY'S OWN BOOK: a Complete Encyclopædia of all the Diversions, Athletic, Scientific, and Recreative, of Boyhood and Youth. New and enlarged edition, with numerous additional illustrations. 1 thick vol., extra cloth, $2.

Juvenile Works.

CHILDREN'S HOLIDAYS. A Story Book for the whole Year. 18mo, illustrated. Cloth, 50 cents.

CHILD'S FIRST HISTORY OF AMERICA. By the author of "Little Dora." Square 18mo, engravings. Half cloth, 25 cents.

CHILDREN'S (The) PICTURE GALLERY. Engravings from one hundred paintings by eminent English artists. 1 vol. 4to, $1 50.

DOUGLASS FARM. A Juvenile Story of Life in Virginia. By MARY E. BRADLEY. 16mo, illustrated. Cloth, 75 cents.

EDGAR CLIFTON; or, RIGHT and WRONG. 16mo. illus. 75 cents.

ELLEN LESLIE; or, the REWARD of SELF-CONTROL. By MARIA J. MCINTOSH. 1 vol. square 16mo, 38 cents.

EMILY HERBERT; or, THE HAPPY HOME. By MARIA J. MCINTOSH. 1 vol. square 12mo, 38 cents.

ENTOMOLOGY in SPORT and ENTOMOLOGY in EARNEST. By Two Lovers of the Science. 1 vol. 12mo. $1 25.

FAGGOTS for THE FIRESIDE; or, FACTS and FANCY. By Peter Parley. 1 vol. 12mo, beautifully illustrated, $1 12.

FLORENCE ARNOTT; or, IS SHE GENEROUS? By MARIA J. MCINTOSH. 1 vol. square 16mo, 38 cents.

FUNNY STORY BOOK; A LAUGHTER PROVOKING BOOK FOR YOUNG FOLKS. 16mo, illustrated, cloth, 75c. Extra cloth, gilt edges, $1.

GEORGE READY; or, HOW TO LIVE FOR OTHERS. By ROBERT O'LINCOLN. 16mo, illustrated. Cloth, 75 cents.

GOOD IN EVERY THING. By Mrs. BARWELL. Square 16mo. illustrated, 50 cents.

GRACE AND CLARA; or, BE JUST, as WELL AS GENEROUS. 1 vol. square 16mo, 38 cents.

GRANDMAMMA EASY'S TOY BOOKS. 8vo. colored. Per dozen, $1 50.

HEWET'S ILLUMINATED HOUSEHOLD STORIES FOR LITTLE FOLKS. Beautifully illustrated.

    No. 1. CINDERELLA,
    "   2. JACK THE GIANT KILLER.
    "   3. PUSS IN BOOTS.
    "   4. LITTLE RED RIDING HOOD.
    "   5. JACK AND THE BEAN STALK.
    "   6. TOM THUMB.
    "   7. BEAUTY AND THE BEAST.   In fancy paper
covers, each 25 cents. In fancy boards, each 50 cents.

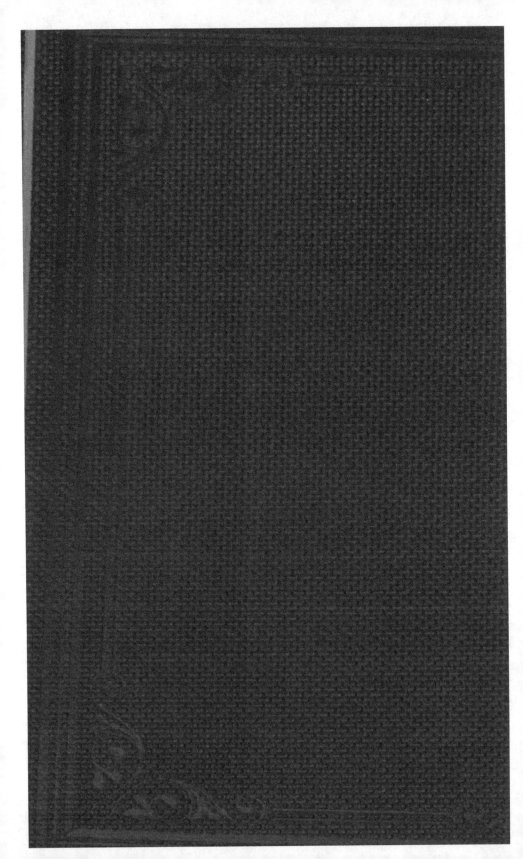

CPSIA information can be obtained
at www.ICGtesting.com
Printed in the USA
BVHW081818220819
556561BV00020B/4515/P